Student Solutions Manual
for use with

College Physics

Alan Giambattista
Cornell University

Betty McCarthy Richardson
Cornell University

Robert C. Richardson
Cornell University

Prepared by

Laurel Tech
Integrated Publishing Services

 **Higher Education**

Boston   Burr Ridge, IL   Dubuque, IA   Madison, WI   New York   San Francisco   St. Louis
Bangkok   Bogotá   Caracas   Kuala Lumpur   Lisbon   London   Madrid   Mexico City
Milan   Montreal   New Delhi   Santiago   Seoul   Singapore   Sydney   Taipei   Toronto

The McGraw·Hill Companies

Student Solutions Manual for use with
COLLEGE PHYSICS
GIAMBATTISTA/RICHARDSON/RICHARDSON

Published by McGraw-Hill Higher Education, an imprint of The McGraw-Hill Companies, Inc.,
1221 Avenue of the Americas, New York, NY 10020. Copyright © The McGraw-Hill Companies,
Inc., 2004. All rights reserved.

This book is printed on acid-free paper.

1 2 3 4 5 6 7 8 9 0 BKM BKM 0 9 8 7 6 5 4 3

ISBN 0-07-052497-1

www.mhhe.com

TABLE OF CONTENTS

Chapter 1

INTRODUCTION

Problems

1. The area of the surface of a sphere is given by $S = 4\pi r^2$.

$$S_1 = 4\pi r_1^2$$
$$S_2 = 4\pi r_2^2 = 1.160 S_1 = 1.160(4\pi r_1^2)$$
$$4\pi r_2^2 = 1.160(4\pi r_1^2)$$
$$r_2^2 = 1.160 r_1^2$$
$$\left(\frac{r_2}{r_1}\right)^2 = 1.160$$
$$\frac{r_2}{r_1} = \sqrt{1.160}$$
$$= 1.077$$

The radius of the balloon increases by $\boxed{7.7\%}$.

3. The area of a circle is $A = \pi r^2$.

$$A_1 = \pi r_1^2$$
$$A_2 = \pi r_2^2 = \pi(2r_1)^2 = 4\pi r_1^2$$

Form a proportion.

$$\frac{A_2}{A_1} = \frac{4\pi r_1^2}{\pi r_1^2} = 4$$

The cross-sectional area of the artery increases by a factor of $\boxed{4}$.

5. If s is the speed of the molecule, then $s \propto \sqrt{T}$ where T is the temperature. Form a proportion.

$$\frac{s_{cold}}{s_{warm}} = \frac{\sqrt{T_{cold}}}{\sqrt{T_{warm}}}$$

Find s_{cold}.

$$s_{cold} = s_{warm}\sqrt{\frac{T_{cold}}{T_{warm}}} = \left(475\frac{m}{s}\right)\sqrt{\frac{250.0\ K}{300.0\ K}} = \boxed{434\ m/s}$$

9. (a) $3.783\times10^6 + 1.25\times10^8 = 0.03783\times10^8 + 1.25\times10^8 = \boxed{1.29\times10^8}$

(b) $(3.783\times10^6) \div (3.0\times10^{-2}) = \boxed{1.3\times10^8}$

13. $\dfrac{1.00 \text{ km}}{1 \text{ h}} \times \dfrac{1 \text{ h}}{3600 \text{ s}} \times \dfrac{1000 \text{ m}}{1 \text{ km}} = \boxed{0.278 \text{ m/s}}$

17. $\dfrac{1.4 \text{ kW}}{1 \text{ m}^2} \times \dfrac{1000 \text{ W}}{1 \text{ kW}} \times \left(\dfrac{1 \text{ m}}{100 \text{ cm}}\right)^2 = \boxed{0.14 \text{ W/cm}^2}$

19. $C = \pi d$

$d = \dfrac{C}{\pi}$

(a) $d = \dfrac{300(0.35 \text{ nm})}{\pi} \times \dfrac{10^{-9} \text{ m}}{1 \text{ nm}} = \boxed{3.3 \times 10^{-8} \text{ m}}$

(b) $d = \dfrac{300(0.35 \text{ nm})}{\pi} \times \dfrac{10^{-3} \text{ μm}}{1 \text{ nm}} = \boxed{3.3 \times 10^{-2} \text{ μm}}$

(c) $d = \dfrac{300(0.35 \text{ nm})}{\pi} \times \dfrac{10^{-7} \text{ cm}}{1 \text{ nm}} \times \dfrac{1 \text{ in}}{2.54 \text{ cm}} = \boxed{1.3 \times 10^{-6} \text{ in}}$

21. $\dfrac{1.36 \times 10^4 \text{ kg}}{1 \text{ m}^3} \times \dfrac{1000 \text{ g}}{1 \text{ kg}} \times \left(\dfrac{1 \text{ m}}{100 \text{ cm}}\right)^3 = \boxed{13.6 \text{ g/cm}^3}$

25. (a) By inspection of the units of G, c, and h, and by trial-and-error, we find that $\boxed{\sqrt{\dfrac{hG}{c^5}}}$.

(b) $\sqrt{\dfrac{hG}{c^5}} = \sqrt{\dfrac{(6.6 \times 10^{-34} \text{ J} \cdot \text{s})\left(6.7 \times 10^{-11} \frac{\text{m}^3}{\text{kg} \cdot \text{s}^2}\right)}{\left(3.0 \times 10^8 \frac{\text{m}}{\text{s}}\right)^5}} = \sqrt{\dfrac{\left(6.6 \times 10^{-34} \frac{\text{kg} \cdot \text{m}^2}{\text{s}^2} \cdot \text{s}\right)\left(6.7 \times 10^{-11} \frac{\text{m}^3}{\text{kg} \cdot \text{s}^2}\right)}{\left(3.0 \times 10^8 \frac{\text{m}}{\text{s}}\right)^5}} = \boxed{1.3 \times 10^{-43} \text{ s}}$

29. (a) a has dimensions $\dfrac{[L]}{[T]^2}$; v has dimensions $\dfrac{[L]}{[T]}$; r has dimension $[L]$. If we square v and divide by r, we have

$\dfrac{v^2}{r} \rightarrow \dfrac{[L]^2}{[T]^2} \cdot \dfrac{1}{[L]} = \dfrac{[L]}{[T]^2}$, which are the dimensions for a. Therefore, we can write $\boxed{a = K \dfrac{v^2}{r}}$, where K is a

dimensionless constant.

(b) $\dfrac{a_2}{a_1} = \dfrac{K \frac{v_2^2}{r}}{K \frac{v_1^2}{r}} = \left(\dfrac{v_2}{v_1}\right)^2 = \left(\dfrac{1.100 v_1}{v_1}\right)^2 = 1.100^2 = 1.210$

$1.210 - 1 = 0.210$, so the centripetal acceleration increases by $\boxed{21.0\%}$.

33. $(1+x)^n = (1+x)^{1/2} \approx 1 + \dfrac{1}{2}x$ for $|x| \ll 1$ and $n = \dfrac{1}{2}$.

(a) $1.008^{1/2} \approx 1 + \dfrac{1}{2}(0.008) = \boxed{1.004 \quad (1.00399)}$

(b) $1.04^{1/2} \approx 1 + \dfrac{1}{2}(0.04) = \boxed{1.02 \ \ (1.0198)}$

(c) $1.4^{1/2} \approx 1 + \dfrac{1}{2}(0.4) = \boxed{1.2 \ \ (1.183)}$

(d) $1.66^{1/2} \approx 1 + \dfrac{1}{2}(0.66) = \boxed{1.33 \ \ (1.288)}$

35.

θ (degrees)	40	30	20	10
θ (radians)	0.698	0.524	0.349	0.1745
$\tan\theta$	0.839	0.577	0.364	0.1763
difference	0.141	0.053	0.015	0.0018

(a) $\dfrac{0.053}{0.524} \approx 0.1$, so the answer is $\boxed{30°}$.

(b) $\dfrac{0.0018}{0.1745} \approx 0.01$, so the answer is $\boxed{10°}$.

37. One story is about 3 m high.

$(3 \text{ m})(40) \sim \boxed{100 \text{ m}}$

41.

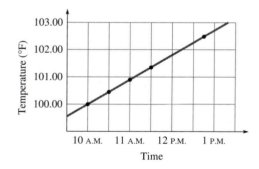

(a) By inspection of the graph, it appears that the temperature at noon was $\boxed{101.8°\text{F}}$.

(b) Estimate the slope of the line.

$$m = \frac{102.6°\text{F} - 100.0°\text{F}}{1{:}00 \text{ P.M.} - 10{:}00 \text{ A.M.}} = \frac{2.6°\text{F}}{3 \text{ h}} = \boxed{0.9 \, °\text{F/h}}$$

(c) In twelve hours, the temperature would, according to the trend, be approximately

$$T = \left(0.9 \frac{°\text{F}}{\text{h}}\right)(12 \text{ h}) + 102.5°\text{F} = 113°\text{F}.$$

The patient would be dead before the temperature reached this level. So, the answer is $\boxed{\text{no}}$.

43. Put the equation that describes the line in slope-intercept form, $y = ax + b$.

$$at = v - v_0$$
$$v = at + v_0$$

(a) v is the dependent variable, and t is the independent variable, so $\boxed{a}$ is the slope of the line.

(b) $y = mx + b$; $v \leftrightarrow y$, $t \leftrightarrow x$, $a \leftrightarrow m$, so $v_0 \leftrightarrow b$.

$\boxed{+v_0}$ is the "y"-intercept of the line.

45. **(a)**

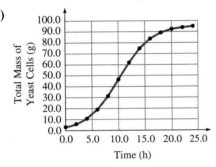

(b) Answers will vary. According to the graph, the carrying capacity is $\boxed{\text{about 100 g}}$.

(c)

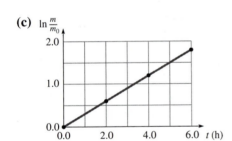

From the plot of $\ln \dfrac{m}{m_0}$ vs. t, the slope r appears to be

$$r = \frac{1.8 - 0.0}{6.0 \text{ s} - 0.0 \text{ s}} = \frac{1.8}{6.0 \text{ s}} = \boxed{0.30 \text{ s}^{-1}}.$$

47. The area of a circle is $A = \pi r^2$.
Calculate the percentage increase of the area of the garden plot.

$$
\begin{aligned}
\frac{\Delta A}{A} \times 100\% &= \frac{\pi r_2^2 - \pi r_1^2}{\pi r_1^2} \times 100\% \\
&= \frac{r_2^2 - r_1^2}{r_1^2} \times 100\% \\
&= \frac{1.25^2 \, r_1^2 - r_1^2}{r_1^2} \times 100\% \\
&= \frac{1.25^2 - 1}{1} \times 100\% \\
&= \boxed{56\%}
\end{aligned}
$$

49. $26 \text{ mi} \times \dfrac{5280 \text{ ft}}{1 \text{ mi}} \times \dfrac{1 \text{ m}}{3.28 \text{ ft}} \times \dfrac{1 \text{ km}}{1000 \text{ m}} = \boxed{42 \text{ km}}$

53. $90,000,000,000 has a precision of 10 billion dollars. $100 has a precision of 100 dollars, so the net worth is the same to one significant figure.

$$\$90,000,000,000 - \$100 = \boxed{\$90,000,000,000}$$

57.   Find the rate of temperature change with respect to time (the slope of the graph of temperature vs. time).

$$m = \frac{\Delta T}{\Delta t} = \frac{101.0°F - 97.0°F}{4.0 \text{ h}} = 1.0°F/h$$

Use the slope-intercept form of a graph of temperature vs. time to find the temperature at 3:35 P.M.

$$T = mt + T_0 = \left(1.0 \frac{°F}{h}\right)(3.5 \text{ h}) + 101.0°F = \boxed{104.5°F}$$

Chapter 2

FORCES AND INTRODUCTION TO VECTORS

Problems

1. The increase in the force is F, and the length that the tendon increases is x if the tendon is modeled as a spring and Hooke's law is used.

$$k = \frac{F}{x} = \frac{4800 \text{ N} - 3200 \text{ N}}{0.50 \text{ cm}} = \frac{1600 \text{ N}}{0.50 \text{ cm}} = \boxed{3200 \text{ N/cm}}$$

5. $175 \text{ lb} \times \dfrac{1 \text{ N}}{0.2248 \text{ lb}} = \boxed{778 \text{ N}}$

9. Let the subscripts be the following:

p = system of plant, soil, pot   h = hook
c = cord   C = ceiling
e = Earth   s = system of plant, soil, pot, cord, hook

(a) 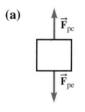   **(b)**   **(c)** 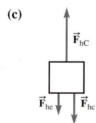   **(d)**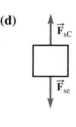

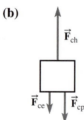

11. The force of the lake on the boat must be equal in magnitude and opposite in direction to the weight of the boat. The force of the wind on the boat must be equal in magnitude and opposite in direction to that of the line.

Let the subscripts be the following:

s = sailboat   e = Earth   w = wind   l = lake   m = mooring line

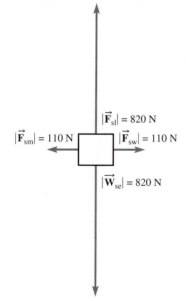

13. (a) 10 N left + 40 N right = −10 N right + 40 N right = $\boxed{\text{30 N to the right}}$

(b) The forces balance, so the net force is $\boxed{0}$.

(c) The horizontal forces balance, so the net force is due only to the downward force. The net force is $\boxed{\text{18 N downward}}$.

17. The two external forces acting on the skydiver and parachute system are $\boxed{\text{the upwardly directed drag due to the air}}$ and $\boxed{\text{the downwardly directed force due to gravity.}}$

19. (a) $W = mg = (40.0 \text{ kg})\left(9.81\dfrac{\text{N}}{\text{kg}}\right) = \boxed{392 \text{ N}}$

(b) $(392.4 \text{ N})\left(\dfrac{0.2248 \text{ lb}}{1.0 \text{ N}}\right) = \boxed{88.2 \text{ lb}}$

21. (a) Set the weight of the mass equal to the force in Hooke's law.

$$W = F$$
$$mg = kx$$
$$k = \frac{mg}{x}$$
$$= \frac{(1.4 \text{ kg})\left(9.8\frac{\text{N}}{\text{kg}}\right)}{7.2 \text{ cm}}$$
$$= \boxed{1.9 \text{ N/cm}}$$

(b) Solve for m in the equation for k found in part (a).

$$m_2 = \frac{kx_2}{g} = \left(\frac{m_1 g}{x_1}\right)\frac{x_2}{g} = \frac{x_2}{x_1}m_1 = \frac{12.2 \text{ cm}}{7.2 \text{ cm}}(1.4 \text{ kg}) = \boxed{2.4 \text{ kg}}$$

25. (a) Sum the forces on the brick. The brick is in static equilibrium, so $\vec{F}_{net} = \vec{0}$.

$$\vec{F}_{bs} + \vec{F}_{bw} + \vec{W}_{be} = \vec{0}$$
$$\vec{F}_{bw} = -\vec{F}_{bs} - \vec{W}_{be}$$
$$= -(-\vec{F}_{sb}) - m\vec{g}$$
$$= 14.0 \text{ N down} - (2.00 \text{ kg})\left(9.79\frac{\text{N}}{\text{kg}} \text{ down}\right)$$
$$= -14.0 \text{ N up} + (2.00 \text{ kg})\left(9.79\frac{\text{N}}{\text{kg}} \text{ up}\right)$$
$$= \boxed{5.6 \text{ N up}}$$

(b) The reading of the pan scale is the sum of the weight of the water and the beaker together, 12.0 N, and the force of the water on the brick, 5.6 N.

$$12.0 \text{ N} + 5.6 \text{ N} = \boxed{17.6 \text{ N}}$$

27. (a) $W = mg = \dfrac{GM_E m}{r^2} = \dfrac{\left(6.673\times10^{-11}\frac{\text{N·m}^2}{\text{kg}^2}\right)(5.975\times10^{24} \text{ kg})(320 \text{ kg})}{(6.371\times10^6 \text{ m} + 16{,}000\times10^3 \text{ m})^2} = \boxed{250 \text{ N}}$

(b) $W = mg = (320 \text{ kg})\left(9.8\dfrac{\text{N}}{\text{kg}}\right) = \boxed{3100 \text{ N}}$

(c) According to Newton's third law, the satellite exerts a force on the Earth equal and opposite to the force the Earth exerts on it, that is, $\boxed{250 \text{ N toward the satellite}}$.

29. (a) $F = \dfrac{GM_EM_M}{r^2} = \dfrac{\left(6.673\times10^{-11} \frac{\text{N·m}^2}{\text{kg}^2}\right)(5.975\times10^{24} \text{ kg})(7.35\times10^{22} \text{ kg})}{(3.85\times10^8 \text{ m})^2} = \boxed{1.98\times10^{20} \text{ N}}$

(b) According to Newton's third law, the magnitude of the gravitational force that the moon exerts on the Earth is $\boxed{\text{the same}}$ as the force that the Earth exerts on the moon.

33. The force required to start the block moving is that needed to overcome static friction. The force required to keep it moving is that needed to overcome kinetic friction. At the instant the block starts to slide, the net force on the block is the difference between the forces required to overcome static and kinetic friction.

$F_{\text{net}} = f_s - f_k = \mu_s mg - \mu_k mg = (\mu_s - \mu_k)mg = (0.40 - 0.15)(5.0 \text{ kg})\left(9.8\dfrac{\text{m}}{\text{s}^2}\right) = \boxed{12 \text{ N}}$

35. (a) To just get the block to move, the force must be equal to the maximum force of static friction.

$F = f_{\text{max}}$
$\quad = \mu_s N$
$\quad = \mu_s mg$
$\mu_s = \dfrac{F}{mg}$
$\quad = \dfrac{12.0 \text{ N}}{(3.0 \text{ kg})\left(9.8\frac{\text{N}}{\text{kg}}\right)}$
$\quad = \boxed{0.41}$

(b) The maximum static frictional force is now proportional to the total mass of the two blocks.

$F = \mu_s mg = 0.41(3.0 \text{ kg} + 7.0 \text{ kg})\left(9.8\dfrac{\text{N}}{\text{kg}}\right) = \boxed{40 \text{ N}}$

37. (a) The force static friction is greater than the applied force, so

$f_s > F$
$\mu_s N > F$
$\mu_s > \dfrac{F}{N}$
$\mu_s > \dfrac{120 \text{ N}}{250 \text{ N}}$
$\boxed{\mu_s > 0.48}$

(b) $\mu_s = \dfrac{F}{N} = \dfrac{150 \text{ N}}{250 \text{ N}} = \boxed{0.60}$

(c) $\mu_k = \dfrac{F}{N} = \dfrac{120 \text{ N}}{250 \text{ N}} = \boxed{0.48}$

39. Let the subscripts be the following:

t = table   e = Earth   1 = block 1
2 = block 2   3 = block 3   4 = block 4
h = horizontal force   1234 = system of blocks
(The blocks are numbered from left to right.)

(a)

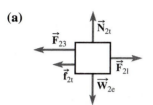

(b)

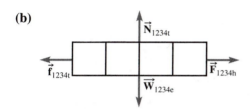

41. The forces acting on the sailboat are:

1) the force of gravity
2) the vertical force of the water opposing gravity and the forces of the water's currents (if any)
3) the force of the wind
4) the force of the line tied to the mooring

43. The tension in the rope is the same along its length. It is equal to the weight at the end of the rope, 120 N. Therefore, scale A reads 120 N.

There are two forces pulling downward on the pulley due to the tension of 120 N in each part of the rope. Therefore,

$T_B = T_A + T_A = 2T_A = 240$ N.

Scale B reads 240 N, since it supports the pulley.

45. Scale B reads 120 N due to the weight attached to it. According to Newton's third law, scale A also reads 120 N, since B is attached directly below it, which is attached to the weight.

49. Let the subscripts be the following:

i = ice   e = Earth   s = stone   o = opponent's stone
Assume the ice is frictionless.

(a) The only forces on the stone are gravity due to the Earth and the normal force due to the ice.

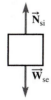

(b)

(c) The additional force is that due to the opponent's stone.

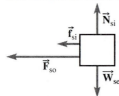

51. (a) The interactions between the magnet and other objects are:

1) The gravitational forces between the magnet and the Earth
2) The contact forces, normal and frictional, between the magnet and the photo
3) The magnetic forces between the magnet and the refrigerator

(b) Let the subscripts be the following:

m = magnet   p = photo   e = Earth   r = refrigerator

The magnet is in static equilibrium, so the horizontal pair of forces and the vertical pair of forces are equal in magnitude and opposite in direction.

(c) The long-range forces are gravity and magnetism. The contact forces are friction and the normal force.

(d) W_{me} and F_{mr} are given.

$$W_{me} = 0.14 \text{ N}$$
$$F_{mr} = 2.10 \text{ N}$$
$$f_{mp} = W_{me} = 0.14 \text{ N}$$
$$N_{mp} = F_{mr} = 2.10 \text{ N}$$

53. (a) The system with the two weights:

Sum the vertical forces on the masses. The masses are in static equilibrium. (The masses are identical.)

The left weight:

$$\sum F_y = T - W = 0$$
$$T = W = 550 \text{ N}$$

The right weight:

$$\sum F_y = T - W = 0$$
$$T = W = 550 \text{ N}$$

So, since the tension is 550 N, the scale reads 550 N.

The system with the single weight:

$$\sum F_y = T - W = 0$$
$$T = W = 550 \text{ N}$$

In both cases the two ropes pull on the scale with forces of 550 N in opposite directions, so the scales give the same reading.

(b) $T = W = \boxed{550 \text{ N}}$

57. (a) The boy must push with a horizontal force equal to the maximum force of static friction on the bottom block due to the floor.

$$F = f_s = \mu_s N = \mu_{\text{lower}} m_{\text{Total}} g = (0.22)(5.0 \text{ kg} + 2.0 \text{ kg})\left(9.8 \frac{\text{N}}{\text{kg}}\right) = \boxed{15 \text{ N}}$$

(b) The limit of the force is the maximum force of static friction on the top block due to the bottom block.

$$F_{\text{max}} = f_{\text{max}} = \mu_{\text{between}} m_{\text{upper}} g = (0.40)(5.0 \text{ kg})\left(9.8 \frac{\text{N}}{\text{kg}}\right) = \boxed{20 \text{ N}}$$

59.

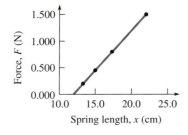

(a) Determine the slope of the line to find k, since $F = kx$.

$$k = \frac{1.20 \text{ N} - 0 \text{ N}}{20.0 \text{ cm} - 12.0 \text{ cm}} = \frac{1.20 \text{ N}}{8.0 \text{ cm}} = \boxed{0.15 \text{ N/cm}}$$

(b) The force on the spring is zero when the spring is relaxed, so from the figure, $x_0 = \boxed{12 \text{ cm}}$.

61. According to Hooke's law, $F_1 = k_1 x_1$ and $F_2 = k_2 x_2$.

Imagine that one spring (1) is suspended from a ceiling and the other (2), attached to the bottom of the first, has a mass m attached to its bottom end. Assume that the masses of the springs are negligible, and that the system is in static equilibrium. The mass connected to the lower spring exerts a force on the lower spring equal to its weight, W. The spring stretches an amount $x_2 = F_2/k_2 = W/k_2$. The lower spring exerts a force on the upper spring equal to $F_2 = W$, and causes it to stretch by $x_1 = F_1/k_1 = F_2/k_1 = W/k_1$. So, $F_1 = F_2$, thus $k_1 x_1 = k_2 x_2$. Let $F_1 = F_2 = F$ and $x = x_1 + x_2$, and imagine the two springs in series as only one spring which stretches an amount x in response to a force F. Find the effective spring constant, k.

$$x = x_1 + x_2 = \frac{F_1}{k_1} + \frac{F_2}{k_2} = \frac{F}{k_1} + \frac{F}{k_2} = F\left(\frac{1}{k_1} + \frac{1}{k_2}\right)$$

So, $F = \left(\dfrac{1}{k_1} + \dfrac{1}{k_2}\right)^{-1} x = \dfrac{k_1 k_2}{k_1 + k_2} x = kx.$

The effective spring constant is $k = \boxed{\dfrac{k_1 k_2}{k_1 + k_2}}$.

65. The Earth exerts a force on the mass, which then exerts a force on the scale, which then exerts a force on the hook, which then exerts a force on the ceiling. All these forces are equal (assuming that the masses of the spring scale and hook are negligible). In addition, each body which has a force exerted on it, exerts an equal and opposite force on the other object. So, the ceiling exerts a force on the hook, the hook on the scale, etc. One person replaces the force on the mass due to the Earth, and the other person replaces the force on the scale due to the hook. So, each person must exert a force of $\boxed{98 \text{ N}}$.

Chapter 3

FORCES AND MOTION ALONG A LINE

Problems

1. When the Porsche catches the Honda, the displacement of the Porsche will be $\Delta r + 186$ m and the displacement for the Honda will be Δr. Δt for both cars will be the same.

$$v_{av} = \frac{\Delta r_{car}}{\Delta t}, \text{ so for the Porsche,}$$

$$v_{av,P} = \frac{\Delta r + 186 \text{ m}}{\Delta t}$$

$$\Delta t v_{av,P} = \Delta r + 186 \text{ m}$$

$$\Delta r = \Delta t v_{av,P} - 186 \text{ m}$$

For the Honda,

$$v_{av,H} = \frac{\Delta r}{\Delta t}$$

$$\Delta r = \Delta t v_{av,H}$$

Equate the two expressions for Δr.

$$\Delta t v_{av,H} = \Delta t v_{av,P} - 186 \text{ m}$$

$$\Delta t (v_{av,H} - v_{av,P}) = -186 \text{ m}$$

$$\Delta t = \frac{186 \text{ m}}{v_{av,P} - v_{av,H}}$$

$$= \frac{186 \text{ m}}{24.4 \frac{m}{s} - 18.6 \frac{m}{s}}$$

$$= \frac{186 \text{ m}}{5.8 \frac{m}{s}}$$

$$= \boxed{32 \text{ s}}$$

3. The displacement of the elevator, Δy, is given by the area under the v_y vs. t curve. From $t = 0$ s to $t = 10$ s, there are 8 squares. From $t = 14$ s to $t = 20$ s, there are 4 squares. Each square represents $(1 \text{ m/s})(2 \text{ s}) = 2$ m. The displacement from t = 14 s to t = 20 s is negative ($v_y < 0$). So, the total displacement is

$\Delta y = 8(2 \text{ m}) + (-4)(2 \text{ m}) = 8$ m, and the elevator is $\boxed{8 \text{ m}}$ above its starting point.

5. The displacement of the car is given by the area under the v_x vs. t curve. Under the curve, there are 16 squares and each square represents $(5 \text{ m/s})(2 \text{ s}) = 10$ m, so the car moves $16(10 \text{ m}) = \boxed{160 \text{ m}}$.

7. (a) $v_{av, x} = \frac{\Delta x}{\Delta t} = \frac{6.0 \text{ m} - 0}{4.0 \text{ s}} = \boxed{1.5 \text{ m/s}}$

   (b) $v_{av, x} = \frac{6.0 \text{ m} - 0}{5.0 \text{ s}} = \boxed{1.2 \text{ m/s}}$

9. Let the positive *x*-direction be to the right.

   (a) $\Delta x = 80 \text{ cm} - 30 \text{ cm} + 90 \text{ cm} - 310 \text{ cm} = -170 \text{ cm}$, so $\Delta \vec{\mathbf{r}} = \boxed{170 \text{ cm to the left}}$.

   (b) The average speed is the distance traveled divided by the time elapsed, so
   $$v_{av} = \frac{\left|80 \text{ cm}\right| + \left|-30 \text{ cm}\right| + \left|90 \text{ cm}\right| + \left|-310 \text{ cm}\right|}{18 \text{ s}} = \boxed{28 \text{ cm/s}}.$$

   (c) $\vec{\mathbf{v}}_{av} = \dfrac{170 \text{ cm to the left}}{18 \text{ s}} = \boxed{9.4 \text{ cm/s to the left}}$

13. Use $v = at$ and solve for *t*.
   $$t = \frac{v}{a} = \frac{22\frac{\text{m}}{\text{s}}}{1.7\frac{\text{m}}{\text{s}^2}} = \boxed{13 \text{ s}}$$

17. The magnitude of the acceleration is the absolute value of the slope of the graph at $t = 7.0$ s.
   $$\left|a_x\right| = \left|\frac{\Delta v_x}{\Delta t}\right| = \left|\frac{0 - 20.0\frac{\text{m}}{\text{s}}}{12.0 \text{ s} - 4.0 \text{ s}}\right| = \boxed{2.5 \text{ m/s}^2}$$

21. Let the direction of motion be +*x*. Let *F* be the magnitude of the force exerted by the locomotive on the caboose. $\sum F_y = 0$, since the vertical component of the acceleration is zero.
   $$\sum F_x = F - f = ma_x$$
   $$F = ma_x + f = (1.0 \text{ kg})\left(3.0\frac{\text{m}}{\text{s}^2}\right) + 0.50 \text{ N} = \boxed{3.5 \text{ N}}$$

23. Use Newton's second law for the vertical direction.
   $$\sum F_y = T - mg = ma_y$$
   Solve for *T*.
   $$T = m(a_y + g) = (2010 \text{ kg})\left(-1.5\frac{\text{m}}{\text{s}^2} + 9.8\frac{\text{m}}{\text{s}^2}\right) = \boxed{17 \text{ kN}}$$

25. (a) The weight of the glider is equal and opposite to the force due to the air, 3.0 kN downward. The force on the Earth due to the glider is equal and opposite to the weight of the glider, $\boxed{3.0 \text{ kN upward}}$.

   (b) The net force is 3.0 kN downward + 2.0 kN upward = 1.0 kN downward. Use Newton's second law and solve for the acceleration.
   $$\vec{\mathbf{a}} = \frac{\vec{\mathbf{F}}}{m} = \frac{\vec{\mathbf{F}}}{\frac{W}{g}} = \frac{\vec{\mathbf{F}}g}{W} = \frac{(1.0 \text{ kN downward})\left(9.8\frac{\text{m}}{\text{s}^2}\right)}{3.0 \text{ kN}} = \boxed{3.3 \text{ m/s}^2 \text{ downward}}$$

29. (a) $\Delta x = v_{0x}t + \dfrac{1}{2}a_x t^2 = (0)t + \dfrac{1}{2}a_x t^2 = \dfrac{1}{2}a_x t^2 = \dfrac{1}{2}\left(1.20\dfrac{\text{m}}{\text{s}^2}\right)(12.0 \text{ s})^2 = \boxed{86.4 \text{ m}}$

(b) $v_x - v_{0x} = a_x \Delta t$

$$v_x - 0 = a_x \Delta t$$

$$v_x = \left(1.20 \frac{\text{m}}{\text{s}^2}\right)(12.0 \text{ s})$$

$$= \boxed{14.4 \text{ m/s}}$$

33. Graphical analysis:

The displacement of the body is given by the area under the v_x vs. t curve between $t = 9.0$ s and

$t = 13.0$ s. The area is a triangle, $A = \frac{1}{2}bh$.

$$\Delta x = \frac{1}{2}(13.0 \text{ s} - 9.0 \text{ s})\left(40 \frac{\text{m}}{\text{s}}\right) = 80 \text{ m}$$

Algebraic solution:

Use the definition of average velocity.

$$\Delta x = v_{\text{av}, x} \Delta t = \frac{v_{0x} + v_x}{2} \Delta t = \frac{40 \frac{\text{m}}{\text{s}} + 0}{2}(13.0 \text{ s} - 9.0 \text{ s}) = 80 \text{ m}$$

The body goes $\boxed{80 \text{ m}}$.

37.
$$\Delta x = v_{\text{av}, x} t$$

$$= \frac{v_{0x} + v_x}{2} t$$

$$= \frac{v_{0x} + (v_{0x} + \Delta v_x)}{2} t$$

$$= \frac{2v_{0x}t}{2} + \frac{1}{2}\Delta v_x t$$

$$= v_{0x}t + \frac{1}{2}(a_x t)t$$

$$\Delta x = x - x_0 = v_{0x}t + \frac{1}{2}a_x t^2$$

41. Find the final speed.

$$v_y^2 - v_{0y}^2 = -2g\Delta y$$

$$v_y^2 - 0 = -2g\Delta y$$

$$v_y = \sqrt{-2g\Delta y}$$

$$= \sqrt{-2\left(9.8 \frac{\text{m}}{\text{s}^2}\right)(0 \text{ m} - 369 \text{ m})}$$

$$= 85 \text{ m/s}$$

So, $\vec{v} = \boxed{85 \text{ m/s down}}$.

45. $v_y{}^2 - v_{0y}{}^2 = -2g\Delta y$

$$v_y{}^2 = v_{0y}{}^2 - 2g\Delta y$$

$$v_y = \sqrt{v_{0y}{}^2 - 2g\Delta y}$$

$$= \sqrt{\left(10.0\frac{m}{s}\right)^2 - 2\left(9.80\frac{m}{s^2}\right)(-40.8\ m)}$$

$$= \boxed{30.0\ m/s}$$

49. (a) $\dfrac{v_t v}{g}$ has dimensions of meters.

For $v \approx v_t$,

$$\frac{v_t v}{g} = \frac{v_t{}^2}{g} = \frac{\left(7\frac{m}{s}\right)^2}{9.8\frac{m}{s^2}} = \boxed{5\ m}.$$

(b)

$$\frac{\left(100\frac{m}{s}\right)^2}{9.8\frac{m}{s^2}} = \boxed{1\ km}$$

51. (a) At terminal velocity, the drag force is equal in magnitude and opposite in direction to the weight, so

$$\vec{F}_d = \boxed{72\ N\ up}.$$

(b) $F_d \propto v^2$

Form a proportion.

$$\frac{F_{d75}}{F_{dt}} = \frac{(0.75v_t)^2}{v_t{}^2} = 0.75^2$$

So, $\vec{F}_{d75} = 0.75^2(72\ N\ up) = \boxed{41\ N\ up}$.

(c) At terminal velocity, the velocity is constant, so $\vec{a} = \boxed{0}$.

(d) Use Newton's second law. Up is the positive direction.

$$\Sigma F_y = F_d - W = ma_y = \frac{W}{g}a_y$$

Solve for a_y.

$$a_y = \frac{F_d - W}{\frac{W}{g}} = \left(\frac{F_d}{W} - 1\right)g = \left(\frac{40.5\ N}{72\ N} - 1\right)\left(9.8\frac{m}{s^2}\right) = -4.3\ m/s^2$$

So, $\vec{a} = \boxed{4.3\ m/s^2\ down}$.

53. (a) The elevator is accelerating downward, so $a_y = -0.50\ m/s^2$.

$$W' = \frac{W}{g}(g + a_y) = W\left(1 + \frac{a_y}{g}\right) = (598\ N)\left(1 + \frac{-0.50\frac{m}{s^2}}{9.80\frac{m}{s^2}}\right) = \boxed{567\ N}$$

(b) The elevator is accelerating upward, so $a_y = 0.50 \text{ m/s}^2$.

$$W' = \frac{W}{g}(g + a_y) = W\left(1 + \frac{a_y}{g}\right) = (598 \text{ N})\left(1 + \frac{0.50\frac{\text{m}}{\text{s}^2}}{9.80\frac{\text{m}}{\text{s}^2}}\right) = \boxed{629 \text{ N}}$$

55. Up is the positive direction.

$$W' = W\left(1 + \frac{a_y}{g}\right)$$

$$W = \frac{W'}{1 + \frac{a_y}{g}}$$

$$= \frac{750 \text{ N}}{1 + \frac{2.0\frac{\text{m}}{\text{s}^2}}{9.8\frac{\text{m}}{\text{s}^2}}}$$

$$= \boxed{620 \text{ N}}$$

57. Calculate the time it takes for an electron to travel a distance x_d.

$$x_d = v_d t$$

$$t = \frac{x_d}{v_d}$$

Find the distance traveled.

$$\text{total distance} = vt = v\frac{x_d}{v_d} = \frac{\left(10^6\frac{\text{m}}{\text{s}}\right)(1 \text{ m})}{\left(10\frac{\text{cm}}{\text{h}}\right)\left(\frac{1 \text{ m}}{100 \text{ cm}}\right)\left(\frac{1 \text{ h}}{3600 \text{ s}}\right)} = \boxed{4 \times 10^{10} \text{ m}}$$

61. Each car has traveled the same distance, x, in the same time, t, when they meet.

$$x = \frac{1}{2}at^2 = v_0 t, \text{ so } t = \frac{2v_0}{a}.$$

The speed of the police car is

$$v = at = a\left(\frac{2v_0}{a}\right) = \boxed{2v_0}.$$

65. (a) $v_y{}^2 - v_{0y}{}^2 = -2g\Delta y$

$$v_y{}^2 - 0 = -2g\Delta y$$

$$-\Delta y = \frac{v_y{}^2}{2g}$$

$$h = \frac{\left(30.0\frac{\text{m}}{\text{s}}\right)^2}{2\left(9.8\frac{\text{m}}{\text{s}^2}\right)}$$

$$= \boxed{46 \text{ m}}$$

(b) $\vec{a} = \frac{\Delta\vec{v}}{\Delta t} = \frac{0 - \left(30.0\frac{\text{m}}{\text{s}} \text{ down}\right)}{1.00 \text{ s}} = \boxed{30.0 \text{ m/s}^2 \text{ up}}$

69. The positive y-direction is up.

$$W' = m(g + a_y)$$

$$W' = mg + ma_y$$

$$a_y = \frac{W' - mg}{m}$$

$$= \frac{W'}{m} - g$$

$$= \frac{408 \text{ N}}{51 \text{ kg}} - 9.8 \frac{\text{m}}{\text{s}^2}$$

$$= -1.8 \text{ m/s}^2$$

So, $\vec{\mathbf{a}} = \boxed{1.8 \text{ m/s}^2 \text{ down}}$.

73. Find v_{x1}.

$$v_{x1} = a_{x1}t_1 = \left(1.0 \frac{\text{m}}{\text{s}^2}\right)(10.0 \text{ s}) = 1.0 \times 10^1 \text{ m/s}$$

Find Δx_1, Δx_3, and t_3.

$$\Delta x_1 = \frac{1}{2}a_{x1}t_1^2 = \frac{1}{2}\left(1.0 \frac{\text{m}}{\text{s}^2}\right)(10.0 \text{ s})^2 = 5.0 \times 10^1 \text{ m}$$

$$\Delta x_3 = \frac{v_{x3}^2 - v_{0x3}^2}{2a_3} = \frac{0 - v_{x1}^2}{2a_3} = \frac{-\left(1.0 \times 10^1 \frac{\text{m}}{\text{s}}\right)^2}{2\left(-2.0 \frac{\text{m}}{\text{s}^2}\right)} = 25 \text{ m}$$

$$\Delta x_3 = v_{0x3}t_3 + \frac{1}{2}a_3t_3^2$$

$$= v_{x1}t_3 + \frac{1}{2}a_3t_3^2$$

$$0 = \frac{1}{2}a_3t_3^2 + v_{x1}t_3 - \Delta x_3$$

$$= \frac{1}{2}\left(-2.0 \frac{\text{m}}{\text{s}^2}\right)t_3^2 + \left(1.0 \times 10^1 \frac{\text{m}}{\text{s}}\right)t_3 - 25 \text{ m}$$

$$= \left(1.0 \frac{\text{m}}{\text{s}^2}\right)t_3^2 - \left(1.0 \times 10^1 \frac{\text{m}}{\text{s}}\right)t_3 + 25 \text{ m}$$

Solve for t_3 using the quadratic formula.

$$t_3 = \frac{1.0 \times 10^1 \frac{\text{m}}{\text{s}} \pm \sqrt{\left(1.0 \times 10^1 \frac{\text{m}}{\text{s}}\right)^2 - 4\left(1.0 \frac{\text{m}}{\text{s}^2}\right)(25 \text{ m})}}{2\left(1.0 \frac{\text{m}}{\text{s}^2}\right)} = 5.0 \text{ s}$$

Find Δx_2.

$$\Delta x_2 = v_{x2}t_2$$

$$= v_{x1}t_2$$

$$t_2 = \frac{\Delta x_2}{v_{x1}}$$

Find the total time.

$$t = t_1 + t_2 + t_3 = t_1 + \frac{\Delta x_2}{v_{x1}} + t_3 = 10.0 \text{ s} + \frac{0.60 \times 10^3 \text{ m} - 5.0 \times 10^1 \text{ m} - 25 \text{ m}}{1.0 \times 10^1 \frac{\text{m}}{\text{s}}} + 5.0 \text{ s} = \boxed{68 \text{ s}}$$

77. **(a)** Since the downward speed is decreasing at a rate of $0.10g$, the acceleration of the truck is $0.10g$ upwards. Use Newton's second law.

$$\Sigma F_x = 0$$
$$\Sigma F_y = T - mg = ma_y = m(0.10g)$$

So, $T = \boxed{1.10mg}$.

(b) Although the motion of the helicopter has changed, the dynamics of the truck are the same as in part (a), so the tension is the same, $\boxed{1.10mg}$.

81. $v_{1x}^2 - v_{10x}^2 = 2a_1d_1$, where $a_1 = 10.0 \text{ ft/s}^2$ and d_1 is the distance to the point of no return. $v_{2x}^2 - v_{20x}^2 = 2a_2d_2$, where $a_2 = -7.00 \text{ ft/s}^2$ and d_2 is the distance from the point of no return to the end of the runway.

The initial speed v_{10x} and the final speed v_{2x} are zero. The speed at the point of no return is $v_{1x} = v_{20x}$. Let $v_{1x} = v_{20x} = v$ for simplicity. Also, $d = d_1 + d_2$ is the length of the runway. So, we have

$v^2 = 2a_1d_1$ and $-v^2 = 2a_2d_2 = 2a_2(d - d_1)$.

Eliminate v^2.

$$2a_1d_1 = 2a_2(d_1 - d)$$
$$a_1d_1 = a_2d_1 - a_2d$$
$$(a_1 - a_2)d_1 = -a_2d$$
$$d_1 = \frac{a_2}{a_2 - a_1}d$$
$$= \frac{-7.00\frac{\text{ft}}{\text{s}^2}}{-7.00\frac{\text{ft}}{\text{s}^2} - 10.0\frac{\text{ft}}{\text{s}^2}}(1.50 \text{ mi})\left(\frac{5280 \text{ ft}}{1 \text{ mi}}\right)$$
$$= \boxed{3260 \text{ ft}}$$

Find the time to d_1.

$$d_1 = \frac{1}{2}a_1t^2$$
$$t^2 = \frac{2d_1}{a_1}$$
$$t = \sqrt{\frac{2d_1}{a_1}}$$
$$= \sqrt{\frac{2(3260 \text{ ft})}{10.0\frac{\text{ft}}{\text{s}^2}}}$$
$$= \boxed{25.5 \text{ s}}$$

Chapter 4

FORCES AND MOTION IN TWO DIMENSIONS

Problems

1. (a)

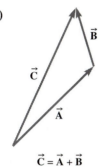

$$\vec{C} = \vec{A} + \vec{B}$$

$$\vec{D} = \vec{A} - \vec{B} = \vec{A} + (-\vec{B})$$

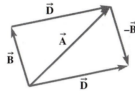

(b)

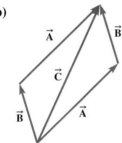

$$\vec{C} = \vec{A} + \vec{B} = \vec{B} + \vec{A}$$

5. x-comp = (20.0 m) cos (90.0° + 60.0°) = $\boxed{-17.3 \text{ m}}$

   y-comp = (20.0 m) sin (90.0° + 60.0°) = $\boxed{10.0 \text{ m}}$

7. (a) Find the magnitude.

   $$\left| \mathbf{A} + \mathbf{B} \right| = \sqrt{[(A+B)_x]^2 + [(A+B)_y]^2} = \sqrt{(-1.0)^2 + \left(\sqrt{3.0}\right)^2} = 2.0 \text{ units}$$

   Find the direction.

   $$\theta = \tan^{-1} \frac{\sqrt{3.0}}{-1.0} = 30° \text{ CCW from the } +y\text{-axis}$$

   So, $\vec{A} + \vec{B} = \boxed{2.0 \text{ units at } 30° \text{ CCW from the } +y\text{-axis}}$.

   (b) Find the magnitude.

   $$\left| \vec{A} + \vec{B} \right| = \sqrt{[(A+B)_x]^2 + [(A+B)_y]^2} = \sqrt{(-1.0)^2 + \left(-\sqrt{3.0}\right)^2} = 2.0 \text{ units}$$

   Find the direction.

   $$\theta = \tan^{-1} \frac{-\sqrt{3.0}}{-1.0} = 30° \text{ CW from the } +y\text{-axis}$$

   So, $\vec{A} + \vec{B} = \boxed{2.0 \text{ units at } 30° \text{ CW from the } +y\text{-axis}}$.

(c) $x\text{-comp} = B_x = \boxed{-1.0 \text{ unit}}$

$\quad y\text{-comp} = -A_y = \boxed{-\sqrt{3.0} \text{ units}}$

9. Let the $+x$-direction be up the incline. Use Newton's second law.
$$\sum F_y = 0$$
$$\sum F_x = F - W\sin\theta = 0, \text{ since the speed is constant } (a = 0).$$
$$F = W\sin\theta$$
$$= mg\sin\left(\tan^{-1}\frac{\Delta y}{\Delta x}\right)$$
$$= (400.0 \text{ kg})\left(9.8\frac{\text{m}}{\text{s}^2}\right)\sin\left(\tan^{-1}\frac{3.0 \text{ m}}{100.0 \text{ m}}\right)$$
$$= \boxed{120 \text{ N}}$$

13. Let east be the $+x$-direction and north be the $+y$-direction.
$$\Delta r_{1x} = 1.2 \text{ km}$$
$$\Delta r_{1y} = 0$$
$$\Delta r_{2x} = (2.7 \text{ km})\cos 135° = -1.9 \text{ km}$$
$$\Delta r_{2y} = (2.7 \text{ km})\sin 135° = 1.9 \text{ km}$$
$$\Delta r_x = \Delta r_{1x} + \Delta r_{2x} = 1.2 \text{ km} - 1.9 \text{ km} = -0.7 \text{ km}$$
$$\Delta r_y = \Delta r_{1y} + \Delta r_{2y} = 1.9 \text{ km}$$
$$|\Delta \vec{r}| = \sqrt{(\Delta r_x)^2 + (\Delta r_y)^2} = \sqrt{(-0.7 \text{ km})^2 + (1.9 \text{ km})^2} = 2.0 \text{ km}$$

The direction of the return trip is opposite the displacement vector found.
$\Delta r_x' = 0.7 \text{ km}$ and $\Delta r_y' = -1.9 \text{ km}$.
$$\theta = \tan^{-1}\frac{-1.9}{0.7} = 70° \text{ south of east}$$

So, they must travel $\boxed{2.0 \text{ km, at } 70° \text{ south of east}}$.

17. Without a machine, the force is equal to the weight of the object W. According to Newton's second law and Figure 4.14, with a frictionless plane, the force is equal to $W\sin\phi = W\dfrac{h}{d}$. So,
$$\frac{W}{W\frac{h}{d}} = \frac{d}{h}.$$

21. Let the $+y$-direction be up and the $+x$-direction be to the right.

(a) Use Newton's second law.
$$\sum F_x = F - T\cos\theta = 0, \text{ so } F = T\cos\theta.$$
$$\sum F_y = T\sin\theta - mg = 0, \text{ so}$$
$$T\sin\theta = mg$$
$$T = \frac{mg}{\sin\theta}$$

Thus, $F = \dfrac{mg}{\sin\theta}\cos\theta = \dfrac{mg}{\tan\theta} = \dfrac{(2.0 \text{ kg})\left(9.8\frac{\text{m}}{\text{s}^2}\right)}{\tan 30.0°} = \boxed{34 \text{ N}}$.

(b) $T = \dfrac{(2.0 \text{ kg})\left(9.8\,\frac{\text{m}}{\text{s}^2}\right)}{\sin 30.0°} = \boxed{39 \text{ N}}$

25. Let the +x-direction be up the incline and the +y-direction by perpendicular to and away from the top surface of the ramp.

   (a) Use Newton's second law.
   $\sum F_y = N - W\cos\theta = 0$, so
   $N = W\cos\theta = (80.0 \text{ N})\cos 20.0° = \boxed{75.2 \text{ N}}$.

   (b) Use Newton's second law.
   $\sum F_x = f_s - W\sin\theta = 0$
   $f_s = W\sin\theta = (80.0 \text{ N})\sin 20.0° = \boxed{27.4 \text{ N}}$

   (c) $f = \mu_{s,\,min} N = W\sin\theta$
   $\mu_{s,\,min} = \dfrac{W\sin\theta}{N} = \dfrac{W\sin\theta}{W\cos\theta} = \tan\theta = \tan 20.0° = \boxed{0.364}$

   (d) Find the magnitude.
   $F = \sqrt{f^2 + N^2} = \sqrt{(27.4 \text{ N})^2 + (75.2 \text{ N})^2} = 80.0 \text{ N}$
   Find the direction.
   $\theta = \tan^{-1}\dfrac{N}{f} = \tan^{-1}\dfrac{W\cos\theta}{W\sin\theta} = \tan^{-1}\dfrac{1}{\tan 20.0°} = 70.0°$ or upward
   So, $\vec{F} = \boxed{80.0 \text{ N upward}}$.
   The answer is the same as that found for Practice Problem 2.6.

29. $\vec{v}_{av} = \dfrac{\Delta \vec{r}}{\Delta t}$

   Find $\Delta\vec{r}$. Let east be in the +x-direction and north be in the +y-direction.
   $|\Delta\vec{r}| = \sqrt{(3.2 \text{ km} + 3.2 \text{ km})^2 + (4.8 \text{ km})^2} = 8.0 \text{ km}$
   $\theta = \tan^{-1}\dfrac{4.8 \text{ km}}{6.4 \text{ km}} = 37°$ north of east
   So, $|\vec{v}_{av}| = \dfrac{\Delta r}{\Delta t} = \dfrac{8.0 \text{ km}}{0.10 \text{ h} + 0.15 \text{ h} + 0.10 \text{ h}} = 23 \text{ km/h}$ and $\vec{v}_{av} = \boxed{23 \text{ km/h at } 37° \text{ north of east}}$.

31. **(a)** $\vec{v}_{av} = \dfrac{\Delta\vec{r}}{\Delta t}$

   Let the center of the circle be the origin, then $\Delta\vec{r} = \vec{r}_f - \vec{r}_0 = 20.0$ m east $- 20.0$ m south.
   $|\Delta\vec{r}| = \sqrt{(20.0 \text{ m})^2 + (-20.0 \text{ m})^2} = 28.3 \text{ m}$
   Let east be the +x-direction and north the +y-direction.
   $\theta = \tan^{-1}\dfrac{20.0}{20.0} = 45.0°$ north of east
   So, $|\vec{v}_{av}| = \dfrac{\Delta r}{\Delta t} = \dfrac{28.3 \text{ m}}{3.0 \text{ s}} = 9.4 \text{ m/s}$ and $\vec{v}_{av} = \boxed{9.4 \text{ m/s at } 45° \text{ north of east}}$.

(b) $\vec{\mathbf{a}}_{av} = \dfrac{\Delta\vec{\mathbf{v}}}{\Delta t} = \dfrac{\vec{\mathbf{v}}_f - \vec{\mathbf{v}}_0}{\Delta t}$

$|\vec{\mathbf{v}}_f| = |\vec{\mathbf{v}}_0| = \dfrac{2\pi r\left(\frac{3}{4}\right)}{\Delta t} = \dfrac{3\pi r}{2\Delta t}$

So, $\vec{\mathbf{a}}_{av} = \dfrac{3\pi r}{2(\Delta t)^2}$ (south − west).

$|\vec{\mathbf{a}}_{av}| = \dfrac{3\pi r}{2(\Delta t)^2}\sqrt{1^2 + 1^2} = \dfrac{3\pi r}{\sqrt{2}(\Delta t)^2}$

$\theta = \tan^{-1}\dfrac{-1}{1} = 45°$ south of east, thus

$\vec{\mathbf{a}}_{av} = \dfrac{3\pi(20.0 \text{ m})}{\sqrt{2}(3.0 \text{ s})^2}$ at 45° south of east = $\boxed{15 \text{ m/s}^2 \text{ at } 45° \text{ south of east}}$

(c) Although the magnitude of the velocity is constant, its direction must change continuously for the car to travel in a circle; $\boxed{\text{changing the direction of the velocity requires an acceleration}}$.

33. (a)

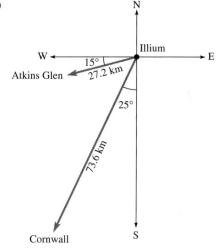

Atkins Glen   15°   27.2 km   Illium

25°

73.6 km

Cornwall

(b) $\Delta\vec{\mathbf{r}} = \vec{\mathbf{r}}_f - \vec{\mathbf{r}}_0$

$\Delta x = x_f - x_0 = r_f\cos\theta_f - r_0\cos\theta_0$

$\Delta y = y_f - y_0 = r_f\sin\theta_f - r_0\sin\theta_0$

Find the magnitude of the displacement.

$\begin{aligned}|\Delta\vec{\mathbf{r}}| &= \sqrt{(\Delta x)^2 + (\Delta y)^2}\\ &= \sqrt{[(27.2 \text{ km})\cos 195° - (73.6 \text{ km})\cos 245°]^2 + [(27.2 \text{ km})\sin 195° - (73.6 \text{ km})\sin 245°]^2}\\ &= 59.9 \text{ km}\end{aligned}$

Find the direction of the displacement.

$\theta = \tan^{-1}\dfrac{(27.2 \text{ km})\sin 195° - (73.6 \text{ km})\sin 245°}{(27.2 \text{ km})\cos 195° - (73.6 \text{ km})\cos 245°} = 85°$ north of east

So, $\Delta\vec{\mathbf{r}} = \boxed{59.9 \text{ km at } 85° \text{ north of east}}$.

(c) $\vec{\mathbf{v}}_{av} = \dfrac{\Delta\vec{\mathbf{r}}}{\Delta t} = \dfrac{59.9 \text{ km at } 85° \text{ north of east}}{(45 \text{ min})\left(\frac{1 \text{ h}}{60 \text{ min}}\right)} = \boxed{80 \text{ km/h at } 85° \text{ north of east}}$

37. (a) $\Delta y = (v_0 \sin \theta)t - \dfrac{1}{2}gt^2$

$x = (v_0 \cos \theta)t$

When a projectile returns to its original height, $\Delta y = 0$.

$$0 = (v_0 \sin \theta)t - \frac{1}{2}gt^2$$

$$0 = v_0 \sin \theta - \frac{1}{2}gt$$

$$\frac{1}{2}gt = v_0 \sin \theta$$

$$t = \frac{2v_0 \sin \theta}{g}$$

Substitute this value for t into $R = x = (v_0 \cos \theta)t$.

$$R = (v_0 \cos \theta)t$$

$$R = v_0 \cos \theta \left(\frac{2v_0 \sin \theta}{g} \right)$$

$$\boxed{R = \frac{2v_0^2 \sin \theta \cos \theta}{g}}$$

(b) $R = \dfrac{2\left(50.0\frac{m}{s}\right)^2 \sin 30.0° \cos 30.0°}{9.80\frac{m}{s^2}} = \boxed{221 \text{ m}}$

(c) Find the time of flight in terms of v_0, x, and θ.

$$x = (v_0 \cos \theta)t$$

$$t = \frac{x}{v_0 \cos \theta}$$

Find the height at which the cannonball strikes.

$$y = y_0 + (v_0 \sin \theta)t - \frac{1}{2}gt^2$$

$$= y_0 + v_0 \sin \theta \left(\frac{x}{v_0 \cos \theta} \right) - \frac{1}{2}g\left(\frac{x}{v_0 \cos \theta} \right)^2$$

$$= y_0 + x \tan \theta - \frac{gx^2}{2v_0^2 \cos^2 \theta}$$

$$= 1.10 \text{ m} + (215 \text{ m})\tan 30.0° - \frac{\left(9.80\frac{m}{s^2}\right)(215 \text{ m})^2}{2\left(50.0\frac{m}{s}\right)^2 \cos^2 30.0°}$$

$$= \boxed{4 \text{ m}}$$

41. (a) $\Delta y = v_{0y}t - \dfrac{1}{2}gt^2$

$\qquad\qquad = (0)t - \dfrac{1}{2}gt^2$

$\qquad\qquad = -\dfrac{1}{2}gt^2$

$\qquad t^2 = -\dfrac{2\Delta y}{g}$

$\qquad t = \sqrt{-\dfrac{2\Delta y}{g}}$

$\qquad\quad = \sqrt{-\dfrac{2(0 - 20.0 \text{ m})}{9.8\frac{\text{m}}{\text{s}^2}}}$

$\qquad\quad = \boxed{2.0 \text{ s}}$

(b) It would still take $\boxed{2.0 \text{ s}}$, since $v_y = 0$ for both cases.

(c) $\Delta y = (v_0 \sin\theta)t - \dfrac{1}{2}gt^2$

$\qquad 0 = \dfrac{1}{2}gt^2 - (v_0 \sin\theta)t + \Delta y$

$\qquad\quad = \left(4.9\dfrac{\text{m}}{\text{s}^2}\right)t^2 - \left(20.0\dfrac{\text{m}}{\text{s}}\right)\sin(-18°)t - 20.0 \text{ m}$

Solve for t using the quadratic formula.

$$t = \dfrac{\left(20.0\frac{\text{m}}{\text{s}}\right)\sin(-18°) \pm \sqrt{\left(20.0\frac{\text{m}}{\text{s}}\right)^2 \sin^2(-18°) - 4\left(4.9\frac{\text{m}}{\text{s}^2}\right)(-20.0 \text{ m})}}{2\left(4.9\frac{\text{m}}{\text{s}^2}\right)}$$

$\qquad = 1.5 \text{ s or } -2.7 \text{ s}$

$t > 0$, so $t = \boxed{1.5 \text{ s}}$.

45. (a) x increases linearly.

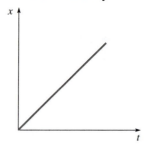

y is parabolic.

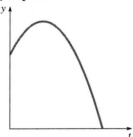

v_x is constant.

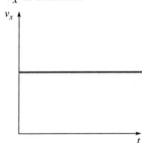

v_y starts positive and decreases linearly.

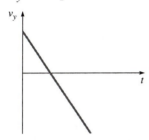

(b) Find v_0 in terms of x, t, and θ.

$$x = (v_0 \cos \theta)t$$

$$v_0 = \frac{x}{t \cos \theta}$$

$$= \frac{105 \text{ m}}{(4.20 \text{ s}) \cos 25.0°}$$

$$= 27.6 \text{ m/s}$$

So, the initial velocity is $\boxed{27.6 \text{ m/s at } 25.0° \text{ above the horizontal}}$.

(c) Find h using the result for v_0 found in part (a).

$$\Delta y = (v_0 \sin \theta)t - \frac{1}{2}gt^2$$

$$= \left(\frac{x}{t \cos \theta} \sin \theta \right)t - \frac{1}{2}gt^2$$

$$= x \tan \theta - \frac{1}{2}gt^2$$

$$= (105 \text{ m}) \tan 25.0° - \frac{1}{2}\left(9.8 \frac{\text{m}}{\text{s}^2} \right)(4.20 \text{ s})^2$$

$$= -37 \text{ m}$$

So, $h = \boxed{37 \text{ m}}$.

(d) Set $v_y = 0$ to find the time when the stone reaches its maximum height.

$$v_y = v_0 \sin\theta - gt = 0, \text{ so } t = \frac{v_0 \sin\theta}{g}.$$

Find H.

$$H = h + (v_0 \sin\theta)t - \frac{1}{2}gt^2$$

$$= h + v_0 \sin\theta\left(\frac{v_0 \sin\theta}{g}\right) - \frac{1}{2}g\left(\frac{v_0 \sin\theta}{g}\right)^2$$

$$= h + \frac{v_0^2 \sin^2\theta}{g} - \frac{v_0^2 \sin^2\theta}{2g}$$

$$= h + \frac{v_0^2 \sin^2\theta}{2g}$$

$$= 37 \text{ m} + \frac{\left(27.6\frac{m}{s}\right)^2 \sin^2 25.0°}{2\left(9.8\frac{m}{s^2}\right)}$$

$$= \boxed{44 \text{ m above the ground}}$$

49. Let north be in the +*y*-direction and east be in the +*x*-direction.

$v_x = 60 \text{ m/s}$

$v_y = a_y t$

Use the Pythagorean theorem.

$$v^2 = v_x^2 + v_y^2$$

$$v_y^2 = v^2 - v_x^2$$

$$v_y = \sqrt{v^2 - v_x^2}$$

$$a_y t = \sqrt{v^2 - v_x^2}$$

$$t = \frac{\sqrt{v^2 - v_x^2}}{a_y}$$

$$= \frac{\sqrt{\left(100\frac{m}{s}\right)^2 - \left(60\frac{m}{s}\right)^2}}{100\frac{m}{s^2}}$$

$$= \boxed{0.8 \text{ s}}$$

51. Let the +*x*-direction be up the incline. Use Newton's second law.

$$\Sigma F_x = -mg\sin\theta = ma_x$$

(a) $F_{net} = -mg\sin\theta = -(10.0 \text{ kg})\left(9.8\frac{m}{s^2}\right)\sin 45° = -69 \text{ N}$

So, $\vec{F}_{net} = \boxed{69 \text{ N directed down the incline}}$.

(b) $ma_x = -mg \sin\theta$

$a_x = -g \sin\theta$

$= -\left(9.8\frac{m}{s^2}\right)\sin 45°$

$= -6.9 \ m/s^2$

So, $\bar{a} = \boxed{6.9 \ m/s^2 \text{ directed down the incline}}$.

(c) $v = at$, so $t = \dfrac{v}{a} = \dfrac{10.0\frac{m}{s}}{6.9\frac{m}{s^2}} = \boxed{1.4 \ s}$.

53. Let the +x-direction be up the incline. Use Newton's second law.

(a) $\sum F_x = F' - mg \sin\theta = 0$

$F' = mg \sin\theta$

The angle between F' and the horizontal force F is θ, so $F' = F \cos\theta$.

$F \cos\theta = mg \sin\theta$

$F = \boxed{mg \tan\theta}$

(b) To roll the crate up at constant speed, the net force is zero, so the force is that from part (a), $\boxed{mg \tan\theta}$.

(c) $\sum F_x = F \cos\theta - mg \sin\theta = ma$

$F \cos\theta = mg \sin\theta + ma$

$F = \boxed{mg \tan\theta + \dfrac{ma}{\cos\theta}}$

57. Let the +x-direction be up the incline for the crate (1), and the +y-direction away from the surface of the incline. For the box (2), let the +y-direction be up. Use Newton's second law.

(a) Crate:

$\sum F_x = T + f_k - m_1 g \sin\theta = m_1 a_x$

$\sum F_y = N - m_1 g \cos\theta = 0$

Box:

$\sum F_x = 0$

$\sum F_y = T - m_2 g = m_2 a_y$

The way the problem is set up, $a_x = -a_y$.

Solve for a_x.

$m_1 a_x = T + \mu_k N - m_1 g \sin\theta$

$= T + \mu_k m_1 g \cos\theta - m_1 g \sin\theta$

$a_x = \dfrac{T}{m_1} + \mu_k g \cos\theta - g \sin\theta$

$= -a_y$

Solve for a_y.

$m_2 a_y = T - m_2 g$

$a_y = \dfrac{T}{m_2} - g$

Eliminate a_x and a_y and solve for T.

$$\frac{T}{m_1} + \mu_k g \cos\theta - g \sin\theta = g - \frac{T}{m_2}$$

$$T\left(\frac{1}{m_1} + \frac{1}{m_2}\right) = g(1 + \sin\theta - \mu_k \cos\theta)$$

$$T = \frac{m_1 m_2 g}{m_1 + m_2}(1 + \sin\theta - \mu_k \cos\theta)$$

$$= \frac{(15 \text{ kg})(8.0 \text{ kg})\left(9.8\frac{\text{m}}{\text{s}^2}\right)}{15 \text{ kg} + 8.0 \text{ kg}}(1 + \sin 60.0° - 0.30\cos 60.0°)$$

$$= \boxed{88 \text{ N}}$$

(b) $a_x = -a_y = g - \dfrac{T}{m_2}$

The crate begins at rest, so $v_0 = 0$.

$$\Delta x = -\frac{1}{2}a_x t^2$$

$$t^2 = -\frac{2\Delta x}{a_x}$$

$$t = \sqrt{-\frac{2\Delta x}{a_x}}$$

$$= \sqrt{-\frac{2\Delta x}{g - \dfrac{T}{m_2}}}$$

$$= \sqrt{-\frac{2(-2.00 \text{ m})}{9.8\frac{\text{m}}{\text{s}^2} - \dfrac{88 \text{ N}}{8.0 \text{ kg}}}}$$

$$= \boxed{2 \text{ s}}$$

(c) Crate:

$$\Sigma F_x = T + P - f_k - m_1 g \sin\theta = 0$$

$$P = f_k + m_1 g \sin\theta - T$$

Box:

$$\Sigma F_y = T - m_2 g = 0$$

$$T = m_2 g$$

Substitute for T and f_k.

$$P = f_k + m_1 g \sin\theta - T$$

$$= \mu_k m_1 g \cos\theta + m_1 g \sin\theta - m_2 g$$

$$= g[m_1(\mu_k \cos\theta + \sin\theta) - m_2]$$

$$= \left(9.8\frac{\text{m}}{\text{s}^2}\right)[(15 \text{ kg})(0.30\cos 60.0° + \sin 60.0°) - 8.0 \text{ kg}]$$

$$= \boxed{70 \text{ N}}$$

(d) Crate:

$$\Sigma F_x = T + f_s - m_1 g \sin\theta = 0$$
$$\Sigma F_y = N - m_1 g \cos\theta = 0$$

Box:

$$\Sigma F_x = 0$$
$$\Sigma F_y = T - m_2 g = 0$$

So, $m_2 = \dfrac{T}{g}$.

Find T.

$$T = m_1 g \sin\theta - f_s = m_1 g \sin\theta - \mu_s m_1 g \cos\theta$$

Thus, $m_2 = m_1 \sin\theta - \mu_s m_1 \cos\theta = m_1(\sin\theta - \mu_s \cos\theta) = (15 \text{ kg})(\sin 60.0° - 0.40 \cos 60.0°) = \boxed{10 \text{ kg}}$

59. Let north be in the $+x$-direction.

v_{JRx} = the velocity of the Jeep relative to the road = 82 km/h

v_{RFx} = the velocity of the road relative to the Ford = $-v_{FRx}$ = 48 km/h

v_{JFx} = the velocity of the Jeep relative to the (observer in the) Ford

$$= v_{JRx} + v_{RFx}$$

$$= 82\frac{\text{km}}{\text{h}} + 48\frac{\text{km}}{\text{h}}$$

$$= 130 \text{ km/h}$$

So, $\vec{v}_{JFx} = \boxed{130 \text{ km/h north}}$.

61. The relative speeds are:

$$v_{upstream} = v_{ship} - v_{water} = v_{up} = v_s - v_w$$

$$v_{downstream} = v_{ship} + v_{water} = v_d = v_s + v_w$$

Find the speed of the current, v_w.

$$x = v_{up} t_{up} = (v_s - v_w)t_{up}, \text{ so } \frac{x}{t_{up}} = v_s - v_w. \quad (1)$$

$$x = v_d t_d = (v_s + v_w)t_d, \text{ so } \frac{x}{t_d} = v_s + v_w. \quad (2)$$

Subtract (1) from (2).

$$\frac{x}{t_d} - \frac{x}{t_{up}} = 2v_w$$

$$v_w = \frac{x}{2}\left(\frac{1}{t_d} - \frac{1}{t_{up}}\right)$$

$$= \frac{208 \text{ km}}{2}\left(\frac{1}{19.2 \text{ h}} - \frac{1}{20.8 \text{ h}}\right)$$

$$= \boxed{0.42 \text{ km/h}}$$

65. (a) The east-west components of the airplane's and the wind's velocities must be equal in magnitude for the plane to travel north.
Let the +y-direction be north and the +x-direction be east.

$$v_{px} = v_{air,\,x}$$

$$v_p \cos\theta = v_{air} \cos\frac{\pi}{4}$$

$$\cos\theta = \frac{v_{air}}{v_p\sqrt{2}}$$

$$\theta = \cos^{-1}\frac{v_{air}}{v_p\sqrt{2}}$$

$$= \cos^{-1}\frac{100.0\frac{km}{h}}{\left(300.0\frac{km}{h}\right)\sqrt{2}}$$

$$= \boxed{76.37°\ \text{N of E}}$$

(b) The northern or y-component of the plane's velocity relative to the ground is the y-component of its velocity relative to the air minus the y-component of the air's velocity relative to the ground.

$$t = \frac{y}{v_y} = \frac{y}{v_p\sin\theta - v_{air}\sin\frac{\pi}{4}} = \frac{600.0\ \text{km}}{\left(300.0\frac{km}{h}\right)\sin\left[\cos^{-1}\frac{100.0\frac{km}{h}}{300.0\frac{km}{h}\sqrt{2}}\right] - \left(100.0\frac{km}{h}\right)\sin\frac{\pi}{4}} = \boxed{2.717\ \text{h}}$$

69. Let the +x-direction be west and the +y-direction be north.
d = dolphin   b = bay   w = water
$\vec{v}_{db} = \vec{v}_{dw} + \vec{v}_{wb}$; calculate the components.

$$v_{dbx} = v_{dwx} + v_{wbx} = v_{dw}\cos\theta - v_{wb}\cos 45° = v_{dw}\cos\theta - \frac{v_{wb}}{\sqrt{2}}$$

$$v_{dby} = v_{dwy} + v_{wby} = v_{dw}\sin\theta - v_{wb}\sin 45° = v_{dw}\sin\theta - \frac{v_{wb}}{\sqrt{2}}$$

(a) Set $v_{dby} = 0$ to find θ.

$$v_{dw}\sin\theta - \frac{v_{wb}}{\sqrt{2}} = 0$$

$$\sin\theta = \frac{v_{wb}}{v_{dw}\sqrt{2}}$$

$$\theta = \sin^{-1}\frac{v_{wb}}{v_{dw}\sqrt{2}}$$

$$= \sin^{-1}\frac{2.83\frac{m}{s}}{\left(4.00\frac{m}{s}\right)\sqrt{2}}$$

$$= \boxed{30.0°\ \text{N of W}}$$

(b) $t = \dfrac{x}{v_{dbx}} = \dfrac{0.80 \times 10^3 \text{ m}}{\left(4.00 \frac{\text{m}}{\text{s}}\right)\cos 30.0° - \dfrac{2.83\frac{\text{m}}{\text{s}}}{\sqrt{2}}}\left(\dfrac{1 \text{ min}}{60 \text{ s}}\right) = \boxed{9.1 \text{ min}}$

73. Let north be $+y$ and east be $+x$.

(a) Sum the distances.

$$100.0 \text{ m} + 200.0 \text{ m} + 75.0 \text{ m} = \boxed{375.0 \text{ m}}$$

(b) Determine the magnitude and direction of the displacement.

$\Delta x = 200.0 \text{ m} + (75.0 \text{ m})\cos 45.0° = 253.0 \text{ m}$

$\Delta y = -100.0 \text{ m} + (75.0 \text{ m})\sin 45.0° = -47.0 \text{ m}$

$\Delta r = \sqrt{(253.03 \text{ m})^2 + (-46.97 \text{ m})^2} = 257.4 \text{ m}$

$\theta = \tan^{-1}\dfrac{-47.0}{253.0} = 10.5° \text{ S of E}$

To return, the rider must travel opposite the original displacement.

So, $\Delta \vec{r}_{\text{return}} = \boxed{257.4 \text{ m at } 10.5° \text{ N of W}}$.

77. **(a)** $x = v_{0x}t = v_0 t$, so $t = \dfrac{x}{v_0}$.

Relate the distance to the initial height.

$$y = y_0 + v_{0y}t - \frac{1}{2}gt^2$$

$$0 = y_0 + (0)t - \frac{1}{2}gt^2$$

$$= y_0 - \frac{1}{2}g\left(\frac{x}{v_0}\right)^2$$

$$\frac{1}{2}g\frac{x^2}{v_0^2} = y_0$$

$$x^2 = \frac{2v_0^2 y_0}{g}$$

$$x = v_0\sqrt{\frac{2y_0}{g}}$$

$$= \left(6.00\frac{\text{m}}{\text{s}}\right)\sqrt{\frac{2(8.00 \text{ m})}{9.80\frac{\text{m}}{\text{s}^2}}}$$

$$= \boxed{7.67 \text{ m}}$$

(b) $v_y = -gt = -g\dfrac{x}{v_0}$ and $v_x = v_0$.

$$v = \sqrt{v_x^2 + v_y^2} = \sqrt{v_0^2 + \frac{g^2 x^2}{v_0^2}} = \sqrt{\left(6.00\frac{\text{m}}{\text{s}}\right)^2 + \frac{\left(9.80\frac{\text{m}}{\text{s}^2}\right)^2 (7.67 \text{ m})^2}{\left(6.00\frac{\text{m}}{\text{s}}\right)^2}} = \boxed{13.9 \text{ m/s}}$$

(c) v_x relative to the seagull is zero.

$$\left|v_y\right| = g\frac{x}{v_0} = \left(9.80\frac{m}{s^2}\right)\frac{7.67\ m}{6.00\frac{m}{s}} = \boxed{12.5\ m/s}$$

81. (a)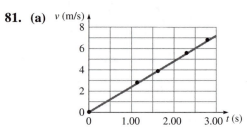

(b) The points appear to lie upon a line, so $\boxed{\text{yes,}}$ it is plausible that the acceleration is constant.

$$a = \frac{\Delta v}{\Delta t} = \frac{7.0\ \frac{m}{s} - 0}{2.88\ s - 0} = \boxed{2.43\ m/s^2}$$

(c) Use Newton's second law.
Let $+x$ be down the incline and $+y$ be away from and perpendicular to the slope.
$\Sigma F_x = mg\sin\theta = ma$, so

$$a = g\sin\theta$$

$$\sin\theta = \frac{a}{g}$$

$$\theta = \sin^{-1}\frac{a}{g}$$

$$= \sin^{-1}\frac{2.43}{9.8}$$

$$= \boxed{14°}$$

(d) If friction is significant, the acceleration is less for the same incline. So, the angle of incline is $\boxed{\text{larger}}$.

85. (a) At the maximum height,

$$v_y = 0 = v_0\sin\theta - gt$$

So, $t = \dfrac{v_0\sin\theta}{g}$.

Also,

$$x = (v_0\cos\theta)t,\ \text{so } t = \frac{x}{v_0\cos\theta}.\quad (x\text{ is half of 0.800 m.})$$

Equate the expressions for t.

$$\frac{v_0\sin\theta}{g} = \frac{x}{v_0\cos\theta}$$

$$v_0^2 = \frac{gx}{\sin\theta\cos\theta}$$

From Problem 83,

$$H = \frac{v_0^2 \sin^2 \theta}{2g}, \text{ so}$$

$$H = \frac{gx\sin^2 \theta}{2g\sin\theta\cos\theta} = \frac{x}{2}\tan\theta = \frac{\left(\frac{0.800\text{ m}}{2}\right)}{2}\tan 55.0° = \boxed{28.6\text{ cm}}$$

(b) Since $H \propto \tan\theta$, and since $\tan\theta$ increases if θ increases $(0 \le \theta \le 90)$, the maximum height would be $\boxed{\text{smaller}}$ $(45.0° < 55.0°)$.

(c) The range would be $\boxed{\text{larger}}$, since the range is maximized for $\theta = 45°$.

(d) Calculate v_0^2.

$$v_0^2 = \frac{\left(9.80\frac{\text{m}}{\text{s}^2}\right)\left(\frac{0.800\text{ m}}{2}\right)}{\sin 55.0°\cos 55.0°} = 8.34\ \text{m}^2/\text{s}^2$$

Calculate the maximum height and range for 45.0°.

$$H = \frac{\left(8.34\frac{\text{m}^2}{\text{s}^2}\right)\sin^2 45.0°}{2\left(9.80\frac{\text{m}}{\text{s}^2}\right)} = \boxed{21.3\text{ cm}}$$

From Problem 82,

$$R = \frac{v_0^2 \sin 2\theta}{g} = \frac{\left(8.34\frac{\text{m}^2}{\text{s}^2}\right)\sin 90.0°}{9.80\frac{\text{m}}{\text{s}^2}} = \boxed{85.1\text{ cm}}$$

89. (a) a = air, w = water, s = sailboat

Case (1):

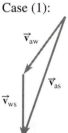

Case (2):

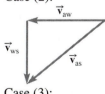

Case (3):

(b) According to the vector diagrams, the apparent wind speed is greater than the true wind speed in cases 1 and 2 .

(c) According to the vector diagrams, the apparent wind direction is forward of the true wind in all three cases.

93. **(a)** Since the bullet will travel not only along the direction of the barrel of the gun, but also at 25.0 m/s in the direction of the train, the guard should aim in front of the hat.

(b) Let $+y$ be in the direction of the motion of the train, and let $+x$ be to the right. m = muzzle velocity and t = train.
Find the time for the bullet to travel 0.300 km.

$$x = v_m t$$

$$t = \frac{x}{v_m}$$

Find the distance before the point at which the guard is directly opposite Jesse.

$$y = v_t t = v_t \left(\frac{x}{v_m}\right) = \frac{25.0 \frac{m}{s}}{0.350 \times 10^3 \frac{m}{s}}(0.300 \times 10^3 \text{ m}) = \boxed{21.4 \text{ m}}$$

(c) The bullet will fall due to the force of gravity.

$$\Delta y = v_{0y}t - \frac{1}{2}gt^2 = 0 - \frac{1}{2}g\left(\frac{x}{v_m}\right)^2 = -\frac{1}{2}\left(9.8\frac{m}{s^2}\right)\left(\frac{0.300 \text{ km}}{0.350 \frac{km}{s}}\right)^2 = -3.6 \text{ m}$$

The guard should aim 3.6 m above Jesse's hat.

(d) Since 0.350 km/s > 120 m/s, drag will slow the bullet, so the guard should fire earlier .

Chapter 5

CIRCULAR MOTION

Problems

1. $s = r\theta = (8.0 \text{ m})(120°)\left(\dfrac{2\pi \text{ rad}}{360°}\right) = \boxed{17 \text{ m}}$

5. $\omega = \dfrac{v}{r} = \dfrac{9.0 \frac{\text{m}}{\text{s}}}{0.35 \text{ m}} = \boxed{26 \text{ rad/s}}$

7. **(a)** $\left(\dfrac{33.3 \text{ rev}}{\text{min}}\right)\left(\dfrac{2\pi \text{ rad}}{\text{rev}}\right)\left(\dfrac{1 \text{ min}}{60 \text{ s}}\right) = \boxed{3.49 \text{ rad/s}}$

  (b) $v = r\omega = (0.13 \text{ m})(3.49 \text{ rad/s}) = \boxed{0.45 \text{ m/s}}$

9. $s = r\theta$, where $s = 100.0$ ft, $\theta = 1.5°$, and r is the radius of curvature.

  $r = \dfrac{s}{\theta} = \dfrac{100.0 \text{ ft}}{1.5°}\left(\dfrac{360°}{2\pi \text{ rad}}\right) = \boxed{3800 \text{ ft}}$

13. The angular speed of the Earth is $\omega = \dfrac{2\pi \text{ rad}}{86,400 \text{ s}}$.

  $a_c = \omega^2 r = \left(\dfrac{2\pi \text{ rad}}{86,400 \text{ s}}\right)^2 (6.371 \times 10^6 \text{ m}) = \boxed{3.37 \text{ cm/s}^2}$

17. **(a)** Use Newton's second law.
  $\Sigma F_y = T_y - mg = 0$, so
  $T_y = T\cos\phi = mg$, or $T = \boxed{\dfrac{mg}{\cos\phi}}$.

(b) $\Sigma F_c = T_c = ma_c = m\omega^2 r = m\omega^2 L \sin\phi = T \sin\phi$, so $T = m\omega^2 L$.

And, from part (a), $T = \dfrac{mg}{\cos\phi}$.

Eliminate T.

$$m\omega^2 L = \frac{mg}{\cos\phi}$$

$$\omega^2 L = \frac{g}{\cos\phi}$$

$$\left(\frac{2\pi}{T}\right)^2 L = \frac{g}{\cos\phi} \quad \text{where } T \text{ is now the period, not the tension}$$

$$\frac{1}{T^2} = \frac{g}{(2\pi)^2 L\cos\phi}$$

$$T = \boxed{2\pi\sqrt{\frac{L\cos\phi}{g}}}$$

19. Let the x-axis point toward the center of curvature and the y-axis point upward. Use Newton's second law.

$$\Sigma F_y = N\cos\theta - mg = 0$$

$$\Sigma F_x = N\sin\theta = ma_c = m\frac{v^2}{r}$$

$$\frac{N\sin\theta}{N\cos\theta} = \frac{m\frac{v^2}{r}}{mg}$$

$$\tan\theta = \frac{v^2}{rg}$$

$$v^2 = rg\tan\theta$$

$$v = \sqrt{rg\tan\theta}$$

$$= \sqrt{(120\text{ m})\left(9.8\ \frac{\text{m}}{\text{s}^2}\right)\tan 3.0°}$$

$$= \boxed{7.9\ \text{m/s}}$$

21. Let the x-axis point toward the center of curvature and the y-axis point upward. Use Newton's second law.

$$\Sigma F_x = N\sin\theta = ma_c = m\frac{v^2}{r}$$
$$\Sigma F_y = N\cos\theta - mg = 0$$

$$\frac{N\sin\theta}{N\cos\theta} = \frac{m\frac{v^2}{r}}{mg}$$

$$\tan\theta = \frac{v^2}{rg}$$

$$\theta = \tan^{-1}\frac{v^2}{rg}$$

$$= \tan^{-1}\frac{\left(18\ \frac{m}{s}\right)^2}{(20.0\ m)\left(9.8\ \frac{m}{s^2}\right)}$$

$$= \boxed{59°}$$

23. Let the x-axis point toward the center of curvature and the y-axis point upward. Use Newton's second law.

(a) $\Sigma F_y = N\cos\theta - mg - f\sin\theta = 0$

$$\Sigma F_x = N\sin\theta + f\cos\theta = m\frac{v^2}{r}$$

Solve for N in the first equation and substitute into the second.

$$N = \frac{f\sin\theta + mg}{\cos\theta},\ \text{so}$$

$$\frac{f\sin\theta + mg}{\cos\theta}\sin\theta + f\cos\theta = m\frac{v^2}{r}$$

$$f\sin^2\theta + mg\sin\theta + f\cos^2\theta = m\frac{v^2}{r}\cos\theta$$

$$f(\sin^2\theta + \cos^2\theta) = m\frac{v^2}{r}\cos\theta - mg\sin\theta$$

$$f(1) = m\left(\frac{v^2}{r}\cos\theta - g\sin\theta\right)$$

$$f = (1400\ kg)\left[\frac{\left(32\ \frac{m}{s}\right)^2}{410\ m}\cos 5.0° - \left(9.8\ \frac{m}{s^2}\right)\sin 5.0°\right]$$

$$= \boxed{2300\ N}$$

(b) $f = 0 = m\left(\dfrac{v^2}{r}\cos\theta - g\sin\theta\right)$

$$\dfrac{v^2}{r}\cos\theta = g\sin\theta$$

$$v^2 = gr\tan\theta$$

$$v = \sqrt{gr\tan\theta}$$

$$= \sqrt{\left(9.8\ \dfrac{m}{s^2}\right)(410\ m)\tan 5.0°}$$

$$= \boxed{19\ m/s}$$

25. Let the x-axis point toward the radius of curvature and the y-axis point upward. θ is measured from the vertical axis. Use Newton's second law.

$$\Sigma F_y = L_y - mg = 0$$

$$\Sigma F_x = L_x = m\dfrac{v^2}{r}$$

$$L_y = L\cos\theta = mg$$

$$L_x = L\sin\theta = m\dfrac{v^2}{r}$$

$$\dfrac{L\sin\theta}{L\cos\theta} = \dfrac{m\dfrac{v^2}{r}}{mg}$$

$$\tan\theta = \dfrac{v^2}{rg}$$

$$\theta = \boxed{\tan^{-1}\dfrac{v^2}{rg}}$$

27. According to Kepler's third law, $r^3 \propto T^2$.

$$\left(\dfrac{4.0r}{r}\right)^3 = \left(\dfrac{T_{4.0}}{T}\right)^2$$

$$64 = \dfrac{T_{4.0}{}^2}{T^2}$$

$$T_{4.0}{}^2 = 64T^2$$

$$T_{4.0} = 8.0T$$

$$= 8.0(16\ h)$$

$$= \boxed{130\ h}$$

29. Use Newton's law of universal gravitation.

$$F_g = \frac{GMm}{r^2} = \frac{\left(6.673\times10^{-11}\ \frac{\text{N·m}^2}{\text{kg}^2}\right)(2.0\times10^{30}\ \text{kg})(6.0\times10^{24}\ \text{kg})}{(1.5\times10^{11}\ \text{m})^2} = 3.6\times10^{22}\ \text{N}$$

Use Newton's second law.

$$\Sigma F_c = ma_c = m\frac{v^2}{r} = (6.0\times10^{24}\ \text{kg})\frac{\left(3.0\times10^4\ \frac{\text{m}}{\text{s}}\right)^2}{1.5\times10^{11}\ \text{m}} = 3.6\times10^{22}\ \text{N}$$

The magnitude of the force is $\boxed{3.6\times10^{22}\ \text{N}}$.

31. Use Newton's second law and law of universal gravitation.

$$\Sigma F_c = \frac{GmM_J}{(3.0\ R_J)^2} = \frac{mv^2}{3.0R_J}$$

Now, $g_J = \dfrac{GM_J}{R_J^2}$, so

$$\frac{mv^2}{3.0R_J} = \frac{mg_J}{9.0}$$

$$v^2 = \frac{g_J R_J}{3.0}$$

$$\left(\frac{2\pi r}{T}\right)^2 =$$

$$\frac{4\pi^2(3.0R_J)^2}{T^2} =$$

$$\frac{4\pi^2(27)R_J}{g_J} = T^2$$

$$T = 2\pi\sqrt{\frac{27R_J}{g_J}}$$

$$= 2\pi\sqrt{\frac{27(71,500\times10^3\ \text{m})}{23\ \frac{\text{N}}{\text{kg}}}}\left(\frac{1\ \text{h}}{3600\ \text{s}}\right)$$

$$= \boxed{16\ \text{h}}$$

33. (a) Use Newton's second law.

$$\Sigma F_c = T - mg = ma_c,\ \text{so}$$

$$T = m(g + a_c) = m\left(g + \frac{v^2}{r}\right) = (1.0\ \text{kg})\left[9.8\ \frac{\text{m}}{\text{s}^2} + \frac{\left(1.6\ \frac{\text{m}}{\text{s}}\right)^2}{0.80\ \text{m}}\right] = \boxed{13\ \text{N}}.$$

(b) If the bob were at rest, the tension would be equal to the weight of the bob. Since the bob is moving and its velocity is changing—its vertical component is increasing from zero—the tension must be greater than the weight. Thus,

$\boxed{\text{the bob has an upward acceleration, so the net } F_y \text{ must be upward and greater than the weight of the bob.}}$

35. If the $+y$-direction is centripetal and the $+x$-direction is tangential to the left, according to Newton's second law, $\Sigma F_t = mg \sin \theta = ma_t$, or $a_t = \boxed{g \sin \theta}$.

37.
$$\Delta \theta = \omega_0 t + \frac{1}{2}\alpha t^2$$
$$= (0)t + \frac{1}{2}\alpha t^2$$
$$\frac{2\Delta\theta}{t^2} = \alpha$$
$$\alpha = \frac{2(8.0 \text{ rev})\left(\frac{2\pi \text{ rad}}{\text{rev}}\right)}{(5.0 \text{ s})^2}$$
$$= \boxed{4.0 \text{ rad/s}^2}$$

41. (a) $v_0 = r\omega_0 = (0.200 \text{ m})\left(5.0 \times 10^5 \, \frac{\text{rad}}{\text{s}}\right) = \boxed{1.0 \times 10^5 \text{ m/s}}$

(b) $a_t = r\alpha = (0.200 \text{ m})\left(0.40 \, \frac{\text{rad}}{\text{s}^2}\right) = \boxed{0.080 \text{ m/s}^2}$

(c) $a_c = \frac{v^2}{r} = \frac{\left(1.0 \times 10^5 \, \frac{\text{m}}{\text{s}}\right)^2}{(0.200 \text{ m})} = \boxed{5.0 \times 10^{10} \text{ m/s}^2}$

45. (a) At the top of the Ferris wheel, $\vec{g}$ and $\vec{a}$ are in the same direction, so the apparent weight $W' = m|\vec{g} - \vec{a}| = m(g - a_y)$ is less than the true weight by ma_y. Thus, the lower weight, $\boxed{518.5 \text{ N}}$, is measured at the top.

(b) At the bottom of the Ferris wheel, $\vec{g}$ and $\vec{a}$ are opposite, so the apparent weight $W' = m|\vec{g} - \vec{a}| = m(g + a_y)$ is greater than the true weight by ma_y. Thus, the higher weight, $\boxed{521.5 \text{ N}}$, is measured at the bottom.

(c)
$$W'_{\text{top}} = W\left(1 - \frac{a_y}{g}\right)$$
$$\frac{W'_{\text{top}}}{W} - 1 = -\frac{a_y}{g}$$
$$g\left(1 - \frac{W'_{\text{top}}}{W}\right) = a_y$$
$$= \omega^2 r$$
$$r = \frac{g}{\omega^2}\left(1 - \frac{W'_{\text{top}}}{W}\right)$$
$$= \frac{9.8 \, \frac{\text{m}}{\text{s}^2}}{\left(0.025 \, \frac{\text{rad}}{\text{s}}\right)^2}\left(1 - \frac{518.5 \text{ N}}{520.0 \text{ N}}\right)$$
$$= \boxed{45 \text{ m}}$$

49. $v = \omega r = \left(\dfrac{2\pi \text{ rad}}{24.0 \text{ h}}\right)\left(\dfrac{1 \text{ h}}{3600 \text{ s}}\right)(6.378\times10^6 \text{ m} + 5895 \text{ m}) = \boxed{464 \text{ m/s}}$

53. (a) The apparent angular speed of the Sun is approximately the angular speed of the Earth.

$$\omega = \left(\frac{2\pi \text{ rad}}{24 \text{ h}}\right)\left(\frac{1 \text{ h}}{3600 \text{ s}}\right) = \boxed{7.3\times10^{-5} \text{ rad/s}}$$

(b) Estimate for arm-length: 1 m
Estimate the finger-width: 2 cm

Use $s = r\theta$ to estimate the angle subtended. Then $s \approx 2$ cm and $r \approx 1$ m, and $\theta = \dfrac{s}{r} \approx \dfrac{0.02 \text{ m}}{1 \text{ m}} = \boxed{0.02 \text{ rad}}$.

(c) $\dfrac{0.02 \text{ rad}}{2\pi \text{ rad}}(24 \text{ h})\left(\dfrac{60 \text{ min}}{\text{h}}\right) = \boxed{5 \text{ min}}$

57. Distance $\pi r = vt$ and $a_c = \dfrac{v^2}{r}$, so $v = \sqrt{a_c r}$. $t = \dfrac{\pi r}{v} = \dfrac{\pi r}{\sqrt{a_c r}} = \pi\sqrt{\dfrac{r}{a_c}}$, so the larger the radius the greater the time

to complete the U-turn. The $\boxed{\text{smallest}}$ possible radius should be used.

$$t_{\min} = \pi\sqrt{\frac{5.0 \text{ m}}{3.0 \frac{\text{m}}{\text{s}^2}}} = \boxed{4.1 \text{ s}}$$

61. (a) $v = \omega r = \left(\dfrac{45 \text{ rev}}{\text{min}}\right)\left(\dfrac{2\pi \text{ rad}}{\text{rev}}\right)\left(\dfrac{1 \text{ min}}{60 \text{ s}}\right)(5.0 \text{ in.})\left(\dfrac{0.0254 \text{ m}}{\text{in.}}\right) = \boxed{0.60 \text{ m/s}}$

(b) Use Newton's second law.

$\Sigma F_c = f \geq ma_c$
$\Sigma F_y = N - mg = 0$

$$f \geq ma_c$$
$$\mu mg \geq m\omega^2 r$$
$$\mu g \geq \omega^2 r$$

$$0.13\left(9.8 \frac{\text{m}}{\text{s}^2}\right) \geq \left(45 \frac{\text{rev}}{\text{min}}\right)^2 \left(\frac{2\pi \text{ rad}}{\text{rev}}\right)^2 \left(\frac{1 \text{ min}}{60 \text{ s}}\right)^2 (5.0 \text{ in.})\left(\frac{0.0254 \text{ m}}{\text{in.}}\right)$$

$$1.3 \frac{\text{m}}{\text{s}^2} \geq 2.8 \frac{\text{m}}{\text{s}^2} \text{ False}$$

$\boxed{\text{The dolls do not stay on the record.}}$

65. For each revolution of the flagellum, the bacterium moves the distance of the pitch.

$(1.0 \text{ μm})\left(110 \dfrac{\text{rev}}{\text{s}}\right) = \boxed{110 \text{ μm/s}}$

Chapter 6

ENERGY

Problems

1. $W = F\Delta r \cos\theta = (30.0 \text{ N})(5.0 \text{ m})\cos 60.0° = \boxed{75 \text{ J}}$

3. Since the book undergoes no displacement, $\boxed{\text{no work is done}}$ *on the book* by Hilda.

5. The x-axis is parallel to the canal and the y-axis is perpendicular. Use Newton's second law.

   $\Sigma F_y = T\sin\theta - T\sin\theta = 0$

   $\Sigma F_x = T\cos\theta + T\cos\theta = F_x$

   $W = F_x\Delta x = 2T\cos\theta\Delta x = 2(1.0 \text{ kN})\cos 45°(150 \text{ m}) = \boxed{210 \text{ kJ}}$

7. $K = \dfrac{1}{2}mv^2 = \dfrac{1}{2}(1600 \text{ kg})\left(30.0 \ \dfrac{\text{m}}{\text{s}}\right)^2 = \boxed{720 \text{ kJ}}$

9. (a) $\qquad\qquad \Delta K = W$

   $\qquad\qquad \dfrac{1}{2}m(v^2 - v_0^2) = F\Delta r\cos\theta$

   $\qquad\qquad\qquad \dfrac{1}{2}mv^2 = F\Delta r\cos\theta$

   $\qquad\qquad\qquad\qquad K = (2.0 \text{ N})(0.35 \text{ m})$

   $\qquad\qquad\qquad\qquad\quad = \boxed{0.70 \text{ J}}$

   (b) $v = \sqrt{\dfrac{2K}{m}} = \sqrt{\dfrac{2(0.70 \text{ J})}{10.0 \text{ kg}}} = \boxed{0.37 \text{ m/s}}$

13. $K_{\text{meteor}} = \dfrac{1}{2}mv^2 = \dfrac{1}{2}(0.0050 \text{ kg})\left(48\times10^3 \ \dfrac{\text{m}}{\text{s}}\right)^2 = \boxed{5.8 \text{ MJ}}$

    $K_{\text{car}} = \dfrac{1}{2}(1100 \text{ kg})\left(29 \ \dfrac{\text{m}}{\text{s}}\right)^2 = \boxed{0.46 \text{ MJ}}$

    $\dfrac{K_{\text{meteor}}}{K_{\text{car}}} = \dfrac{5.8 \text{ MJ}}{0.46 \text{ MJ}} > 12$

    $\boxed{\text{The meteor has more than 12 times the kinetic energy of the car.}}$

15. $W = \dfrac{1}{2}kx^2 = \dfrac{1}{2}\left(20.0 \ \dfrac{\text{N}}{\text{m}}\right)(0.40 \text{ m})^2 = \boxed{1.6 \text{ J}}$

17. Since the displacement of the model airplane is zero, $\boxed{\text{zero}}$ work has been done on it by the string.

21. (a) Since the floor is level, the change in the desk's gravitational potential energy is $\boxed{\text{zero}}$.

(b) $W = F_x \Delta x = (340 \text{ N})(10.0 \text{ m}) = \boxed{3.4 \text{ kJ}}$

(c) The energy has been $\boxed{\text{dissipated as heat}}$ by friction between the bottom of the desk and the floor.

23. (a) Since the work done by gravity on the orange on the way up is the opposite of the work done on the way down, the total work done is $\boxed{\text{zero}}$.

(b) $W = -mg\Delta y = -(0.30 \text{ kg})\left(9.8 \dfrac{\text{N}}{\text{kg}}\right)(0-1.0 \text{ m}) = \boxed{2.9 \text{ J}}$

25. $\dfrac{U_{\text{perigee}}}{U_{\text{apogee}}} = \dfrac{-\dfrac{GmM_E}{2R_E}}{-\dfrac{GmM_E}{4R_E}} = \dfrac{4}{2} = \boxed{2}$

28. Find k. Use Newton's second law.

$\Sigma F_y = kx_1 - mg = 0,$ so

$kx_1 = mg$

$k = \dfrac{mg}{x_1}$

Find v_{max}.

$$K_i + K_f = U_i + U_f$$

$$0 + \frac{1}{2}mv_{\text{max}}^2 = \frac{1}{2}kx_{\text{max}}^2 + 0$$

$$\frac{1}{2}mv_{\text{max}}^2 = \frac{1}{2}kx_{\text{max}}^2$$

$$v_{\text{max}} = x_{\text{max}}\sqrt{\frac{k}{m}}$$

$$= x_{\text{max}}\sqrt{\frac{g}{x_1}}$$

$$= (0.100 \text{ m} - 0.050 \text{ m})\sqrt{\frac{9.8 \frac{\text{m}}{\text{s}^2}}{0.060 \text{ m} - 0.050 \text{ m}}}$$

$$= \boxed{1.6 \text{ m/s}}$$

30. (a) $E_1 = \dfrac{1}{2}mv_1^2$ if $y_1 = 0$ and $E_3 = \dfrac{1}{2}mv_3^2 + mgy_3$.

$$E_f = E_i$$

$$E_3 = E_1$$

$$\frac{1}{2}mv_3^2 + mgy_3 = \frac{1}{2}mv_1^2$$

$$v_3^2 + 2gy_3 = v_1^2$$

$$v_3 = \sqrt{v_1^2 - 2gy_3}$$

$$= \sqrt{\left(20.0 \frac{\text{m}}{\text{s}}\right)^2 - 2\left(9.81 \frac{\text{m}}{\text{s}^2}\right)(10.0 \text{ m})}$$

$$= \boxed{14.3 \text{ m/s}}$$

(b) $v_4 = \sqrt{v_1^2 - 2gy_4} = \sqrt{\left(20.0 \ \frac{m}{s}\right)^2 - 2\left(9.81 \ \frac{m}{s^2}\right)(20.0 \ m)} = 3 \ m/s$

Yes, the cart will reach position 4.

32. The initial height of the rope is $l\cos\theta$ where l is the length of the rope and θ is the angle it makes with the vertical. Then $\Delta y = l\cos\theta - l = l(\cos\theta - 1)$.

$$\Delta K = -\Delta U$$

$$\frac{1}{2}mv^2 - 0 = -mg\Delta y$$

$$\frac{1}{2}mv^2 = -mg\Delta y$$

$$v = \sqrt{-2g\Delta y}$$

$$= \sqrt{2gl(1 - \cos\theta)}$$

$$= \sqrt{2\left(9.8 \ \frac{m}{s^2}\right)(20.0 \ m)(1 - \cos 35.0°)}$$

$$= \boxed{8.4 \ m/s}$$

36. The escape speed for Zoroaster is given by $v_{esc} = \sqrt{\dfrac{2GM_Z}{R_Z}}$.

$$\Delta K = -\Delta U$$

$$\frac{1}{2}mv_f^2 - \frac{1}{2}mv_i^2 = \frac{GM_Z m}{R_Z}.$$

$$v_f^2 - v_i^2 = \frac{2GM_Z}{R_Z}$$

$$v_f = \sqrt{v_i^2 + \frac{2GM_Z}{R_Z}}$$

$$= \sqrt{v_i^2 + v_{esc}^2}$$

$$= \sqrt{\left(5.0 \ \frac{km}{s}\right)^2 + \left(12.0 \ \frac{km}{s}\right)^2}$$

$$= \boxed{13.0 \ km/s}$$

41. (a) The total kinetic energy required for the bob to travel the full circle is equal to the gravitational potential energy difference between the bottom and the top of the circle, $mgh = mg[2(L-d)] = 2mg(L-d)$ plus the kinetic energy required for the bob to have enough speed at the top of the circle to complete it. The centripetal acceleration must be equal to that due to gravity at the top of the circle for the bob to just complete the circle. So, $a_c = v_{top}^2/r = g$, or $v_{top} = \sqrt{gr} = \sqrt{g(L-d)}$. So, the total kinetic energy of the bob at the bottom of the circle is

$$K_{\text{total}} = \frac{1}{2}mv^2 = 2mg(L-d) + \frac{1}{2}mv_{\text{top}}^2 = 2mg(L-d) + \frac{1}{2}mg(L-d).$$

$$\frac{1}{2}mv^2 = \frac{5}{2}mg(L-d)$$

$$v^2 = 5g(L-d)$$

$$v = \boxed{\sqrt{5g(L-d)}}$$

(b) $h = L(1-\cos\theta)$ since $\theta = 0°$ gives $h = L(1-1) = 0$ and $\theta = 90°$ gives $h = L(1-0) = L$. Use conservation of energy.

$$U_i + K_i = U_f + K_f$$

$$mgh + 0 = 0 + \frac{1}{2}mv^2$$

$$mgL(1-\cos\theta) = \frac{1}{2}m[5g(L-d)]$$

$$1-\cos\theta = \frac{5}{2}\left(\frac{L-d}{L}\right)$$

$$= \frac{5}{2}\left(1-\frac{d}{L}\right)$$

$$-\cos\theta = \frac{5}{2} - \frac{5d}{2L} - 1$$

$$= -\frac{5d}{2L} + \frac{3}{2}$$

$$\cos\theta = \frac{5d}{2L} - \frac{3}{2}$$

$$\theta = \boxed{\cos^{-1}\left(\frac{5d}{2L} - \frac{3}{2}\right)}$$

45. (a)

$$K_i + U_i = K_f + U_f$$

$$0 + \frac{1}{2}kd^2 = \frac{1}{2}mv^2 + 0$$

$$v = \boxed{d\sqrt{\frac{k}{m}}}$$

(b)

$$K_i + U_i = K_f + U_f$$

$$\frac{1}{2}mv^2 + 0 = 0 + \frac{1}{2}kx^2$$

$$x = v\sqrt{\frac{m}{k}}$$

$$= d\sqrt{\frac{k}{m}}\sqrt{\frac{m}{k}}$$

$$= \boxed{d}$$

49. $\text{kW}\cdot\text{h} = 10^3\,\dfrac{\text{J}}{\text{s}}\cdot\text{h}\cdot\dfrac{3600\text{ s}}{1\text{ h}} = 3.6\times10^6\text{ J} = 3.6\text{ MJ}$

53. $P_{av} = \dfrac{\Delta E}{\Delta t} = \dfrac{\frac{1}{2}m(v_f{}^2 - v_i{}^2)}{\Delta t} = \dfrac{(1200 \text{ kg})\left[\left(30.0 \frac{m}{s}\right)^2 - \left(20.0 \frac{m}{s}\right)^2\right]}{2(5.0 \text{ s})} = \boxed{60 \text{ kW}}$

57. (a) $P_a + P_c = 0$ since $\dfrac{\Delta U}{\Delta t} = 0$.

$P_a = F_a v \cos\theta$

$F_a = \dfrac{P_a}{v \cos\theta}$

$= \dfrac{-120 \text{ W}}{\left(6.0 \frac{m}{s}\right)\cos 180°}$ ($\vec{v}$ is antiparallel to $\vec{F}_a$.)

$= \boxed{20 \text{ N}}$

(b) $v = \dfrac{P_c}{F_c \cos\theta} = \dfrac{120 \text{ W}}{(-18 \text{ N})\cos 180°} = \boxed{6.7 \text{ m/s}}$

61. $W_{total} = W_c + W_{nc} = \Delta K = \dfrac{1}{2}mv_f{}^2$, so

$W_{nc} = \dfrac{1}{2}mv_f{}^2 - W_c = \dfrac{1}{2}mv_f{}^2 - mgh = \dfrac{1}{2}(75 \text{ kg})\left(12 \frac{m}{s}\right)^2 - (75 \text{ kg})\left(9.8 \frac{N}{kg}\right)(78 \text{ m}) = \boxed{-52 \text{ kJ}}$.

65. $\dfrac{GM}{R^2} = 30.0 \text{ m/s}^2$, and

$v_{esc} = \sqrt{\dfrac{2GM}{R}} = \sqrt{2\left(\dfrac{GM}{R^2}\right)R} = \sqrt{2\left(30.0 \frac{m}{s^2}\right)(6.00\times10^7 \text{ m})} = \boxed{60.0 \text{ km/s}}$

69. $R_{E\text{-}S} =$ Earth-Sun distance

$E_i = E_f$

$\dfrac{1}{2}mv_i{}^2 - \dfrac{GM_Em}{R_E} - \dfrac{GM_Sm}{R_{E\text{-}S}} = 0 + 0$

$v_i{}^2 = 2G\left(\dfrac{M_E}{R_E} + \dfrac{M_S}{R_{E\text{-}S}}\right)$

$v_i = \sqrt{2G\left(\dfrac{M_E}{R_E} + \dfrac{M_S}{R_{E\text{-}S}}\right)}$

$= \sqrt{2\left(6.67\times10^{-11} \frac{N\cdot m^2}{kg^2}\right)\left(\dfrac{5.98\times10^{24} \text{ kg}}{6.37\times10^6 \text{ m}} + \dfrac{1.99\times10^{30} \text{ kg}}{1.50\times10^{11} \text{ m}}\right)}$

$= \boxed{43.5 \text{ km/s}}$

73.

$$K_i + U_i = K_f + U_f$$

$$\frac{1}{2}mv^2 + mgh_0 = 0 + mgh$$

$$\frac{1}{2}mv^2 = mg(h - h_0)$$

$$h = \frac{v^2}{2g} + h_0$$

$$= \frac{\left(10.0\ \frac{m}{s}\right)^2}{2\left(9.8\ \frac{m}{s^2}\right)} + 1.0\ m$$

$$= \boxed{6.1\ m}$$

75. (a) $BMR = \left(\dfrac{1\ kcal}{0.010\ mol}\right)\left(\dfrac{0.015\ mol}{min}\right)\left(\dfrac{1440\ min}{day}\right) = \boxed{2200\ kcal/day}$

(b) $\dfrac{2160\ \frac{kcal}{day}}{9.3\ \frac{kcal}{g}}\left(\dfrac{2.2\ lb}{10^3\ g}\right) = 0.51\ lb$

Since Jermaine is not resting the entire time, he loses $\boxed{\text{more than } 0.51\ lb}$.

77. $d = 8.0\ m$, $d_1 = 5.0\ m$, and $d_2 = 8.0\ m - 5.0\ m = 3.0\ m$.

$W_{total} = W_c + W_{nc} = \Delta K = 0$, since the speeds at top and bottom of the incline are zero.

Also, $W_c = -\Delta U$ and $W_{nc} = Td_2$.

$$W_{nc} = -W_c$$

$$Td_2 = \Delta U$$

$$T = \frac{\Delta U}{d_2}$$

$$= \frac{mg\Delta y}{d_2}$$

$$= \frac{mg(0 - d\sin\theta)}{d_2}$$

$$= -\frac{mgd\sin\theta}{d_2}$$

$$= -\frac{(4.0\ kg)\left(9.8\ \frac{m}{s^2}\right)(8.0\ m)\sin 15°}{3.0\ m}$$

$$= -27\ N$$

The sign is negative because the work done by the tension is opposite the box's motion. So, the magnitude of the tension is $\boxed{27\ N}$.

Find the speed of the block just before the person grasps the cord.

Use Newton's second law. $+y$ is perpendicular to the incline and $+x$ is down the incline.

$$\Sigma F_y = N - mg\cos\theta = 0$$

$$\Sigma F_x = mg\sin\theta = ma$$

$$v_f^2 - v_i^2 = 2g\sin\theta d_1$$

$$v_f^2 - 0 = 2g\sin\theta d_1$$

Let $v_f = v$.

Find the tension.

$$\Sigma F_x = -T + mg\sin\theta = ma_x, \text{ so } a_x = -\left(\frac{T}{m} - g\sin\theta\right).$$

$$v_f^2 - v_i^2 = -2\left(\frac{T}{m} - g\sin\theta\right)d_2$$

$$0 - v^2 =$$

$$v^2 = 2\left(\frac{T}{m} - g\sin\theta\right)d_2$$

$$2g\sin\theta d_1 =$$

$$\frac{g\sin\theta d_1}{d_2} = \frac{T}{m} - g\sin\theta$$

$$g\sin\theta\left(1 + \frac{d_1}{d_2}\right) = \frac{T}{m}$$

$$T = mg\sin\theta\left(\frac{d_1 + d_2}{d_2}\right)$$

$$= mg\sin\theta\frac{d}{d_2}$$

$$= (4.0 \text{ kg})\left(9.8 \ \frac{\text{m}}{\text{s}^2}\right)\sin 15°\left(\frac{8.0 \text{ m}}{3.0 \text{ m}}\right)$$

$$= 27 \text{ N}$$

81. Find the distance that the tendon stretches. Use Newton's second law.

$$\Sigma F = T - kx = 0$$

$$T = kx$$

$$x = \frac{T}{k}$$

$$= \frac{4.7 \text{ kN}}{350 \ \frac{\text{kN}}{\text{m}}}$$

$$= \boxed{1.3 \text{ cm}}$$

Find the stored elastic energy.

$$E = \frac{1}{2}kx^2 = \frac{1}{2}k\frac{T^2}{k^2} = \frac{T^2}{2k} = \frac{(4.7\times10^3 \text{ N})^2}{2\left(350\times10^3 \ \frac{\text{N}}{\text{m}}\right)} = \boxed{32 \text{ J}}$$

85. The area between the two graphs in Figure 6.41 represents the dissipated elastic energy.
The area under the upper graph has approximately 71–71.5 rectangles.
The area under the lower graph has approximately 68–69 rectangles.

$$\frac{71 - 69}{71}\times100\% = 3\% \text{ and } \frac{71.5 - 68}{71.5}\times100\% = 5\%$$

So, $\boxed{\text{approximately } 3\%\text{–}5\%}$ of the elastic energy is dissipated.

Chapter 7

LINEAR MOMENTUM

Problems

1. Use conservation of momentum.

$$\Delta p_2 = -\Delta p_1$$
$$p_{2f} - p_{2i} = p_{1i} - p_{1f}$$
$$p_{1f} + p_{2f} = p_{1i} + p_{2i}$$
$$(m_1 + m_2)v_f = m_1 v_{1i} + m_2 v_{2i}$$
$$p_f = (2.0 \text{ kg})\left(1.0 \ \frac{\text{m}}{\text{s}}\right) + (1.0 \text{ kg})(0)$$
$$= 2.0 \text{ kg} \cdot \text{m/s}$$
$$= p_{1i}$$

Since p_{1i} was directed to the right, and $p_f = p_{1i}$, the total momentum of the two blocks after the collision is $\boxed{2.0 \text{ kg} \cdot \text{m/s to the right}}$.

5.
$$\vec{\mathbf{p}}_{\text{tot}} = \vec{\mathbf{p}}_1 + \vec{\mathbf{p}}_2 + \vec{\mathbf{p}}_3$$
$$= m_1 \vec{\mathbf{v}}_1 + m_2 \vec{\mathbf{v}}_2 + m_3 \vec{\mathbf{v}}_3$$
$$= m_1 v_1 \text{ north} + m_2 v_2 \text{ south} + m_3 v_3 \text{ north}$$
$$= (m_1 v_1 - m_2 v_2 + m_3 v_3) \text{ north}$$
$$= \left[(3.0 \text{ kg})\left(3.0 \ \frac{\text{m}}{\text{s}}\right) - (4.0 \text{ kg})\left(5.0 \ \frac{\text{m}}{\text{s}}\right) + (7.0 \text{ kg})\left(2.0 \ \frac{\text{m}}{\text{s}}\right)\right] \text{ north} = \boxed{3 \text{ kg} \cdot \text{m/s north}}$$

7. $\Delta p = p_f - p_i = m v_f - m v_i = m(v_f - v_i) = (5.0 \text{ kg})\left(-2.0 \ \frac{\text{m}}{\text{s}} - 2.0 \ \frac{\text{m}}{\text{s}}\right) = -20 \text{ kg} \cdot \text{m/s}$

So, $\Delta \vec{\mathbf{p}} = \boxed{20 \text{ kg} \cdot \text{m/s in the } -x\text{-direction}}$.

9. $v_y = v_{0y} - gt = -gt$, since the object starts from rest.
Find Δp.

$$\Delta p = p_f - p_i = m(v_f - v_i) = m(-gt - 0) = -mgt = -(3.0 \text{ kg})\left(9.8 \ \frac{\text{m}}{\text{s}^2}\right)(3.4 \text{ s}) = -1.0 \times 10^2 \text{ kg} \cdot \text{m/s}$$

So, $\Delta \vec{\mathbf{p}} = \boxed{1.0 \times 10^2 \text{ kg} \cdot \text{m/s downward}}$.

11. Use the impulse-momentum theorem.

$$\Delta t = \frac{\Delta p}{F_{\text{av}}} = \frac{m \Delta v}{F_{\text{av}}} = \frac{(3800 \text{ kg})\left(1.1 \times 10^4 \ \frac{\text{m}}{\text{s}} - 2.6 \times 10^4 \ \frac{\text{m}}{\text{s}}\right)}{-1.8 \times 10^5 \text{ N}} = \boxed{320 \text{ s}}$$

13. Use the impulse-momentum theorem.

$$F_{av} = \frac{\Delta p}{\Delta t} = \frac{m(v_f - v_i)}{\Delta t} = \frac{(1.0 \times 10^3 \text{ kg})\left(0 - 30.0 \frac{m}{s}\right)}{5.0 \text{ s}} = -6.0 \times 10^3 \text{ N}$$

So, $\vec{F}_{av} = \boxed{6.0 \times 10^3 \text{ N opposite the car's direction of motion}}$.

17. Use conservation of momentum.

$$\vec{p}_{rf} + \vec{p}_{bf} = \vec{p}_{ri} + \vec{p}_{bi}$$

$$\vec{p}_{rf} = 0 + 0 - \vec{p}_{bf}$$

$$m_r \vec{v}_{rf} = -m_b \vec{v}_{bf}$$

$$\left| \vec{v}_{rf} \right| = \frac{m_b}{m_r} \left| -\vec{v}_{bf} \right|$$

$$= \frac{0.0100 \text{ kg}}{4.5 \text{ kg}} \left(820 \frac{m}{s} \right)$$

$$= \boxed{1.8 \text{ m/s}}$$

21. $\vec{p}_i = 0 = -\vec{p}_f$, and since we are only concerned with the horizontal direction, we have:

$$m_{mc} v_{mc} = m_b v_b$$

$$m_{mc} = \frac{v_b}{v_{mc}} m_b$$

$$= \frac{\left(173 \frac{m}{s} \right) \cos 30.0°}{1.0 \times 10^{-3} \frac{m}{s}} (0.010 \text{ kg})$$

$$= \boxed{1500 \text{ kg}}$$

23. Find x_{CM} and y_{CM}.

$$x_{CM} = \frac{m_A x_A + m_B x_B}{m_A + m_B} = \frac{(5.0 \text{ g})(0) + (1.0 \text{ g})(25 \text{ cm})}{5.0 \text{ g} + 1.0 \text{ g}} = 4.2 \text{ cm}$$

$$y_{CM} = \frac{m_A y_A + m_B y_B}{m_A + m_B} = \frac{(5.0 \text{ g})(0) + (1.0 \text{ g})(0)}{5.0 \text{ g} + 1.0 \text{ g}} = 0$$

So, the location of the center of mass is $(x_{CM}, y_{CM}) = \boxed{(4.2 \text{ cm}, 0)}$.

25. Find x_{CM} and y_{CM}.

$$x_{CM} = \frac{m_1 x_1 + m_2 x_2 + m_3 x_3}{m_1 + m_2 + m_2} = \frac{(4.0 \text{ kg})(4.0 \text{ m}) + (6.0 \text{ kg})(2.0 \text{ m}) + (3.0 \text{ kg})(-1.0 \text{ m})}{4.0 \text{ kg} + 6.0 \text{ kg} + 3.0 \text{ kg}} = 1.9 \text{ m}$$

$$y_{CM} = \frac{m_1 y_1 + m_2 y_2 + m_3 y_3}{m_1 + m_2 + m_2} = \frac{(4.0 \text{ kg})(0) + (6.0 \text{ kg})(4.0 \text{ m}) + (3.0 \text{ kg})(-2.0 \text{ m})}{4.0 \text{ kg} + 6.0 \text{ kg} + 3.0 \text{ kg}} = 1.4 \text{ m}$$

So, the location of the center of mass is $(x_{CM}, y_{CM}) = \boxed{(1.9 \text{ m}, 1.4 \text{ m})}$.

27. $\vec{p} = M\vec{v}_{CM} = m_A\vec{v}_A + m_B\vec{v}_B$ since $\vec{p} = \vec{p}_A + \vec{p}_B$. Thus, $\vec{v}_{CM} = \dfrac{m_A\vec{v}_A + m_B\vec{v}_B}{m_A + m_B}$.

Find the components of $\vec{v}_{CM}$.

$$v_{CMx} = \frac{m_A v_{Ax} + m_B v_{Bx}}{m_A + m_B} = \frac{(3 \text{ kg})\left(14 \frac{m}{s}\right) + (4 \text{ kg})(0)}{3 \text{ kg} + 4 \text{ kg}} = 6 \text{ m/s}$$

$$v_{CMy} = \frac{(3 \text{ kg})(0) + (4 \text{ kg})\left(-7 \frac{m}{s}\right)}{3 \text{ kg} + 4 \text{ kg}} = -4 \text{ m/s}$$

So, the components are $(v_{CMx}, v_{CMy}) = \boxed{(6 \text{ m/s}, -4 \text{ m/s})}$.

29. $\sum \vec{F}_{ext} = \lim\limits_{\Delta t \to 0} \dfrac{\Delta \vec{p}}{\Delta t} = \lim\limits_{\Delta t \to 0} \dfrac{\vec{p}_f - \vec{p}_i}{\Delta t} = \lim\limits_{\Delta t \to 0} \dfrac{M\vec{v}_{CMf} - M\vec{v}_{CMi}}{\Delta t} = M \lim\limits_{\Delta t \to 0} \dfrac{\Delta \vec{v}_{CM}}{\Delta t} = M\vec{a}_{CM}$ since $\vec{a}_{CM} = \lim\limits_{\Delta t \to 0} \dfrac{\Delta \vec{v}_{CM}}{\Delta t}$.

31. Let east be in the $+x$-direction. Use momentum conservation. The block is initially at rest, so $v_{2i} = 0$.

$$m_1 v_{1f} + m_2 v_{2f} = m_1 v_{1i} + m_2 v_{2i}$$
$$m_2 v_{2f} = m_1 v_{1i} + m_2(0) - m_1 v_{1f}$$
$$v_{2f} = \frac{m_1(v_{1i} - v_{1f})}{m_2}$$
$$= \frac{0.020 \text{ kg}}{2.0 \text{ kg}}\left[200.0 \frac{m}{s} - \left(-100.0 \frac{m}{s}\right)\right]$$
$$= 3.0 \text{ m/s}$$

So, $\vec{v}_{block} = \boxed{3.0 \text{ m/s east}}$.

33. The spring imparts the same (in magnitude) impulse to each block. (The same magnitude force is exerted on each block by the ends of the spring for the same amount of time.) So, each block has the same final magnitude of momentum. (The initial momentum is zero.)

$$m_B v_B = m_A v_A$$
$$m_B = \frac{v_A}{v_B} m_A$$
$$= \frac{\frac{x_A}{t}}{\frac{x_B}{t}} m_A$$
$$= \frac{x_A}{x_B} m_A$$
$$= \frac{1.0 \text{ m}}{3.0 \text{ m}}(0.60 \text{ kg})$$
$$= \boxed{0.20 \text{ kg}}$$

37. Use momentum conservation. The collision is perfectly inelastic, so $v_{1f} = v_{2f} = v_f$. Let the positive direction be the initial direction of motion.

$$m_1 v_f + m_2 v_f = m_1 v_{1i} + m_2 v_{2i}$$
$$v_f = \frac{m_1(0) + m_2 v_{2i}}{m_1 + m_2}$$
$$= \frac{3.0 \text{ kg}}{2.0 \text{ kg} + 3.0 \text{ kg}}\left(8.0 \frac{m}{s}\right)$$
$$= \boxed{4.8 \text{ m/s}}$$

41. Momentum conservation:

$m_1 v_{1f} + m_2 v_{2f} = m_1 v_{1i} + m_2 v_{2i}$ and $p_{1i} = -p_{2i}$. So, $m_1 v_{1i} = -m_2 v_{2i}$ and $m_1 v_{1f} + m_2 v_{2f} = 0$, or $m_1 v_{1f} = -m_2 v_{2f}$.

$K_i = K_f$, since the collision is elastic.

$$\frac{1}{2} m_1 v_{1i}^2 + \frac{1}{2} m_2 v_{2i}^2 = \frac{1}{2} m_1 v_{1f}^2 + \frac{1}{2} m_2 v_{2f}^2$$

$$m_1 v_{1i}^2 + m_2 v_{2i}^2 = m_1 v_{1f}^2 + m_2 v_{2f}^2$$

Eliminate v_{1i} and v_{1f}.

$$m_1 \left(-\frac{m_2}{m_1} v_{2i} \right)^2 + m_2 v_{2i}^2 = m_1 \left(-\frac{m_2}{m_1} v_{2f} \right)^2 + m_2 v_{2f}^2$$

$$\left(\frac{m_2^2}{m_1} + m_2 \right) v_{2i}^2 = \left(\frac{m_2^2}{m_1} + m_2 \right) v_{2f}^2$$

$$v_{2i}^2 = v_{2f}^2$$

Therefore, the initial and final speeds of object 2 are the same.

Eliminate v_{2i} and v_{2f}.

$$m_1 v_{1i}^2 + m_2 \left(-\frac{m_1}{m_2} v_{1i} \right)^2 = m_1 v_{1f}^2 + m_2 \left(-\frac{m_1}{m_2} v_{1f} \right)^2$$

$$\left(m_1 + \frac{m_1^2}{m_2} \right) v_{1i}^2 = \left(m_1 + \frac{m_1^2}{m_2} \right) v_{1f}^2$$

$$v_{1i}^2 = v_{1f}^2$$

Therefore, the initial and final speeds of object 1 are the same.

45. (a) Use conservation of momentum.

$$\Delta p_{1x} = -\Delta p_{2x} = m_2 v_{2ix} - m_2 v_{2fx} = m_2(0 - v_2) = -m_2 v_2 = -5m_1 \left[\frac{1}{4} v_0 \cos(-36.9°) \right] = \boxed{-1.00 m_1 v_0}$$

$$\Delta p_{1y} = -\Delta p_{2y} = m_2 v_{2iy} - m_2 v_{2fy} = 5m_1(0 - v_{2fy}) = -5m_1 v_{2fy} = -5m_1 \left[\frac{1}{4} v_0 \sin(-36.9°) \right] = \boxed{0.751 m_1 v_0}$$

(b) $\Delta p_{2x} = -\Delta p_{1x} = m_1(v_{1ix} - v_{1fx}) = m_1(v_0 - 0) = \boxed{m_1 v_0}$

$$\Delta p_{2y} = -\Delta p_{1y} = m_1(v_{1iy} - v_{1fy}) = m_1(0 - v_1) = -m_1 v_1 = -m_1(0.751 v_0) = \boxed{-0.751 m_1 v_0}$$

$$\boxed{\text{The momentum changes for each mass are equal and opposite.}}$$

47. Use conservation of momentum.

$$m v_{1fy} + m v_{2fy} = m v_{1iy} + m v_{2iy}$$

$$v_{1fy} + v_{2fy} = 0 + 0$$

$$v_{2fy} = -v_{1fy}$$

$$v_{2f} \sin\theta_2 = -v_{1f} \sin\theta_1$$

$$v_{2f} = \frac{-\sin\theta_1}{\sin\theta_2} v_{1f}$$

$$= \frac{-\sin 60.0°}{\sin(-30.0°)} v_{1f}$$

$$= \boxed{1.73 v_{1f}}$$

49. Use conservation of momentum.

Find v_{dfx}.

$$m_n v_{nix} + m_d v_{dix} = m_n v_{nfx} + m_d v_{dfx}$$

$$m_n v_0 + 0 = 0 + m_d v_{dfx}$$

$$v_{dfx} = \frac{m_n}{m_d} v_0$$

Find v_{dfy}.

$$m_n v_{niy} + m_d v_{diy} = m_n v_{nfy} + m_d v_{dfy}$$

$$0 + 0 = m_n \frac{v_0}{\sqrt{3}} + m_d v_{dfy}$$

$$v_{dfy} = -\frac{1}{\sqrt{3}} v_0 \frac{m_n}{m_d}$$

Find the components, v_{dfx} and v_{dfy}.

$$(v_{dfx}, v_{dfy}) = \left(\frac{m_n}{m_d} v_0, -\frac{1}{\sqrt{3}} v_0 \frac{m_n}{m_d} \right) = \left(\frac{m_n}{2m_n} v_0, -\frac{1}{\sqrt{3}} v_0 \frac{m_n}{2m_n} \right) = \boxed{\left(\frac{v_0}{2}, -\frac{v_0}{2\sqrt{3}} \right)}$$

53. Use the impulse-momentum theorem.

$$F_{av} = \frac{\Delta p}{\Delta t} = \frac{m\sqrt{(\Delta v_x)^2 + (\Delta v_y)^2}}{\Delta t}$$

$$= \frac{0.060 \text{ kg}}{0.065 \text{ s}} \sqrt{\left[\left(53 \frac{\text{m}}{\text{s}} \right) \cos 18° - \left(54 \frac{\text{m}}{\text{s}} \right) \cos(-22°) \right]^2 + \left[\left(53 \frac{\text{m}}{\text{s}} \right) \sin 18° - \left(54 \frac{\text{m}}{\text{s}} \right) \sin(-22°) \right]^2} = \boxed{34 \text{ N}}$$

55. Use the impulse-momentum theorem.

$$F_{av} = \frac{\Delta p}{\Delta t} = \frac{m \Delta v}{\Delta t} = \frac{m}{\Delta t} \Delta v = \left(24 \frac{\text{kg}}{\text{s}} \right) \left(17 \frac{\text{m}}{\text{s}} \right) = \boxed{410 \text{ N}}$$

57. The fly splatters on the windshield, so the collision is perfectly inelastic ($v_{\text{fly, final}} = v_{\text{car, final}} = v_f$).
Use conservation of momentum. Let the positive direction be along the velocity of the automobile.

(a) $\Delta p_{car} = -\Delta p_{fly} = -m_{fly}(v_{\text{fly, f}} - v_{\text{fly, i}}) \approx -m_{fly}(v_{\text{car, i}} - 0) = -(0.1 \times 10^{-3} \text{ kg}) \left(100 \frac{\text{km}}{\text{h}} \right) = -0.01 \text{ kg} \cdot \text{km/h}$

So, the change in the car's momentum due to the fly is $\boxed{0.01 \text{ kg} \cdot \text{km/h} \text{ opposite the car's motion}}$.

(b) $\Delta p_{fly} = -\Delta p_{car} = 0.01 \text{ kg} \cdot \text{km/h}$, or $\boxed{0.01 \text{ kg} \cdot \text{km/h} \text{ along the car's velocity}}$.

(c) $N \Delta p_{fly} = -m_{car} \Delta v_{car}$

$$N = -\frac{m_{car} \Delta v_{car}}{\Delta p_{fly}}$$

$$= -\frac{(1000 \text{ kg}) \left(-1 \frac{\text{km}}{\text{h}} \right)}{0.01 \text{ kg} \cdot \frac{\text{km}}{\text{h}}}$$

$$= \boxed{10^5 \text{ flies}}$$

61. Use conservation of momentum. The collision is perfectly inelastic, so $v_{1f} = v_{2f} = v_f$.

$$m_1 v_{1f} + m_2 v_{2f} = m_1 v_{1i} + m_2 v_{2i}$$
$$(m_1 + m_2)v_f = m_1 v_i + 0$$
$$v_f = \frac{m_1}{m_1 + m_2} v_i$$
$$= \frac{5.0 \text{ kg}}{5.0 \text{ kg} + 1.0 \text{ kg}}(1.0 \text{ m/s})$$
$$= \boxed{0.83 \text{ m/s}}$$

65. $F_{av} = \dfrac{\Delta p}{\Delta t} = \dfrac{m\Delta v}{\Delta t} = \dfrac{(0.01\times10^{-15} \text{ kg})\left(1\times10^{-6} \frac{\text{m}}{\text{s}} - 0\right)}{10\times10^{-6} \text{ s}} = \boxed{10^{-18} \text{ N}}$

67. $2m = m_B = 2m_A$

Find the maximum kinetic energy of A alone, and thus, its speed just before it strikes B. Use conservation of energy.

$$\Delta K = -\Delta U$$
$$\frac{1}{2}mv_1^2 - 0 = mgh - 0$$
$$v_1 = \sqrt{2gh}$$

Use momentum conservation to find the speed of the combined bobs just after impact. The collision is perfectly inelastic, so $v_{Af} = v_{Bf} = v_2$.

$$m_A v_{Af} + m_B v_{Bf} = m_A v_{Ai} + m_B v_{Bi}$$
$$(m + 2m)v_2 = mv_1 + 0$$
$$3mv_2 = mv_1$$
$$v_2 = \frac{1}{3}v_1$$

Find the maximum height.

$$\Delta K = -\Delta U$$
$$0 - \frac{1}{2}mv_2^2 = 0 - mgh_2$$
$$v_2^2 = 2gh_2$$
$$\left(\frac{1}{3}\sqrt{2gh}\right)^2 =$$
$$\frac{2gh}{9} = 2gh_2$$
$$\boxed{\frac{1}{9}h} = h_2$$

69. Momentum conservation:

$$mv_{Af} + mv_{Bf} = mv_{Ai} + mv_{Bi}$$
$$v_{Af} + v_{Bf} = v_{Ai} + 0$$
$$v_{Bf} = v_{Ai} - v_{Af}$$

Perfectly elastic collision ($K_i = K_f$):

$$\frac{1}{2}mv_{Af}^2 + \frac{1}{2}mv_{Bf}^2 = \frac{1}{2}mv_{Ai}^2 + \frac{1}{2}mv_{Bi}^2$$
$$v_{Af}^2 + v_{Bf}^2 = v_{Ai}^2 + 0$$

Energy conservation:

$$\frac{1}{2}mv_{Ai}^2 = mgh$$
$$v_{Ai} = \sqrt{2gh}$$

Find v_{Af} in terms of v_{Ai}.

$$v_{Af}^2 + v_{Bf}^2 = v_{Ai}^2$$
$$v_{Af}^2 + (v_{Ai} - v_{Af})^2 = v_{Ai}^2$$
$$v_{Af}^2 + v_{Ai}^2 - 2v_{Ai}v_{Af} + v_{Af}^2 = v_{Ai}^2$$
$$2v_{Af}^2 - 2v_{Ai}v_{Af} = 0$$
$$v_{Af}(v_{Af} - v_{Ai}) = 0$$

So, $v_{Af} = 0$ or v_{Ai}. The only way v_{Af} could equal v_{Ai} is if bob B didn't exist, so $v_{Af} = 0$.

Calculate v_{Bf}.

$$v_{Bf} = v_{Ai} - v_{Af} = \sqrt{2gh} - 0 = \sqrt{2\left(9.8\ \frac{m}{s^2}\right)(5.1\ m)} = \boxed{10\ m/s}$$

Chapter 8

TORQUE AND ANGULAR MOMENTUM

Problems

1. I has units $\mathrm{kg \cdot m^2}$. ω^2 has units $(\mathrm{rad \cdot s})^2$. So, $\frac{1}{2}I\omega^2$ has units $\mathrm{kg \cdot m^2 \cdot \dfrac{rad^2}{s^2}} = \dfrac{\mathrm{kg \cdot m^2}}{\mathrm{s^2}} = \mathrm{J}$, which is a unit of energy.

3. The rotational inertia of a solid disk is $I = \frac{1}{2}MR^2$.

$$I = \frac{1}{2}MR^2 = \frac{1}{2}(49 \text{ kg})(0.200 \text{ m})^2 = \boxed{0.98 \text{ kg} \cdot \text{m}^2}$$

5. The rotational inertia of a solid disk is $I = \frac{1}{2}MR^2$.

$$W = \Delta K = \frac{1}{2}I(\omega_f^2 - \omega_i^2) = \frac{1}{2}\left(\frac{1}{2}MR^2\right)\left[\left(\frac{v_f}{r}\right)^2 - \left(\frac{v_i}{r}\right)^2\right] = \frac{1}{4}M\left(\frac{R}{r}\right)^2(v_f^2 - v_i^2)$$

$$= \frac{1}{4}(0.0158 \text{ kg})\left(\frac{\frac{0.120 \text{ m}}{2}}{0.0200 \text{ m}}\right)^2\left[\left(1.20 \frac{\text{m}}{\text{s}}\right)^2 - 0\right] = \boxed{0.0512 \text{ J}}$$

9. The total energy required to bring the centrifuge from rest to 420 rad/s is equal to the kinetic energy when it rotates at $\omega = 420$ rad/s.

$$K = \frac{1}{2}I\omega^2 = \frac{1}{2}(6.5 \times 10^{-3} \text{ kg} \cdot \text{m}^2)\left(420 \frac{\text{rad}}{\text{s}}\right)^2 = \boxed{570 \text{ J}}$$

13. The point of application of the force of gravity is at the geometrical center of the door, so $r_\perp = \dfrac{1.0 \text{ m}}{2}$. The force is equal to the weight of the door.

$$\tau = r_\perp F = r_\perp mg = \left(\frac{1.0 \text{ m}}{2}\right)(50.0 \text{ N}) = \boxed{25 \text{ N} \cdot \text{m}}$$

15. $|\tau| = F_\perp r = mgr = (0.124 \text{ kg})\left(9.8 \dfrac{\text{N}}{\text{kg}}\right)(0.25 \text{ m}) = \boxed{0.30 \text{ N} \cdot \text{m}}$

17. The center of gravity is located at the center of mass.

$$x_{\text{CM}} = \frac{m_1 x_1 + m_2 x_2 + m_3 x_3}{M} = \frac{(5.0 \text{ kg})(0.0) + (15.0 \text{ kg})(5.0 \text{ m}) + (10.0 \text{ kg})(10.0 \text{ m})}{5.0 \text{ kg} + 15.0 \text{ kg} + 10.0 \text{ kg}} = \boxed{5.83 \text{ m}}$$

21. $W = \tau\theta = r_\perp F\theta = (0.100 \text{ m})(20.0 \text{ N})(12 \text{ rev})\left(\dfrac{2\pi \text{ rad}}{\text{rev}}\right) = \boxed{150 \text{ J}}$

25. **(a)** Choose the axis of rotation at the point at which the right-hand cable connects to the platform. Let $m_1 = 75$ kg and $m_2 = 20.0$ kg. Let $l = 5.0$ m.
The system is in equilibrium.

$$\tau_{net} = 0 = -Fl + m_1 g(l - d) + m_2 g\left(\frac{l}{2}\right), \text{ so}$$

$$Fl = g\left[m_1(l - d) + m_2 \frac{l}{2}\right]$$

$$F = g\left[m_1\left(1 - \frac{d}{l}\right) + \frac{m_2}{2}\right]$$

$$= \left(9.8 \ \frac{N}{kg}\right)\left[(75 \text{ kg})\left(1 - \frac{2.0 \text{ m}}{5.0 \text{ m}}\right) + \frac{20.0 \text{ kg}}{2}\right]$$

$$= \boxed{540 \text{ N}}.$$

(b) $F_{net} = 0 = -m_1 g - m_2 g + F_L + F_R$, so

$$F_R = (m_1 + m_2)g - F_L = (75 \text{ kg} + 20.0 \text{ kg})\left(9.8 \ \frac{N}{kg}\right) - 539 \text{ N} = \boxed{390 \text{ N}}.$$

27. Choose the axis of rotation at the fulcrum.
$\tau_{net} = 0 = F(3.0 \text{ m}) - (1200 \text{ N})(0.50 \text{ m})$, so

$$F = \frac{(1200 \text{ N})(0.50 \text{ m})}{3.0 \text{ m}} = \boxed{200 \text{ N}}.$$

29. Choose the axis of rotation at the point of contact between the driveway and the ladder.
$F_{net,\ x} = 0 = f - N_w$, so $f = N_w$.

$$\tau_{net} = 0 = N_w(4.7 \text{ m}) - W_1(2.5 \text{ m})\cos\theta - W_p\left(\frac{3.0 \text{ m}}{4.7 \text{ m}}\right)(5.0 \text{ m})\cos\theta, \text{ so}$$

$$N_w = \frac{\cos\theta}{4.7 \text{ m}}\left[W_1(2.5 \text{ m}) + W_p\left(\frac{15 \text{ m}}{4.7}\right)\right].$$

Find θ.
$4.7 \text{ m} = (5.0 \text{ m})\sin\theta$

$$\theta = \sin^{-1}\frac{4.7}{5.0}$$

Calculate f.

$$f = N_w = \frac{\cos\sin^{-1}\frac{4.7}{5.0}}{4.7 \text{ m}}\left[(120 \text{ N})(2.5 \text{ m}) + (680 \text{ N})\left(\frac{15 \text{ m}}{4.7}\right)\right] = 180 \text{ N}$$

So, the force of friction is $\boxed{180 \text{ N toward the wall}}$.

31. Choose the axis of rotation at the hinge.

$$\tau_{\text{net}} = 0 = Wl\cos\theta - Tl\sin\theta + mg\,\frac{l}{2}\cos\theta$$

$$Tl\sin\theta = Wl\cos\theta + mg\,\frac{l}{2}\cos\theta$$

$$\boxed{T = \frac{W + \frac{mg}{2}}{\tan\theta}}$$

$$\boxed{\text{For } \theta = 0, T \to \infty, \text{ and for } \theta = 90°, T \to 0.}$$

33. Palms:

Choose the axis of rotation at the point of contact between the floor and the man's feet.

$$\tau_{\text{net}} = 0 = -F(1.70\text{ m}) + mg(1.00\text{ m})$$

$$F = \frac{mg(1.00\text{ m})}{1.70\text{ m}} = \frac{(68\text{ kg})\left(9.8\ \frac{\text{N}}{\text{kg}}\right)(1.00\text{ m})}{1.70\text{ m}} = \boxed{390\text{ N}}$$

Feet:

Use Newton's second law.

$$F_{\text{net, }y} = 0 = F_{\text{p}} + F_{\text{f}} - mg$$

$$F_{\text{f}} = mg - F_{\text{p}} = (68\text{ kg})\left(9.8\ \frac{\text{N}}{\text{kg}}\right) - 392\text{ N} = \boxed{270\text{ N}}$$

37. Choose the axis of rotation at the elbow.

$$\tau_{\text{net}} = 0 = -W_{\text{m}}(35.0\text{ cm}) - W_{\text{a}}(16.5\text{ cm}) + F_{\text{b}}(5.00\text{ cm})\sin\theta$$

$$F_{\text{b}} = \frac{W_{\text{m}}(35.0\text{ cm}) + W_{\text{a}}(16.5\text{ cm})}{(5.00\text{ cm})\sin\theta} = \frac{(9.9\text{ N})(35.0\text{ cm}) + (18.0\text{ N})(16.5\text{ cm})}{(5.00\text{ cm})\dfrac{30.0\text{ cm}}{\sqrt{(30.0\text{ cm})^2 + (5.00\text{ cm})^2}}} = \boxed{130\text{ N}}$$

41. Use the rotational form of Newton's second law.

$I = \dfrac{1}{2}mr^2$ for a uniform disk.

$$\tau = I\alpha = \frac{1}{2}mr^2\left(\frac{\omega_{\text{f}}^2 - \omega_{\text{i}}^2}{2\Delta\theta}\right) = \frac{mr^2\omega_{\text{f}}^2}{4\Delta\theta} = \frac{(0.22\text{ kg})\left(\frac{0.305\text{ m}}{2}\right)^2\left(3.49\ \frac{\text{rad}}{\text{s}}\right)^2}{4(2.0\text{ rev})\left(\frac{2\pi\text{ rad}}{\text{rev}}\right)} = \boxed{0.0012\text{ N}\cdot\text{m}}$$

45. (a) Use the rotational form of Newton's second law.

$$\tau = I\alpha = \left(\frac{1}{2}MR^2 + 2mR^2\right)\frac{\Delta\omega}{\Delta t}$$

$$= \left[\frac{1}{2}(350.0\text{ kg})\left(\frac{2.50\text{ m}}{2}\right)^2 + 2(30.0\text{ kg})\left(\frac{2.50\text{ m}}{2}\right)^2\right]\left(\frac{25\text{ rpm}}{20.0\text{ s}}\right)\left(\frac{2\pi\text{ rad}}{\text{rev}}\right)\left(\frac{1\text{ min}}{60\text{ s}}\right) = \boxed{48\text{ N}\cdot\text{m}}$$

(b) Let F be the magnitude of the tangential force with which each child must push the rim.

$$FR + FR = \tau$$

$$F = \frac{\tau}{2R}$$

$$= \frac{48\text{ N}\cdot\text{m}}{2\left(\frac{2.50\text{ m}}{2}\right)}$$

$$= \boxed{19\text{ N}}$$

49. Solid sphere:

$$K_{tr} + K_{rot} = \frac{1}{2}mv^2 + \frac{1}{2}I\omega^2 = \frac{1}{2}mv^2 + \frac{1}{2}\left(\frac{2}{5}mr^2\right)\left(\frac{v}{r}\right)^2 = \frac{1}{2}mv^2 + \frac{1}{5}mv^2 = \frac{7}{10}mv^2$$

Solid cylinder:

$$K_{tr} + K_{rot} = \frac{1}{2}mv^2 + \frac{1}{2}I\omega^2 = \frac{1}{2}mv^2 + \frac{1}{2}\left(\frac{1}{2}mr^2\right)\left(\frac{v}{r}\right)^2 = \frac{1}{2}mv^2 + \frac{1}{4}mv^2 = \frac{3}{4}mv^2$$

Hollow cylinder:

$$K_{tr} + K_{rot} = \frac{1}{2}mv^2 + \frac{1}{2}I\omega^2 = \frac{1}{2}mv^2 + \frac{1}{2}mr^2\left(\frac{v}{r}\right)^2 = \frac{1}{2}mv^2 + \frac{1}{2}mv^2 = mv^2$$

$$\boxed{\text{solid sphere: } K = \frac{7}{10}mv^2; \text{ solid cylinder: } K = \frac{3}{4}mv^2; \text{ hollow cylinder: } K = mv^2}$$

53. At the top of the loop, the cylinder's speed must be at least the speed that results in a centripetal acceleration of g.

$$\frac{v^2}{r} = g, \text{ so } v^2 = gr.$$

So, its kinetic energy is $\frac{1}{2}mv^2 + \frac{1}{2}I\omega^2 = \frac{1}{2}mv^2 + \frac{1}{2}mr^2\left(\frac{v}{r}\right)^2 = mv^2$, and it must equal the potential energy

difference $mgh - mg(2r)$.

Thus,

$$mv^2 = mgh - 2mgr$$
$$mgr = mg(h - 2r)$$
$$r = h - 2r$$
$$h = \boxed{3r}$$

57. $L = I\omega = mr^2\omega = (5.6 \times 10^4 \text{ kg})(2.6 \text{ m})^2(350 \text{ rpm})\left(\frac{2\pi \text{ rad}}{\text{rev}}\right)\left(\frac{1 \text{ min}}{60 \text{ s}}\right) = \boxed{1.4 \times 10^7 \text{ kg} \cdot \text{m}^2/\text{s}}$

59. $\tau = \lim\limits_{\Delta t \to 0} \frac{\Delta L}{\Delta t} = \frac{\Delta L}{\Delta t}$, so $\Delta t = \frac{\Delta L}{\tau} = \frac{-6.40 \frac{\text{kg} \cdot \text{m}^2}{\text{s}}}{-4.00 \text{ N} \cdot \text{m}} = \boxed{1.60 \text{ s}}$.

61. Use conservation of angular momentum.

$$L_i = I_i\omega_i = L_f = I_f\omega_f$$

$$\omega_f = \frac{I_i}{I_f}\omega_i = \frac{1}{0.67}\left(1.0 \frac{\text{rev}}{\text{s}}\right) = \boxed{1.5 \text{ rev/s}}$$

63. Use conservation of angular momentum.

$$L_i = I_i\omega_i = L_f = I_f\omega_f$$

$$\omega_i = \frac{I_f}{I_i}\omega_f = \frac{1}{3.00}\left(\frac{2.00 \text{ rev}}{1.33 \text{ s}}\right)\left(\frac{2\pi \text{ rad}}{\text{rev}}\right) = \boxed{3.15 \text{ rad/s}}$$

65. Let $\vec{L}_i = L$ in the +y-direction. Then $\Delta\vec{L}$ has components $\Delta L_x = L\sin\theta$ and $\Delta L_y = L - L\cos\theta = L(1-\cos\theta)$. So,

$$\left|\Delta\vec{L}\right| = \sqrt{(L\sin\theta)^2 + [L(1-\cos\theta)]^2} = L\sqrt{\sin^2 60.0° + (1-\cos 60.0°)^2} = 1.00L.$$

The magnitude of the required torque is

$$\tau = \left|\frac{\Delta\vec{L}}{\Delta t}\right| = \frac{1.00L}{\Delta t} = \frac{1.00I\omega}{\Delta t} = \frac{\frac{1}{2}mr^2\omega}{\Delta t} = \frac{(1.00\times10^5 \text{ kg})(2.00 \text{ m})^2(300.0 \text{ rpm})}{2(3.00 \text{ s})}\left(\frac{2\pi \text{ rad}}{\text{rev}}\right)\left(\frac{1 \text{ min}}{60 \text{ s}}\right)$$

$$= \boxed{2.10\times10^6 \text{ N}\cdot\text{m}}$$

69. (a) $I = \dfrac{1}{2}MR^2 = \dfrac{1}{2}(200.0 \text{ kg})(0.40 \text{ m})^2 = \boxed{16 \text{ kg}\cdot\text{m}^2}$

(b) $K_{\text{rot}} = \dfrac{1}{2}I\omega^2 = \dfrac{1}{2}(16 \text{ kg}\cdot\text{m}^2)\left(3160 \dfrac{\text{rad}}{\text{s}}\right)^2 = \boxed{8.0\times10^7 \text{ J}}$

(c) $\dfrac{K_{\text{rot}}}{K_{\text{tr}}} = \dfrac{K_{\text{rot}}}{\frac{1}{2}mv^2} = \dfrac{2(8.0\times10^7 \text{ J})}{(1000.0 \text{ kg})\left(22.4 \frac{\text{m}}{\text{s}}\right)^2} = \boxed{320}$

(d) Work done by air resistance = stored energy

$$Fd = K_{\text{rot}}$$

$$d = \frac{K_{\text{rot}}}{F}$$

$$= \frac{8.0\times10^7 \text{ J}}{670.0 \text{ N}}$$

$$= \boxed{120 \text{ km}}$$

73. $\tau = F_\perp r = mgr = (10.0 \text{ kg})\left(9.8 \dfrac{\text{N}}{\text{kg}}\right)(1.0 \text{ m}) = \boxed{98 \text{ N}\cdot\text{m}}$

75. Use conservation of energy.

$$\Delta K = -\Delta U$$

$$\frac{1}{2}I\omega^2 = mg(2r)$$

$$\frac{1}{2}\left[\frac{1}{3}m(2r)^2\right]\omega^2 = 2rmg$$

$$\frac{2}{3}r^2\omega^2 = 2rg$$

$$\omega^2 = \frac{3g}{r}$$

$$\omega = \sqrt{\frac{3\left(9.8 \frac{\text{m}}{\text{s}^2}\right)}{1.0 \text{ m}}}$$

$$= \boxed{5.4 \text{ rad/s}}$$

77. (a) Choose the axis of rotation at the point of contact between the ladder and the floor.

$$\tau_{\text{net}} = 0 = mg(4.0 \text{ m})\cos 60.0° - F(6.0 \text{ m})\cos 60.0°$$

$$F = \frac{4.0}{6.0}mg = \frac{4.0}{6.0}(15 \text{ kg})\left(9.8 \ \frac{\text{N}}{\text{kg}}\right) = \boxed{98 \text{ N}}$$

(b) | This does not help the person trying to lift the ladder, since the torque problem is not alleviated by exerting a force at the point of rotation.

81. (a) $\omega_f = 2\omega_{\text{av}} = 2\dfrac{v_{\text{av}}}{r} = 2\left(\dfrac{2\pi}{C}\right)\dfrac{\Delta x}{\Delta t} = \dfrac{4\pi(10.0 \text{ m})}{(2.00 \text{ m})(10.0 \text{ s})} = \boxed{6.28 \text{ rad/s}}$

(b) $L = I\omega = mr^2\omega = m\left(\dfrac{C}{2\pi}\right)^2\omega = (1.50 \text{ kg})\left(\dfrac{2.00 \text{ m}}{2\pi}\right)^2\left(2\pi \ \dfrac{\text{rad}}{\text{s}}\right) = \boxed{0.955 \text{ kg} \cdot \text{m}^2/\text{s}}$

(c) The force of $\boxed{\text{friction}}$ supplied the net torque.

(d) $\tau_{\text{av}} = \dfrac{\Delta L}{\Delta t}$

$fr =$

$f\dfrac{C}{2\pi} =$

$f = \dfrac{2\pi}{C}\dfrac{\Delta L}{\Delta t}$

$= \dfrac{2\pi\left(0.955 \ \frac{\text{kg} \cdot \text{m}^2}{\text{s}}\right)}{(2.00 \text{ m})(10.0 \text{ s})}$

$= \boxed{0.300 \text{ N}}$

85. (a) Use conservation of angular momentum.

$L_i = L_f$

$I_0\omega_0 = (I_0 + mR^2)\omega$

$$\omega = \boxed{\dfrac{I_0\omega_0}{I_0 + mR^2}}$$

(b) Before:

$$K_{\text{rot}} = \boxed{\dfrac{1}{2}I_0\omega_0^2}$$

$L = \boxed{I_0\omega_0}$

After:

$$K_{\text{rot}} = \dfrac{1}{2}I\omega^2 = \dfrac{1}{2}(I_0 + mR^2)\left(\dfrac{I_0\omega_0}{I_0 + mR^2}\right) = \boxed{\dfrac{1}{2}\dfrac{I_0^2\omega_0^2}{I_0 + mR^2}}$$

$L = \boxed{I_0\omega_0}$

89. Since the bike travels with constant velocity, $a_{CM} = 0$ and $\tau_{net} = I\alpha = I\dfrac{a_{CM}}{r_2} = 0$. Also, $\tau_{net} = 0 = fr_2 - F_C r_1$.

So, $F_c = \dfrac{r_2}{r_1} f = 6.0(3.8\ \text{N}) = \boxed{23\ \text{N}}$.

93. (a) Use conservation of angular momentum.

$$L_f = L_i$$
$$I_f \omega_f = I_i \omega_i$$
$$\omega_f = \dfrac{I_i}{I_f} \omega_i$$

$$= \dfrac{(2.40\ \text{kg}\cdot\text{m}^2)\left(0.50\ \tfrac{\text{rev}}{\text{s}}\right)}{\begin{array}{c} 2.40\ \text{kg}\cdot\text{m}^2 - 2\left[\tfrac{1}{3}(3.00\ \text{kg})(0.65\ \text{m})^2\right] - 2(1.00\ \text{kg})(0.65\ \text{m})^2 \\ + 2\left[\tfrac{1}{3}(3.00\ \text{kg})(0.22\ \text{m})^2\right] + 2(1.00\ \text{kg})(0.22\ \text{m})^2 \end{array}}$$

$$= \boxed{1.3\ \text{rev/s}}$$

(b) The rate of rotation $\boxed{\text{stays the same}}$ since no net external torque acts on the system. (The falling dumbbells are no longer part of the system.)

Chapter 9

FLUIDS

Problems

1. $P = \dfrac{F}{A} = \dfrac{500 \text{ N}}{1.0 \text{ cm}^2} \left(\dfrac{100 \text{ cm}}{1 \text{ m}}\right)^2 \left(\dfrac{1 \text{ atm}}{101.3 \times 10^3 \text{ Pa}}\right) = \boxed{50 \text{ atm}}$

5. The gas pushes outward equally on each wall of the cube.

$F = PA = (4.0 \times 10^5 \text{ Pa})(0.10 \text{ m})^2 = 4.0 \text{ kN}$

So, $\vec{\mathbf{F}} = \boxed{4.0 \text{ kN southward}}$.

9. (a) The pressure in the fluid is equal to $P = \dfrac{F_b}{A_b}$. The pressure is also equal to the normal force N divided by the area of the brake pad piston A.

$N = PA = \dfrac{A}{A_b} F_b = \dfrac{12.0 \text{ cm}^2}{3.0 \text{ cm}^2}(7.5 \text{ N}) = \boxed{30 \text{ N}}$

(b) The frictional force due to one pad is μN, so the total force is $2\mu N$.

$\tau = F_\perp r = 2\mu N r = 1.6(3.0 \times 10^1 \text{ N})(0.12 \text{ m}) = \boxed{5.8 \text{ N} \cdot \text{m}}$

11. $P = P_{atm} + \rho g d = 1.0 \text{ atm} + \left(1025 \dfrac{\text{kg}}{\text{m}^3}\right)\left(9.8 \dfrac{\text{m}}{\text{s}^2}\right)(10 \text{ m})\left(\dfrac{1 \text{ atm}}{1.013 \times 10^5 \text{ Pa}}\right) = \boxed{2 \text{ atm}}$

13. (a) $\Delta P = \rho_{water} g d = \left(1.00 \times 10^3 \dfrac{\text{kg}}{\text{m}^3}\right)\left(9.8 \dfrac{\text{m}}{\text{s}^2}\right)(35.0 \text{ m}) = \boxed{343 \text{ kPa}}$

(b) $\Delta P = -\rho_{air} g h = -\left(1.20 \dfrac{\text{kg}}{\text{m}^3}\right)\left(9.8 \dfrac{\text{m}}{\text{s}^2}\right)(35 \text{ m}) = -410 \text{ Pa}$

The pressure decreases by $\boxed{410 \text{ Pa}}$.

17. $V_{Pt} = \dfrac{m_{Pt}}{\rho_{Pt}} = \dfrac{1.00 \text{ kg}}{21{,}500 \dfrac{\text{kg}}{\text{m}^3}} = \boxed{4.65 \times 10^{-5} \text{ m}^3}$

Compare V_{Pt} to V_{Al}.

$\dfrac{V_{Pt}}{V_{Al}} = \dfrac{\frac{m_{Pt}}{\rho_{Pt}}}{\frac{m_{Al}}{\rho_{Al}}} = \left(\dfrac{m_{Pt}}{m_{Al}}\right)\left(\dfrac{\rho_{Al}}{\rho_{Pt}}\right) = 1\left(\dfrac{2702}{21{,}500}\right) = \boxed{0.126}$

19. (a) $\left(32 \dfrac{\text{lb}}{\text{in.}^2}\right)\left(\dfrac{1.013 \times 10^5 \text{ Pa}}{14.7 \frac{\text{lb}}{\text{in.}^2}}\right) = \boxed{2.2 \times 10^5 \text{ Pa}}$

(b) $\left(32 \dfrac{\text{lb}}{\text{in.}^2}\right)\left(\dfrac{760.0 \text{ torr}}{14.7 \frac{\text{lb}}{\text{in.}^2}}\right) = \boxed{1700 \text{ torr}}$

(c) $\left(32 \dfrac{\text{lb}}{\text{in.}^2}\right)\left(\dfrac{1 \text{ atm}}{14.7 \frac{\text{lb}}{\text{in.}^2}}\right) = \boxed{2.2 \text{ atm}}$

21. $P_{\text{abs}} = P_{\text{atm}} + P_{\text{gauge}} = 74.0 \text{ cm Hg} + 40.0 \text{ cm Hg} = \boxed{114.0 \text{ cm Hg}}$

23. (a) The amount the fluid rises is one-half the difference of levels, or $\dfrac{\Delta h_{\text{oil}}}{2}$.

$$\Delta P = \rho_{\text{Hg}} g \Delta h_{\text{Hg}} = \rho_{\text{oil}} g \Delta h_{\text{oil}}, \text{ so } \dfrac{\Delta h_{\text{oil}}}{2} = \dfrac{\rho_{\text{Hg}}}{2\rho_{\text{oil}}} \Delta h_{\text{Hg}} = \dfrac{13.6 \frac{\text{g}}{\text{cm}^3}}{2\left(0.90 \frac{\text{g}}{\text{cm}^3}\right)}(0.74 \text{ cm Hg}) = \boxed{5.6 \text{ cm}}.$$

(b) $\dfrac{\Delta h_{\text{oil}}}{2}\left(\dfrac{\rho_{\text{oil}}}{\rho_{\text{Hg}}}\right) = (5.6 \text{ cm})\dfrac{0.90 \frac{\text{g}}{\text{cm}^3}}{13.6 \frac{\text{g}}{\text{cm}^3}} = \boxed{0.37 \text{ cm}}$

25. Since the goose has 25% of its volume submerged, its density is 25% of water's, or about $\boxed{250 \text{ kg/m}^3}$.

29. Let the $+y$-direction be downward. Use Newton's second law.

$\Sigma F_y = mg - F_B = ma$

$a = g - \dfrac{F_B}{m} = g - \dfrac{\rho_w g V}{m} = g\left(1 - \dfrac{\rho_w V}{\rho V}\right) = g\left(1 - \dfrac{1}{5.0}\right) = 0.80g$

So, $\vec{\mathbf{a}} = \boxed{0.80g \text{ downward}}$.

33. The new density of the fish is $\rho = \dfrac{m_f + m_a}{V_f + V_a} = \dfrac{m_f + \rho_a V_a}{\dfrac{m_f}{\rho_f} + V_a} = \rho_w$.

Solve for V_a.

$m_f + \rho_a V_a = \dfrac{\rho_w}{\rho_f} m_f + \rho_w V_a$

$V_a(\rho_a - \rho_w) = m_f\left(\dfrac{\rho_w}{\rho_f} - 1\right)$

$V_a = m_f \dfrac{1 - \dfrac{\rho_w}{\rho_f}}{\rho_w - \rho_a}$

$= (0.0100 \text{ kg})\dfrac{1 - \dfrac{1060 \frac{\text{kg}}{\text{m}^3}}{1080 \frac{\text{kg}}{\text{m}^3}}}{1060 \frac{\text{kg}}{\text{m}^3} - 1.20 \frac{\text{kg}}{\text{m}^3}}$

$= \boxed{0.17 \text{ cm}^3}$

35. Use the continuity equation for an ideal fluid.

$$A_2 v_2 = A_1 v_1$$

$$v_2 = \frac{A_1}{A_2} v_1$$

$$= \frac{\pi r_1^2}{\pi r_2^2} v_1$$

$$= \left(\frac{2.0 \text{ cm}}{0.40 \text{ cm}}\right)^2 \left(2.0 \ \frac{\text{m}}{\text{s}}\right)$$

$$= \boxed{50 \text{ m/s}}$$

37. (a) Use the continuity equation for an ideal fluid.

$$v_2 = \frac{A_1}{A_2} v_1 = \frac{\pi r_1^2}{\pi r_2^2} v_1 = \left(\frac{r_1}{r_2}\right)^2 v_1 = \left(\frac{1.00 \text{ mm}}{8.00 \text{ mm}}\right)^2 \left(25.0 \ \frac{\text{m}}{\text{s}}\right) = \boxed{39.1 \text{ cm/s}}$$

(b) $\dfrac{\Delta V}{\Delta t} = A_1 v_1 = \pi (1.00 \times 10^{-3} \text{ m})^2 \left(25.0 \ \dfrac{\text{m}}{\text{s}}\right) = \boxed{78.5 \text{ cm}^3/\text{s}}$

(c) $\dfrac{\Delta m}{\Delta t} = \rho A_1 v_1 = \left(1.0 \ \dfrac{\text{g}}{\text{cm}^3}\right)\left(78.5 \ \dfrac{\text{cm}^3}{\text{s}}\right) = \boxed{78.5 \text{ g/s}}$

39. The potential energy difference is relatively small, so Bernoulli's equation becomes

$$P_1 + \frac{1}{2}\rho v_1^2 = P_2 + \frac{1}{2}\rho v_2^2$$

$$P_1 - P_2 = \frac{1}{2}\rho v_2^2 - \frac{1}{2}\rho v_1^2$$

Estimate the force.

$$F = \Delta P A = (P_1 - P_2) A = \left(\frac{1}{2}\rho v_2^2 - \frac{1}{2}\rho v_1^2\right) A = \frac{1}{2} A \rho (v_2^2 - v_1^2) = \frac{1}{2}(28 \text{ m}^2)\left(1.3 \ \frac{\text{kg}}{\text{m}^3}\right)\left[\left(190 \ \frac{\text{m}}{\text{s}}\right)^2 - \left(160 \ \frac{\text{m}}{\text{s}}\right)^2\right]$$

$$= \boxed{1.9 \times 10^5 \text{ N}}$$

41. (a) $\dfrac{\Delta W}{\Delta t} = \dfrac{mg\Delta y}{\Delta t} = \rho g \Delta y \dfrac{\Delta V}{\Delta t} = \left(1.0 \times 10^3 \ \dfrac{\text{kg}}{\text{m}^3}\right)\left(9.8 \ \dfrac{\text{m}}{\text{s}^2}\right)(40.0 \text{ m})\left(2.0 \times 10^{-4} \ \dfrac{\text{m}^3}{\text{s}}\right) = \boxed{78 \text{ W}}$

(b) Assuming that the speed of the water at the top and bottom of the well is zero, Bernoulli's equation gives

$$\Delta P = \rho g \Delta y = \left(1.0 \times 10^3 \ \frac{\text{kg}}{\text{m}^3}\right)\left(9.8 \ \frac{\text{m}}{\text{s}^2}\right)(40.0 \text{ m}) = \boxed{390 \text{ kPa}} \ .$$

(c) Since ΔP is greater than atmospheric pressure, the pump must be $\boxed{\text{at the bottom}}$ so that it can push the water up.

45. (a) Use Poiseuille's law to find the pressure of the fluid in the syringe, P_s.

$$\frac{\Delta V}{\Delta t} = \frac{\pi \Delta P r^4}{8\eta L}$$

$$\left(\frac{8\eta L}{\pi r^4}\right)\frac{\Delta V}{\Delta t} = P_s - P_v$$

$$P_s = (16.0 \text{ mm Hg})\left(\frac{1.013\times10^5 \text{ Pa}}{760.0 \text{ mm Hg}}\right) + \frac{8(2.00\times10^{-3} \text{ Pa}\cdot\text{s})(0.0300 \text{ m})}{\pi(0.000300 \text{ m})^4}\left(0.250 \frac{\text{cm}^3}{\text{s}}\right)\left(\frac{\text{m}}{100 \text{ cm}}\right)^3$$

$$= \boxed{6850 \text{ Pa}}$$

(b) $F = PA = (6850 \text{ Pa})(1.00 \text{ cm}^2)\left(\frac{\text{m}}{100 \text{ cm}}\right)^2 = \boxed{0.685 \text{ N}}$

47.

$$\frac{\frac{\Delta V}{\Delta t}_C}{\frac{\Delta V}{\Delta t}_B} = \frac{4\left[\frac{\pi \Delta P_C r^4}{8\eta\left(\frac{L}{2}\right)}\right]}{2\left(\frac{\pi \Delta P_B r^4}{8\eta L}\right)} = \frac{4\Delta P_C}{\Delta P_B}, \text{ so}$$

$$\frac{\Delta V}{\Delta t}_C = \frac{4\Delta P_C}{\Delta P_B}\left(\frac{\Delta V}{\Delta t}_B\right) = 4\left(\frac{2.0\times10^5 \text{ Pa}}{4.0\times10^5 \text{ Pa}}\right)\left(0.020 \frac{\text{m}^3}{\text{s}}\right) = \boxed{0.040 \text{ m}^3/\text{s}}.$$

49. (a) Use Poiseuille's law and $\frac{\Delta V}{\Delta t} = Av$ to find ΔP.

$$\frac{\pi \Delta P r^4}{8\eta L} = \frac{\Delta V}{\Delta t}$$

$$= Av$$

$$\Delta P = \left(\frac{8\eta L}{\pi r^4}\right)\pi r^2 v$$

$$= \frac{8\eta L v}{r^2}$$

$$= \frac{8(2.1\times10^{-3} \text{ Pa}\cdot\text{s})(0.20 \text{ m})\left(0.060 \frac{\text{m}}{\text{s}}\right)}{(0.0020 \text{ m})^2}$$

$$= \boxed{50 \text{ Pa}}$$

(b) $\Delta P = \dfrac{8(2.1\times10^{-3} \text{ Pa}\cdot\text{s})(0.0010 \text{ m})\left(0.00060 \frac{\text{m}}{\text{s}}\right)}{(3.0\times10^{-6} \text{ m})^2} = \boxed{1100 \text{ Pa}}$

(c) $(100 \text{ torr})\left(\dfrac{101.3 \text{ kPa}}{760.0 \text{ torr}}\right) = 10 \text{ kPa}$

100 torr is approximately $\boxed{10 \text{ kPa}}$, which is much larger than both pressures found in parts (a) and (b).

53. Use Stokes's law and Newton's second law.

$\Sigma F_y = F_D + F_B - W = 0$, so

$$6\pi\eta rv + m_l g - m_s g = 0$$
$$6\pi\eta rv = g(m_s - m_l)$$
$$\eta = \frac{\frac{4}{3}\pi r^3 g(\rho_s - \rho_l)}{6\pi rv}$$
$$= \frac{2r^2 g(\rho_s - \rho_l)}{9v}$$

Find the viscosity of the second liquid by forming a proportion.

$$\frac{\eta_2}{\eta_1} = \frac{\frac{2r^2 g(\rho_s - \rho_l)}{9v_2}}{\frac{2r^2 g(\rho_s - \rho_l)}{9v_1}}$$
$$= \frac{v_1}{v_2}$$
$$\eta_2 = \frac{v_1}{1.2v_1}\eta_1$$
$$= \frac{\eta_1}{1.2}$$
$$= \frac{0.5 \text{ Pa}\cdot\text{s}}{1.2}$$
$$= \boxed{0.4 \text{ Pa}\cdot\text{s}}$$

57.

m (g)	8	12	16	20	24	28
$v_t\left(\dfrac{\text{cm}}{\text{s}}\right)$	1.0	1.5	2.0	2.5	3.0	3.5
$\dfrac{m}{v_t}\left(\dfrac{\text{g}\cdot\text{s}}{\text{cm}}\right)$	8	8.0	8.0	8.0	8.0	8.0
$\dfrac{m}{v_t^2}\left(\dfrac{\text{g}\cdot\text{s}^2}{\text{cm}^2}\right)$	8	5.3	4.0	3.2	2.7	2.3

For a viscous drag force, $v_t \propto m$.

For a turbulent drag force, $v_t \propto \sqrt{m}$.

$\boxed{\text{Since } m/v_t \text{ is constant, the drag force is primarily viscous.}}$

61. (a) γ is the force per unit length with which the surface pulls on its edge, so $W = F\Delta s = \boxed{\gamma L\Delta s}$.

(b) $W = \Delta E$ and $\Delta A = L\Delta s$, so $\boxed{\Delta E = \gamma\Delta A}$, where ΔE is the increase in surface energy.

(c) $\gamma \Delta A = \Delta E$

$$\gamma = \frac{\Delta E}{\Delta A}$$

So, γ can be thought of as the surface energy (ΔE) per unit area (ΔA).

(d) $F \Delta s = \gamma L \Delta s$

$$\frac{F}{L} = \gamma$$

Thus, γ has units N/m.

$\gamma = \dfrac{\Delta E}{\Delta A}$, thus γ has units J/m^2.

65. $\dfrac{\text{mass of fat}}{\text{total mass}} \times 100\% = \dfrac{\rho V}{m} \times 100\% = \dfrac{\left(890 \, \frac{\text{kg}}{\text{m}^3} \right)(0.020 \text{ m}^3)}{90.0 \text{ kg}} \times 100\% = \boxed{20\%}$

69. (a) Let V be the volume of the liquid displaced and V_h be the volume of the hydrometer. Then $V_h - V = Ah$ where A is the cross-sectional area of the stem and h is the height above the liquid.
Use Newton's second law.
$$\Sigma F_y = F_B - W = 0$$

$$F_B = W$$
$$\rho g V = m_h g$$
$$(\text{S.G.}) \rho_w V = m_h$$
$$1.00 \rho_w (V_h - Ah) =$$
$$V_h - Ah = \frac{m_h}{1.00 \rho_w}$$
$$Ah = V_h - \frac{m_h}{1.00 \rho_w}$$
$$h = \frac{1}{A} \left(V_h - \frac{m_h}{1.00 \rho_w} \right)$$
$$= \frac{1}{0.400 \text{ cm}^2} \left[8.80 \text{ cm}^3 - \frac{4.80 \text{ g}}{1.00 \left(1.00 \, \frac{\text{g}}{\text{cm}^3} \right)} \right]$$
$$= \boxed{10.0 \text{ cm}}$$

(b) $(\text{S.G.}) \rho_w (V_h - Ah) = m_h$

$$\text{S.G.} = \frac{m_h}{\rho_w (V_h - Ah)}$$
$$= \frac{4.80 \text{ g}}{\left(1.00 \, \frac{\text{g}}{\text{cm}^3} \right) [8.80 \text{ cm}^3 - (0.400 \text{ cm}^2)(7.25 \text{ cm})]}$$
$$= \boxed{0.814}$$

(c) For the minimum S.G., the volume of the displaced liquid is equal to the volume of the hydrometer, so $(\text{S.G.})\rho_w V_h = m_h$.

$$\text{S.G.}_{\text{min}} = \frac{m_h}{\rho_w V_h} = \frac{4.80 \text{ g}}{\left(1.00 \ \frac{\text{g}}{\text{cm}^3}\right)(8.80 \text{ cm}^3)} = \boxed{0.545}$$

73. $y_1 \approx y_2$ and $v_2 = 0$ (for the opening where the airspeed is zero), so Bernoulli's equation becomes

$$P_1 + \frac{1}{2}\rho_a v_1^2 = P_2$$

$$\frac{1}{2}\rho_a v_1^2 = \Delta P$$

$$v_1 = \sqrt{\frac{2\Delta P}{\rho_a}}$$

$$= \sqrt{\frac{2\rho_m g \Delta y_m}{\rho_a}} \quad (\text{since } \Delta P = \rho_m g \Delta y_m)$$

$$= \sqrt{\frac{2\left(13{,}600 \ \frac{\text{kg}}{\text{m}^3}\right)\left(9.8 \ \frac{\text{m}}{\text{s}^2}\right)(0.25 \text{ m})}{0.90 \ \frac{\text{kg}}{\text{m}^3}}}$$

$$= \boxed{270 \text{ m/s}}$$

77. (a) Use Newton's second law.

$$\Sigma F_y = F_B - F_D - W = 0, \text{ so}$$

$$F_D = F_B - W$$

$$6\pi\eta r v_t = \rho_w g V - \rho_a g V$$

$$v_t = \frac{\frac{4}{3}\pi r^3 g(\rho_w - \rho_a)}{6\pi\eta r}$$

$$= \frac{2r^2 g(\rho_w - \rho_a)}{9\eta}$$

$$= \frac{2(1.0\times10^{-3} \text{ m})^2\left(9.8 \ \frac{\text{m}}{\text{s}^2}\right)\left(1.0\times10^3 \ \frac{\text{kg}}{\text{m}^3} - 1.2 \ \frac{\text{kg}}{\text{m}^3}\right)}{9(1.0\times10^{-3} \text{ Pa}\cdot\text{s})}$$

$$= 2.2 \text{ m/s}$$

So, $\vec{v}_t = \boxed{2.2 \text{ m/s up}}$.

(b) $\Delta P = \rho g \Delta y$

$$\frac{\Delta P}{\Delta t} = \rho g \frac{\Delta y}{\Delta t}$$

$$= \rho g v_t$$

$$= \left(1.0\times10^3 \ \frac{\text{kg}}{\text{m}^3}\right)\left(9.8 \ \frac{\text{m}}{\text{s}^2}\right)\left(2.175 \ \frac{\text{m}}{\text{s}}\right)$$

$$= \boxed{21 \text{ kPa/s}}$$

81. (a) Since a pump maintains a pressure difference between the outflow and intake pressures, the maximum depth is given by $P_{atm} = \rho g d_{max}$.

$$d_{max} = \frac{P_{atm}}{\rho g} = \frac{1.013 \times 10^5 \text{ Pa}}{\left(1.00 \times 10^3 \ \frac{kg}{m^3}\right)\left(9.8 \ \frac{m}{s^2}\right)} = \boxed{10 \text{ m}}$$

(b) A pump at the bottom of a well does not rely on a pressure difference to bring the water to the surface; it pushes the water up from below.

Chapter 10

ELASTICITY AND OSCILLATIONS

Problems

1. The stress is proportional to the strain.

$$Y\frac{\Delta L}{L} = \frac{F}{A}$$

$$\Delta L = \frac{FL}{YA}$$

$$= \frac{(5.8\times10^4 \text{ N})(2.5 \text{ m})}{(200\times10^9 \text{ Pa})(7.5\times10^{-3} \text{ m}^2)}$$

$$= \boxed{0.1 \text{ mm}}$$

3. The stress is proportional to the strain.

$$\Delta L = \frac{FL}{YA} = \frac{(5.0\times10^3 \text{ N})(2.0 \text{ m})}{(9.2\times10^{10} \text{ Pa})(5.0 \text{ mm}^2)\left(\frac{1 \text{ m}}{1000 \text{ mm}}\right)^2} = \boxed{2.2 \text{ cm}}$$

5. (a) The average power required is equal to the kinetic energy change divided by the elapsed time it takes for the flea to reach its peak velocity.

$$P_{av} = \frac{\Delta K}{\Delta t} = \frac{\frac{1}{2}m(v_f^2 - v_i^2)}{\Delta t} = \frac{mv_f^2}{2\Delta t} = \frac{(0.45\times10^{-6} \text{ kg})\left(0.74 \frac{\text{m}}{\text{s}}\right)^2}{2(1.0\times10^{-3} \text{ s})} = \boxed{1.2\times10^{-4} \text{ W}}$$

(b) $\left(60 \frac{\text{W}}{\text{kg}}\right)(0.45\times10^{-6} \text{ kg})(0.2) = 5\times10^{-6} \text{ W} < 1.2\times10^{-4} \text{ W}$

$\boxed{\text{No}}$, the flea's muscle cannot provide the power needed.

(c) There are two pads, so the total energy store is $2U = 2\left(\frac{1}{2}k(\Delta L)^2\right) = k(\Delta L)^2$.

$$U = k(\Delta L)^2 = Y\frac{A}{L}(\Delta L)^2 = Y\frac{L^2}{L}L^2 = YL^3 = \left(1.7\times10^6 \frac{\text{N}}{\text{m}^2}\right)(6.0\times10^{-5} \text{ m})^3 = \boxed{3.7\times10^{-7} \text{ J}}$$

(d) $P_{av} = \frac{\Delta U}{\Delta t} = \frac{3.7\times10^{-7} \text{ J}}{1.0\times10^{-3} \text{ s}} = 3.7\times10^{-4} \text{ W} > 1.2\times10^{-4} \text{ W}$

$\boxed{\text{Yes}}$, enough power is provided for the jump.

9. Tension:
   For tensile stress and strain, the graph is far from being linear, but for relatively small values of stress and strain, it is approximately linear. So, for small values of tensile stress and strain, Young's Modulus is

$$Y = \frac{\text{stress}}{\text{strain}} = \frac{5.0 \times 10^7 \frac{N}{m^2}}{0.0033} = \boxed{1.5 \times 10^{10} \text{ N/m}^2}.$$

   Compression:

   Similarly, for small values of stress and strain $Y = \dfrac{-4.5 \times 10^7 \frac{N}{m^2}}{-0.0050} = \boxed{9.0 \times 10^9 \text{ N/m}^2}.$

11. Set the stress equal to the tensile strength of the hair to find the diameter of the hair.

$$\text{tensile strength} = \frac{F}{A}$$

$$A = \frac{F}{\text{tensile strength}}$$

$$\frac{1}{4}\pi d^2 =$$

$$d = \sqrt{\frac{4F}{\pi(\text{tensile strength})}}$$

$$= \sqrt{\frac{4(1.2 \text{ N})}{\pi(2.0 \times 10^8 \text{ Pa})}}$$

$$= \boxed{8.7 \times 10^{-5} \text{ m}}$$

13. The stress on the copper wire must be less than its elastic limit.

$$\frac{F}{A} < \text{elastic limit}$$

$$F < \pi r^2(\text{elastic limit})$$

$$F < \pi(0.0010 \text{ m})^2(2.0 \times 10^8 \text{ Pa})$$

$$F < \boxed{630 \text{ N}}$$

17. Set the stresses equal to the compressive strengths to determine the effective cross-sectional areas.
    Human:

$$\frac{F}{A} = 1.6 \times 10^8 \text{ Pa}$$

$$A = \frac{5 \times 10^4 \text{ N}}{1.6 \times 10^8 \text{ Pa}}$$

$$= \boxed{3 \text{ cm}^2}$$

   Horse:

$$A = \frac{10 \times 10^4 \text{ N}}{1.4 \times 10^8 \text{ Pa}} = \boxed{7 \text{ cm}^2}$$

21. Set the shear stress equal to the total shear strength to find the maximum shearing force.

$$\frac{F}{4A_{\text{bolt}}} = \text{shear strength}$$

$$F = 4\pi r^2(\text{shear strength}) = 4\pi(0.010 \text{ m})^2(6.0 \times 10^8 \text{ Pa}) = \boxed{7.5 \times 10^5 \text{ N}}$$

23. Use Hooke's law for shear deformations.

$$\frac{F}{A} = S\frac{\Delta x}{L}$$

$$\frac{F}{L^2} =$$

$$F = S\Delta x L$$

$$= (940 \text{ Pa})(0.64 \times 10^{-2} \text{ m})(0.050 \text{ m})$$

$$= \boxed{0.30 \text{ N}}$$

25. At the equilibrium point, the speed is at its maximum, $v_m = \omega A$.

$$v_m = \frac{2\pi}{T}A = \frac{2\pi(0.050 \text{ m})}{0.50 \text{ s}} = \boxed{0.63 \text{ m/s}}$$

29. a has units m/s^2. $-\omega^2 x$ has units $\text{s}^{-2} \cdot \text{m} = \text{m/s}^2$. So, $a = -\omega^2 x$ is consistent for units.

ω has units s^{-1}. $\sqrt{\dfrac{k}{m}}$ has units $\sqrt{\dfrac{\frac{N}{m}}{kg}} = \sqrt{\dfrac{\frac{kg \cdot m}{s^2}}{kg}} = \sqrt{\dfrac{1}{s^2}} = \text{s}^{-1}$. So, $\sqrt{\dfrac{k}{m}}$ has the same units as ω.

33. $v_m = \omega A$, so $\omega = \dfrac{v_m}{A}$. $a_m = \omega^2 A = \dfrac{v_m^2}{A^2}A = \dfrac{v_m^2}{A}$, so $v_m^2 = a_m A$.

35. $v_m = \omega A = 2\pi(25.0 \text{ Hz})(0.00100 \text{ m}) = \boxed{0.157 \text{ m/s}}$

$$a_m = \omega^2 A = 4\pi^2(25.0 \text{ Hz})^2(0.00100 \text{ m}) = \boxed{24.7 \text{ m/s}^2}$$

37. (a) According to Newton's second law, at equilibrium, $\Sigma F_y = 0 = kd - mg$, so $k = \dfrac{mg}{d}$. When the extension of the spring is a maximum, $\Sigma F_y = ma = k(2d) - mg = 2\left(\dfrac{mg}{d}\right)d - mg = mg$. So, $a = \boxed{g}$.

    (b) At maximum extension, $\Sigma F_y = kx - mg = ma$. Solve for x.

    $$kx = mg + ma$$
    $$= m(g + a)$$

    $$x = \frac{m}{k}(g + a)$$

    $$= \frac{(1.0 \text{ kg})\left(9.8 \frac{N}{kg} + 9.8 \frac{N}{kg}\right)}{25 \frac{N}{m}}$$

    $$= \boxed{0.78 \text{ m}}$$

41. Since $y(t) = A\sin\omega t$, $f = \dfrac{\omega}{2\pi} = \dfrac{1.57 \frac{rad}{s}}{2\pi} = \boxed{0.250 \text{ Hz}}$.

45. During the fall:

$$y - y_0 = v_{0y}t - \frac{1}{2}gt^2$$

$$y - h = (0)t - \frac{1}{2}gt^2$$

$$y = h - \frac{1}{2}gt^2$$

At $y = 0$, $t = \sqrt{\frac{2h}{g}}$.

During the rise:

The speed of the ball just before and after it hits the ground is $v = gt = g\sqrt{\frac{2h}{g}} = \sqrt{2gh}$. So, at

$t_0 = \sqrt{\frac{2h}{g}}$, $v_{0y} = \sqrt{2gh}$, and $y = y_0 = 0$.

If $t_0 = 0$ when $y = y_0 = 0$, then $y = v_{0y}t - \frac{1}{2}gt^2$, but $t_0 = \sqrt{\frac{2h}{g}}$. The graph is shifted to the right, so

$$y = \sqrt{2gh}\left(t - \sqrt{\frac{2h}{g}}\right) - \frac{1}{2}g\left(t - \sqrt{\frac{2h}{g}}\right)^2 , \text{ and } y = h \text{ when } t = 2\sqrt{\frac{2h}{g}}.$$

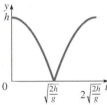

The motion is not SHM, since it is $\boxed{\text{not a sine or cosine function}}$. The graph is always nonnegative and has a parabolic shape.

49. Since $\omega = \sqrt{\frac{g}{L}}$ and $\omega = \frac{2\pi}{T}$, $T = 2\pi\sqrt{\frac{L}{g}}$, which does not depend upon the mass. So, $T = \boxed{1.5 \text{ s}}$.

53. Solve for L using the equation for the period of a pendulum.

$$T = 2\pi\sqrt{\frac{L}{g}}$$

$$\frac{gT^2}{4\pi^2} = L$$

Form a proportion.

$$\frac{L_2}{L_1} = \frac{T_2^2}{T_1^2} = \left(\frac{1.00 \text{ s}}{0.950 \text{ s}}\right)^2 = \boxed{1.11}$$

57. $E = \frac{1}{2}m\omega^2 A^2 \propto A^2$ for a pendulum.

Compare the fractional decrease per cycle. Let n = the number of cycles for E to decrease 5.0%.

$$\frac{\frac{\Delta E}{E}}{n} = \frac{\frac{\Delta A^2}{A^2}}{10 \text{ cycles}}$$

$$\frac{-0.050}{n} = \frac{\frac{0.950^2 - 1^2}{1^2}}{10 \text{ cycles}}$$

$$n = (10 \text{ cycles})\frac{-0.050}{0.950^2 - 1}$$

$$= \boxed{5 \text{ cycles}}$$

61. $T = 2\pi\sqrt{\frac{I}{mgd}}$ for a physical pendulum, where d is the distance from the axis to the center of mass.

(a) $I = \frac{1}{3}mL^2$ for a uniform rod with the axis through its end.

$$T = 2\pi\sqrt{\frac{\frac{1}{3}mL^2}{mgd}} = 2\pi L\sqrt{\frac{1}{3gd}} = \frac{2\pi(1.00 \text{ m})}{\sqrt{3\left(9.80 \text{ } \frac{\text{m}}{\text{s}^2}\right)(0.500 \text{ m})}} = \boxed{1.64 \text{ s}}$$

(b) Treat the meterstick as two rods with lengths 75 cm and 25 cm.

$$I = \frac{1}{3}\left(\frac{m}{4}\right)\left(\frac{L}{4}\right)^2 + \frac{1}{3}\left(\frac{3m}{4}\right)\left(\frac{3L}{4}\right)^2 = \frac{1}{3}mL^2\left(\frac{1}{64} + \frac{27}{64}\right) = \frac{1}{3}mL^2\left(\frac{28}{64}\right) = \frac{7}{48}mL^2$$

$$T = 2\pi\sqrt{\frac{\frac{7}{48}mL^2}{mgd}} = 2\pi\sqrt{\frac{7L^2}{48g\left(\frac{L}{4}\right)}} = 2\pi\sqrt{\frac{7L}{12g}} = 2\pi\sqrt{\frac{7(1.00 \text{ m})}{12\left(9.80 \text{ } \frac{\text{m}}{\text{s}^2}\right)}} = \boxed{1.53 \text{ s}}$$

(c) Treat the meterstick as two rods with lengths 60 cm and 40 cm.

$$I = \frac{1}{3}\left(\frac{4m}{10}\right)\left(\frac{4L}{10}\right)^2 + \frac{1}{3}\left(\frac{6m}{10}\right)\left(\frac{6L}{10}\right)^2 = \frac{1}{3}mL^2\left(\frac{64}{1000} + \frac{216}{1000}\right) = \frac{7}{75}mL^2$$

$$T = 2\pi\sqrt{\frac{\frac{7}{75}mL^2}{mg\left(\frac{L}{10}\right)}} = 2\pi\sqrt{\frac{14L}{15g}} = 2\pi\sqrt{\frac{14(1.00 \text{ m})}{15\left(9.80 \text{ } \frac{\text{m}}{\text{s}^2}\right)}} = \boxed{1.94 \text{ s}}$$

65. (a) The inertia is $I = \frac{1}{3}m_1L^2 + m_2L^2$.

The distance to the center of mass from the rotation axis is $d = \frac{m_1\frac{L}{2} + m_2L}{m_1 + m_2} = \frac{\frac{m_1}{2} + m_2}{m}L$.

Find the period of this physical pendulum.

$$T = 2\pi\sqrt{\frac{I}{mgd}} = 2\pi\sqrt{\frac{\frac{1}{3}m_1L^2 + m_2L^2}{mgd}} = 2\pi\sqrt{\frac{L^2\left(\frac{m_1}{3} + m_2\right)}{mg\left(\frac{\frac{m_1}{2} + m_2}{m}\right)L}} = 2\pi\sqrt{\frac{L\left(\frac{m_1}{3} + m_2\right)}{g\left(\frac{m_1}{2} + m_2\right)}} = 2\pi\sqrt{\frac{2L(m_1 + 3m_2)}{3g(m_1 + 2m_2)}}$$

(b) For each case, replace the smaller mass with zero. Then

for $m_1 \gg m_2$, $T = 2\pi\sqrt{\dfrac{2L}{3g}}$, and for $m_1 \ll m_2$, $T = 2\pi\sqrt{\dfrac{L}{g}}$.

The former is the period for the uniform rod alone and the latter is the period for the block alone.

69. (a) From the figure below, we see that $L\cos\theta + y = L$, or $y = L(1 - \cos\theta)$.

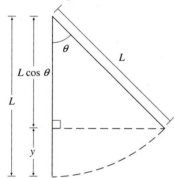

(b) $U = mgy = mgL(1 - \cos\theta) \approx mgL\left[\dfrac{1}{2}\left(\dfrac{x}{L}\right)^2\right] = \dfrac{1}{2}\left(\dfrac{mg}{L}\right)x^2 = \dfrac{1}{2}kx^2$ with $k = \dfrac{mg}{L}$.

73. The angle θ through which the tuning pin must be turned is related to the extension of the wire by the formula for arc length.

$$s = \frac{d_p}{2}\theta = \Delta L$$

Find ΔL using the stress-strain relation.

$$Y\frac{\Delta L}{L} = \frac{F}{A}$$

$$\Delta L = \frac{FL}{AY}$$

$$\frac{2}{d_p}\Delta L = \frac{2FL}{d_p AY}$$

$$\theta = \frac{2FL}{d_p\pi\left(\dfrac{d_w}{2}\right)^2 Y}$$

$$= \frac{8FL}{\pi d_p d_w^2 Y}$$

$$= \frac{8(402\ \text{N} - 381\ \text{N})(0.66\ \text{m})}{\pi(0.0080\ \text{m})(0.00080\ \text{m})^2(2.0\times10^{11}\ \text{Pa})}\left(\frac{360°}{2\pi}\right)$$

$$= \boxed{2.0°}$$

77. (a) $\text{strain} = \dfrac{\Delta L}{L} = \dfrac{L' - L'\cos\theta}{L'\cos\theta} = \dfrac{1}{\cos\theta} - 1 = \dfrac{1}{\cos 0.040} - 1 = \boxed{8\times 10^{-4}}$

(b) According to Newton's second law, $\Sigma F_y = 2T\sin\theta - mg = 0$.

So, $T = \dfrac{mg}{2\sin\theta} = \dfrac{640\text{ N}}{2\sin 0.040} = \boxed{8.0\text{ kN}}$.

(c) Find the cross-sectional area of the cable using the stress-strain relation.

$$\frac{T}{A} = Y\frac{\Delta L}{L}$$

$$\frac{mg}{2A\sin\theta} = Y\left(\frac{1}{\cos\theta} - 1\right)$$

$$A = \frac{mg}{2Y\sin\theta\left(\frac{1}{\cos\theta} - 1\right)}$$

$$= \frac{640\text{ N}}{2(200\times 10^9\text{ Pa})\sin 0.040\left(\frac{1}{\cos 0.040} - 1\right)}$$

$$= \boxed{5\times 10^{-5}\text{ m}^2}$$

(d) $\dfrac{T}{A} = \dfrac{8.0\times 10^3\text{ N}}{5\times 10^{-5}\text{ m}^2} = 1.6\times 10^8\text{ Pa} < 2.5\times 10^8\text{ Pa}$

$\boxed{\text{No}}$, the cable has not been stretched beyond its elastic limit.

81. (a) Find the force using the stress-strain relation.

$$\frac{F}{A} = Y\frac{\Delta L}{L}$$

$$F = \frac{YA\Delta L}{L}$$

$$= \frac{\left(1.7\times 10^6\ \frac{\text{N}}{\text{m}^2}\right)(1.0\times 10^{-6}\text{ m}^2)(4.0\text{ cm} - 1.0\text{ cm})}{1.0\text{ cm}}$$

$$= \boxed{5.1\text{ N}}$$

(b) The energy is elastic potential energy. Use Hooke's law for k.

$$U = \frac{1}{2}kx^2 = \frac{1}{2}\left(\frac{F}{x}\right)x^2 = \frac{1}{2}Fx = \frac{1}{2}(5.1\text{ N})(0.030\text{ m}) = \boxed{7.7\times 10^{-2}\text{ J}}$$

Chapter 11

WAVES

Problems

1. Form a proportion with the intensities treating the Sun as an isotropic source.

$$\frac{I_J}{I_E} = \frac{\frac{P}{4\pi r_J^2}}{\frac{P}{4\pi r_E^2}} = \frac{r_E^2}{r_J^2}$$

$$I_J = \left(\frac{r_E}{r_J}\right)^2 I_E = \left(\frac{1}{5.2}\right)^2 \left(1400 \ \frac{W}{m^2}\right) = \boxed{52 \ W/m^2}$$

3. The power equals the intensity times the area.

$$P = IA = \left(\frac{120 \ m}{8600 \ m}\right)^2 \left(9.2 \ \frac{W}{m^2}\right) 4\pi(8600 \ m)^2 = \boxed{1.7 \ MW}$$

5. (a) $v = \dfrac{\Delta x}{\Delta t} = \dfrac{1.80 \ m - 1.50 \ m}{0.20 \ s} = \boxed{1.5 \ m/s}$

(b) $v = \dfrac{\Delta y}{\Delta t} = \dfrac{8.7 \ cm - 4.5 \ cm}{0.20 \ s} = \boxed{21 \ cm/s}$

7. $v = \sqrt{\dfrac{F}{\mu}} = \sqrt{\dfrac{90.0 \ N}{3.20 \times 10^{-3} \ \frac{kg}{m}}} = \boxed{168 \ m/s}$

9. The weight of the string divided by the load is $\dfrac{0.25 \ N}{1.00 \times 10^3 \ N} = 2.5 \times 10^{-4} = 0.025\%$. The weight of the string is negligible since the result will be limited to two significant figures (by 0.25 N).

$$t = \frac{y}{v} = \frac{L}{\sqrt{\frac{FL}{m}}} = \sqrt{\frac{mL}{F}} = \sqrt{\frac{mgL}{Fg}} = \sqrt{\frac{(0.25 \ N)(10.0 \ m)}{(1.00 \times 10^3 \ N)\left(9.8 \ \frac{N}{kg}\right)}} = \boxed{16 \ ms}$$

11. $\lambda = vT = \left(75.0 \ \dfrac{m}{s}\right)(5.00 \times 10^{-3} \ s) = \boxed{0.375 \ m}$

13. (a) $f = \dfrac{v}{\lambda} = \dfrac{340 \ \frac{m}{s}}{1.0 \ m} = \boxed{340 \ Hz}$

(b) $f = \dfrac{v}{\lambda} = \dfrac{30.0 \times 10^8 \ \frac{m}{s}}{1.0 \ m} = \boxed{3.0 \times 10^8 \ Hz}$

17. $y(x, t) = (3.5 \text{ cm}) \sin \dfrac{\pi}{3.0 \text{ cm}} \left[x - \left(66 \dfrac{\text{cm}}{\text{s}} \right) t \right] = A \sin(kx - \omega t),$ so we have

(a) $A = \boxed{3.5 \text{ cm}}$

(b) $\lambda = \dfrac{2\pi}{k} = \dfrac{2\pi}{\dfrac{\pi}{3.0 \text{ cm}}} = \boxed{6.0 \text{ cm}}$

21. (a) $y(x, t) = (4.0 \text{ cm}) \sin[(378 \text{ s}^{-1})t - (314 \text{ cm}^{-1})x]$

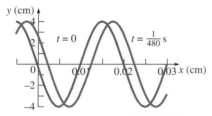

$y_{\max} = 4.0 \text{ cm, so } A = \boxed{4.0 \text{ cm}}.$

$\lambda = \Delta x = 0.020 \text{ cm} - 0 = \boxed{0.020 \text{ cm}}$

$v = \dfrac{\Delta x}{\Delta t} = \dfrac{0.0025 \text{ cm} - 0}{\dfrac{1}{480} \text{ s}} = \boxed{1.2 \text{ cm/s}}$

(b)

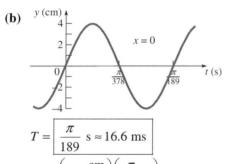

$T = \boxed{\dfrac{\pi}{189} \text{ s} \approx 16.6 \text{ ms}}$

$vT = \left(1.2 \dfrac{\text{cm}}{\text{s}} \right) \left(\dfrac{\pi}{189} \text{ s} \right) = 0.020 \text{ cm} = \lambda$

25.

t (s)	Short Pulse Position	Tall Pulse Position
0.15	$10 \text{ cm} + \left(40 \dfrac{\text{cm}}{\text{s}} \right)(0.15 \text{ s}) = 16 \text{ cm}$	$30 \text{ cm} - \left(40 \dfrac{\text{cm}}{\text{s}} \right)(0.15 \text{ s}) = 24 \text{ cm}$
0.25	$10 \text{ cm} + \left(40 \dfrac{\text{cm}}{\text{s}} \right)(0.25 \text{ s}) = 20 \text{ cm}$	$30 \text{ cm} - \left(40 \dfrac{\text{cm}}{\text{s}} \right)(0.25 \text{ s}) = 20 \text{ cm}$
0.30	$10 \text{ cm} + \left(40 \dfrac{\text{cm}}{\text{s}} \right)(0.30 \text{ s}) = 22 \text{ cm}$	$30 \text{ cm} - \left(40 \dfrac{\text{cm}}{\text{s}} \right)(0.30 \text{ s}) = 18 \text{ cm}$

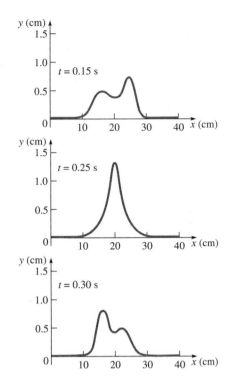

27. Use the trigonometric identity $\sin\alpha + \sin\beta = 2\sin\left(\dfrac{\alpha+\beta}{2}\right)\cos\left(\dfrac{\alpha-\beta}{2}\right)$.

$$y = y_1 + y_2 = A\sin(\omega t + kx) + A\sin(\omega t + kx - \phi) = 2A\sin\left(\omega t + kx - \frac{\phi}{2}\right)\cos\frac{\phi}{2} = A'\sin\left(\omega t + kx - \frac{\phi}{2}\right)$$

where $A' = 2A\cos\dfrac{\phi}{2} = 6.69$ cm.

Find ϕ.

$$\cos\frac{\phi}{2} = \frac{A'}{2A}$$

$$\frac{\phi}{2} = \cos^{-1}\frac{A'}{2A}$$

$$\phi = 2\cos^{-1}\frac{6.69 \text{ cm}}{2(5.00 \text{ cm})}$$

$$= \boxed{96.0°}$$

29. (a)

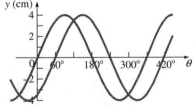

Let $y_1 = A\sin(\omega t + kx)$ and $y_2 = A\sin(\omega t + kx - \phi)$ and use the trigonometric identity

$\sin\alpha + \sin\beta = 2\sin\left(\dfrac{\alpha+\beta}{2}\right)\cos\left(\dfrac{\alpha-\beta}{2}\right)$. Use the principle of superposition.

$$y = y_1 + y_2 = A\sin(\omega t + kx) + A\sin(\omega t + kx - \phi) = 2A\sin\left(\omega t + kx - \frac{\phi}{2}\right)\cos\frac{\phi}{2} = A'\sin\left(\omega t + kx - \frac{\phi}{2}\right)$$

where $A' = 2A\cos\frac{\phi}{2}$.

$$A' = 2(4.0\text{ cm})\cos\frac{60.0°}{2} = \boxed{6.9\text{ cm}}$$

(b)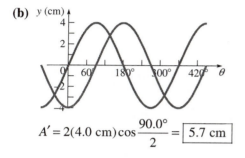

$$A' = 2(4.0\text{ cm})\cos\frac{90.0°}{2} = \boxed{5.7\text{ cm}}$$

33. The pulse moves $1.80\text{ m} - 1.50\text{ m} = 0.30\text{ m}$ in 0.20 s. So, the speed of the wave is $v = \dfrac{0.30\text{ m}}{0.20\text{ s}} = 1.5\text{ m/s}$. When the pulse reaches the right endpoint, it is reflected and inverted. When exactly half of the pulse has been reflected and inverted, the superposition of the incident and reflected waves results in the cancellation of the waves $(y_1 + y_2 = 0)$. Thus, the string looks flat at $t = \dfrac{x}{v} = \dfrac{4.0\text{ m} - 1.5\text{ m}}{1.5\ \frac{\text{m}}{\text{s}}} = \boxed{1.7\text{ s}}$.

35. **(a)** The resulting wave will have its highest intensity when the waves interfere constructively. The phase difference is $\boxed{0°}$. $A = A_1 + A_2 = 6.0\text{ cm} + 3.0\text{ cm} = \boxed{9.0\text{ cm}}$

(b) The resulting wave will have its lowest intensity when the waves interfere destructively. The phase difference is $\boxed{180°}$. $A = |A_1 - A_2| = |6.0\text{ cm} - 3.0\text{ cm}| = \boxed{3.0\text{ cm}}$

(c) $\dfrac{I_1}{I_2} = \left(\dfrac{A_1}{A_2}\right)^2 = \left(\dfrac{9.0\text{ cm}}{3.0\text{ cm}}\right)^2 = 9.0$

The ratio is $\boxed{9:1}$.

37. Intensity is proportional to the amplitude squared.

$$\frac{A_1}{A_2} = \sqrt{\frac{I_1}{I_2}} = \sqrt{\frac{25}{28}}$$

For destructive interference, the resultant amplitude is the difference of the original amplitudes.

$$A = |A_1 - A_2| = A_2\left(1 - \sqrt{\frac{25}{28}}\right)$$

$$\sqrt{\frac{I}{I_2}} = \frac{A}{A_2} = 1 - \sqrt{\frac{25}{28}}$$

$$I = \left(1 - \sqrt{\frac{25}{28}}\right)^2 I_2 = \left(1 - \sqrt{\frac{25}{28}}\right)^2\left(28\times 10^{-3}\ \frac{\text{W}}{\text{m}^2}\right) = \boxed{80\ \mu\text{W/m}^2}$$

41. (a) $\sqrt{\dfrac{FL}{m}}$ has units $\sqrt{\dfrac{\text{N} \cdot \text{m}}{\text{kg}}} = \sqrt{\dfrac{\text{kg} \cdot \frac{\text{m}}{\text{s}^2} \cdot \text{m}}{\text{kg}}} = \text{m/s}$, which are the units of speed.

(b) Set $[F]^a[L]^b[m]^c$ equal to m/s, the units of speed, and determine a, b, and c.

$$[F]^a[L]^b[m]^c = \text{m} \cdot \text{s}^{-1}$$
$$\text{N}^a\text{m}^b\text{kg}^c =$$
$$\frac{\text{kg}^a \cdot \text{m}^a}{\text{s}^{2a}}\text{m}^b\text{kg}^c =$$
$$\text{kg}^{a+c}\text{m}^{a+b}\text{s}^{-2a} = \text{kg}^0 \cdot \text{m}^1 \cdot \text{s}^{-1}$$

Equate exponents.

$a + c = 0$, so $a = -c$.
$a + b = 1$, so $b = 1 - a = 1 + c$.
$-2a = -1$, so $a = \dfrac{1}{2}$, $c = -\dfrac{1}{2}$, and $b = \dfrac{1}{2}$.

Therefore, the only combination of F, L, and m that gives units of speed is $F^{1/2}L^{1/2}m^{-1/2} = \sqrt{FL/m}$, and the speed of transverse waves on the string can only be $\sqrt{FL/m}$ times some dimensionless constant.

45. $f_n = \dfrac{nv}{2L}$ and $v = \sqrt{\dfrac{T}{\mu}}$. Find μ.

$$f_1 = \frac{v}{2L}$$
$$= \frac{1}{2L}\sqrt{\frac{T}{\mu}}$$
$$4L^2 f_1^2 = \frac{T}{\mu}$$
$$\mu = \frac{T}{4L^2 f_1^2}$$
$$= \frac{82 \text{ N}}{4(0.65 \text{ m})^2(329.63 \text{ Hz})^2}$$
$$= \boxed{4.5 \times 10^{-4} \text{ kg/m}}$$

49. $\lambda = \dfrac{v}{f} = \dfrac{3.0 \times 10^8 \ \frac{\text{m}}{\text{s}}}{90 \times 10^6 \text{ Hz}} = \boxed{3 \text{ m}}$

53. λ has units m. g has units m/s^2. $\lambda \cdot g$ has units m^2/s^2. $\sqrt{\lambda g}$ has units m/s. So, $\boxed{v \propto \sqrt{\lambda g}}$.

57. Find a relationship between the distance between frets and the frequencies.

$$f \propto \frac{1}{L}, \text{ so } \frac{L_2}{L_1} = \frac{f_1}{f_2}.$$

$$L_1 - L_2 = L_1 - \frac{f_1}{f_2} L_1$$

$$\Delta L = L_1 \left(1 - \frac{f_1}{f_2} \right)$$

First:

$$\Delta L = (64.8 \text{ cm}) \left(1 - \frac{1}{1.0595} \right) = \boxed{3.64 \text{ cm}}$$

Second:

$$3.64 \text{ cm} + (64.8 \text{ cm} - 3.64 \text{ cm}) \left(1 - \frac{1}{1.0595} \right) = \boxed{7.07 \text{ cm}}$$

Third:

$$7.074 \text{ cm} + (64.8 \text{ cm} - 7.074 \text{ cm}) \left(1 - \frac{1}{1.0595} \right) = \boxed{10.32 \text{ cm}}$$

59. $\Delta x = 1.80 \text{ m} - 1.50 \text{ m} = 0.30 \text{ m}$ in $\Delta t = 0.20 \text{ s}$, so $v = \dfrac{0.30 \text{ m}}{0.20 \text{ s}} = 1.5 \text{ m/s}$.

Find the position of the peak at $t = 2.2$ s.

$$x_{\text{peak}} = 1.5 \text{ m} + \left(1.5 \frac{\text{m}}{\text{s}} \right)(2.2 \text{ s}) = 4.8 \text{ m } (3.2 \text{ m}; \ 4.8 \text{ m} - 4.0 \text{ m} = 0.8 \text{ m to the left})$$

The peak of the pulse is now inverted due to reflection.

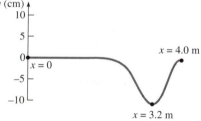

61. Set the stress equal to the strength.

$$\frac{F}{A} = \text{strength} = \frac{\frac{T}{0.93}}{A}, \text{ so } T = 0.93A(\text{strength}).$$

$$f_n = \frac{nv}{2L} \text{ and } v = \sqrt{\frac{TL}{m}}. \text{ Find } f_1.$$

$$f_1 = \frac{v}{2L} = \frac{1}{2L}\sqrt{\frac{TL}{m}} = \frac{1}{2}\sqrt{\frac{TL}{mL^2}} = \frac{1}{2}\sqrt{\frac{0.93A(\text{strength})L}{mL^2}} = \frac{1}{2}\sqrt{\frac{0.93(\text{strength})V}{mL^2}} = \frac{1}{2}\sqrt{\frac{0.93(\text{strength})}{\rho L^2}}$$

$$= \frac{1}{2}\sqrt{\frac{0.93(6.3\times10^8 \text{ Pa})}{\left(8500 \ \frac{\text{kg}}{\text{m}^3}\right)(0.094 \text{ m})^2}} = \boxed{1.4 \text{ kHz}}$$

Chapter 12

SOUND

Problems

1. $\lambda = \dfrac{v}{f}$ and $v = v_0\sqrt{\dfrac{T}{T_0}}$.

$$\lambda = \frac{v}{f} = \frac{v_0}{f}\sqrt{\frac{T}{T_0}} = \frac{331\frac{\text{m}}{\text{s}}}{1.0\times10^5\ \text{Hz}}\sqrt{\frac{273.15\ \text{K} + 15\ \text{K}}{273.15}} = \boxed{3.4\ \text{mm}}$$

5. (a) $v = v_0\sqrt{\dfrac{T}{T_0}} = v_0\sqrt{\dfrac{T_C + 273.15}{273.15}}$

(b) Use the binomial approximation $(1+x)^{1/2} \approx 1 + \dfrac{1}{2}x$ for $x \ll 1$.

$$v = v_0\sqrt{1 + \frac{T_C}{273.15}} \approx \left(331\ \frac{\text{m}}{\text{s}}\right)\left[1 + \frac{T_C}{2(273.15)}\right] = (331 + 0.606 T_C)\ \text{m/s}$$

7. $v = \sqrt{\dfrac{Y}{\rho}}$ for a solid.

$$v = \sqrt{\frac{Y}{\rho}} = \sqrt{\frac{1.1\times10^{11}\ \text{Pa}}{8.92\times10^3\ \frac{\text{kg}}{\text{m}^3}}} = \boxed{3.5\ \text{km/s}}$$

The copper alloy has a slightly lower speed of sound than that listed in Table 12.1 for copper, 3560 m/s.

9. (a) $v = v_0\sqrt{\dfrac{T}{T_0}} = \left(331\ \dfrac{\text{m}}{\text{s}}\right)\sqrt{\dfrac{273.15\ \text{K} + 12\ \text{K}}{273.15\ \text{K}}} = \boxed{338\ \text{m/s}}$

(b) The speed of light is so much faster than the speed of sound in air that the time it takes for light to reach an observer is negligible in this case.

$$d = vt = \left(338\ \frac{\text{m}}{\text{s}}\right)(8.2\ \text{s}) = \boxed{2.8\ \text{km}}$$

13. Solve for the intensity.

$$\beta = (10 \text{ db}) \log \frac{I}{I_0}$$

$$10^{\frac{\beta}{10 \text{ dB}}} = \frac{I}{I_0}$$

$$I = I_0 10^{\frac{\beta}{10 \text{ dB}}}$$

$$\frac{\Delta I}{I} \times 100\% = \frac{I_0 \left(10^{\frac{\beta + 1.00 \text{ dB}}{10 \text{ dB}}} - 10^{\frac{\beta}{10 \text{ dB}}}\right)}{I_0 10^{\frac{\beta}{10 \text{ dB}}}} \times 100\% = \frac{10^{\frac{\beta}{10 \text{ dB}}} \left(10^{\frac{1.00 \text{ dB}}{10 \text{ dB}}} - 1\right)}{10^{\frac{\beta}{10 \text{ dB}}}} \times 100\% = \left(10^{\frac{1.00}{10}} - 1\right) \times 100\% = \boxed{26\%}$$

17. (a) $f_n = \frac{nv}{2L}$ for a pipe open at both ends and $v = v_0 \sqrt{\frac{T}{T_0}}$. Find L.

$$f_1 = \frac{v}{2L}$$

$$L = \frac{v}{2f_1}$$

$$= \frac{v_0}{2f_1} \sqrt{\frac{T}{T_0}}$$

$$= \frac{331 \frac{\text{m}}{\text{s}}}{2(261.5 \text{ Hz})} \sqrt{\frac{273.15 \text{ K} + 20.0 \text{ K}}{273.15 \text{ K}}}$$

$$= \boxed{65.6 \text{ cm}}$$

(b) $f \propto v \propto \sqrt{T}$, so $f_0 = f_{20} \sqrt{\frac{T_0}{T_{20}}} = (261.5 \text{ Hz}) \sqrt{\frac{273.15 \text{ K} + 0.0 \text{ K}}{273.15 \text{ K} + 20.0 \text{ K}}} = \boxed{252.4 \text{ Hz}}$.

19. $f_n = \frac{nv}{2L}$ for a pipe open at both ends. Find L.

$$f_1 = \frac{v}{2L}$$

$$L = \frac{v}{2f_1}$$

$$= \frac{331 \frac{\text{m}}{\text{s}}}{2(382 \text{ Hz})}$$

$$= \boxed{43.3 \text{ cm}}$$

21. (a) The rod is analogous to a pipe open at both ends.

There is a displacement node (pressure antinode) at the center of the rod and displacement antinodes (pressure nodes) at the ends.

(b) For a pipe open at both ends, $\lambda_1 = 2L$, so $v = \lambda_1 f_1 = 2Lf_1 = 2(1.0 \text{ m})(2.55 \times 10^3 \text{ Hz}) = \boxed{5100 \text{ m/s}}$.

(c) $\lambda = \frac{v}{f} = \frac{334 \frac{\text{m}}{\text{s}}}{2.55 \times 10^3 \text{ Hz}} = \boxed{13.1 \text{ cm}}$

(d) The longitudinal motion of the rod is symmetrical about a central axis, so
the ends move in opposite directions and thus, they are out of phase.

25. **(a)** The beat frequency decreased as the tension was increased, so the original frequency was low.

    $f = 293.0 \text{ Hz} - 3.0 \text{ Hz} = \boxed{290.0 \text{ Hz}}$

(b) $F \propto f^2$, so

$$\frac{\Delta F}{F_0} \times 100\% = \frac{F - F_0}{F_0} \times 100\% = \left(\frac{F}{F_0} - 1\right) \times 100\% = \left[\left(\frac{f}{f_0}\right)^2 - 1\right] \times 100\% = \left[\left(\frac{293.0 - 1.0}{290.0}\right)^2 - 1\right] \times 100\%$$

$$= \boxed{1.4\%}.$$

29. **(a)** An observer is moving toward a stationary source $(v_o < 0)$.

    $$f_o = \left(1 - \frac{v_o}{v}\right) f_s = [1 - (-0.50)](1.0 \text{ kHz}) = \boxed{1.5 \text{ kHz}}$$

(b) The observer is now moving away from the source $(v_o > 0)$.

    $$f_o = (1 - 0.50)(1.0 \text{ kHz}) = \boxed{500 \text{ Hz}}$$

33. Toward the spectators: $\dfrac{f_{o1}}{f_s} = \dfrac{1}{1 - \frac{v_s}{v}}$ $(v_s > 0)$

    Away from the spectators: $\dfrac{f_{o2}}{f_s} = \dfrac{1}{1 + \frac{v_s}{v}}$ $(v_s > 0)$

    The observed frequency of the sound as the car recedes from the spectators is 0.75 times that observed during the car's approach, so $f_{o2} = 0.75 f_{o1}$. Find v_s, the speed of the racecar. $v = 343$ m/s for $T = 20.0°$C.

    $$\frac{0.75}{1 - \frac{v_s}{v}} = \frac{1}{1 + \frac{v_s}{v}}$$

    $$0.75\left(1 + \frac{v_s}{v}\right) = 1 - \frac{v_s}{v}$$

    $$0.75 + 0.75\frac{v_s}{v} =$$

    $$\frac{v_s}{v}(0.75 + 1) = 1 - 0.75$$

    $$1.75 v_s = 0.25 v$$

    $$v_s = \frac{v}{7.0}$$

    $$= \frac{343 \frac{\text{m}}{\text{s}}}{7.0}$$

    $$= 49 \text{ m/s}$$

    The race car is moving with a speed of $\boxed{49 \text{ m/s}}$.

35. (a) Use the result of Problem 34, $\sin\theta = \dfrac{v_{sound}}{v_{plane}}$.

$$\sin\theta = \frac{v_{sound}}{v_{plane}}$$

$$\frac{v_{plane}}{v_{sound}} = \frac{1}{\sin\theta}$$

$$\text{Mach number} = \frac{1}{\sin\theta}$$

$$= \frac{1}{\sin 22.0°}$$

$$= 2.67$$

The plane is traveling at $\boxed{\text{Mach } 2.67}$.

(b) $v_{plane} = 2.67 v_{sound} = 2.67 \left(322\ \dfrac{\text{m}}{\text{s}} \right) = \boxed{860\text{ m/s}}$

37. The distance traveled (round trip) by the sound wave in time t is vt, so

$$h = \frac{1}{2}vt = \frac{1}{2}\left(1533\ \frac{\text{m}}{\text{s}} \right)(7.07\text{ s}) = \boxed{5.42\text{ km}}.$$

41. (a) $f_{beat} = \Delta f = f_r - f = \dfrac{1 + \frac{v}{c}}{1 - \frac{v}{c}}f - f = \left(\dfrac{1 + \frac{v}{c}}{1 - \frac{v}{c}} - 1 \right)f = \dfrac{1 + \frac{v}{c} - \left(1 - \frac{v}{c}\right)}{1 - \frac{v}{c}}f = \dfrac{\frac{2v}{c}}{1 - \frac{v}{c}}f = \boxed{\dfrac{2fv}{c - v}}$

(b) From Appendix A.5, the binomial approximation for $(1-x)^{-1}$ is $1 + x$ for $x \ll 1$, so

$$f_{beat} = \Delta f = \frac{\frac{2v}{c}}{1 - \frac{v}{c}}f \approx \frac{2v}{c}\left(1 + \frac{v}{c} \right)f = \left(\frac{2v}{c} + \frac{2v^2}{c^2} \right)f \approx \frac{2v}{c}f = \left(\frac{2f}{c} \right)v,$$

$$\left(\text{since } \frac{2v^2}{c^2} \text{ is extremely small for } v \ll c \right).$$

So, $\Delta f \propto v$ if $v \ll c$.

45. (a) The round-trip distance traveled by the sound waves in a time t is vt, so

$$d = \frac{1}{2}vt = \frac{1}{2}\left(331\ \frac{\text{m}}{\text{s}} \right)(0.06\text{ s}) = \boxed{10\text{ m}}$$

(b) $t = \dfrac{2d}{v} = \dfrac{2(0.3\text{ m})}{331\ \frac{\text{m}}{\text{s}}} = \boxed{2\text{ ms}}$

(c) $\boxed{\text{No}}$; 3 ms to emit the chirp is greater than 2 ms for the echo to arrive, so the bat will still be emitting the first chirp.

49. $3 \times 12 = 36,\ 5 \times 12 = 60,\ 7 \times 12 = 84$

The fundamental frequency is 12 Hz.

$$\lambda = \frac{v}{f} = \frac{180\ \frac{\text{m}}{\text{s}}}{12\text{ Hz}} = \boxed{15\text{ m}}$$

53. Use the result of Problem 34 to find the speed of the plane.

$$\sin\theta = \frac{v_{sound}}{v_{plane}}$$

$$v_{plane} = \frac{v_{sound}}{\sin\theta}$$

$$v_{air} = \frac{343\ \frac{m}{s}}{\sin 40.0°}$$

$$= \boxed{534\ m/s}$$

Chapter 13

TEMPERATURE AND THE IDEAL GAS

Problems

1. (a) $T_C = \dfrac{T_F - 32°F}{1.8 \frac{°F}{°C}} = \dfrac{84°F - 32°F}{1.8 \frac{°F}{°C}} = \boxed{29°C}$

(b) $T = 29\text{ K} + 273.15\text{ K} = \boxed{302\text{ K}}$

5. (a) Since each concrete slab expands along its entire length, only half of the expansion is considered for a particular gap. Two sections meet at a gap, so the gap should be as wide as the expansion of one concrete slab.

$\Delta L = L_0 \alpha \Delta T$

$\qquad = (15\text{ m})(12 \times 10^{-6}\ °C^{-1})(40.0°C - 20.0°C)$

$\qquad = \boxed{3.6\text{ mm}}$

(b) $\Delta L = L_0 \alpha \Delta T$

$\qquad = (15\text{ m})(12 \times 10^{-6}\ °C^{-1})(-20.0°C - 20.0°C)$

$\qquad = -7.2\text{ mm}$

gap width $= 7.2\text{ mm} + 3.6\text{ mm} = \boxed{10.8\text{ mm}}$

7. The hole expands just as if it were a solid brass disk.

$\Delta A = 2\alpha A_0 \Delta T = 2\left(1.9 \times 10^{-5}°C^{-1}\right)(1.00\text{ mm}^2)(30.0°C - 20.0°C) = \boxed{3.8 \times 10^{-4}\text{ mm}^2}$

9. (a) $\dfrac{\Delta V}{V_0} = \beta \Delta T$ and $\dfrac{\Delta \rho}{\rho} = -\dfrac{\Delta V}{V_0}$.

(A decrease in volume for a fixed mass increases the density, and vice versa.)
Thus,

$\dfrac{\Delta \rho}{\rho} = -\beta \Delta T$

$\Delta \rho = -\beta \rho \Delta T$

(b) $\dfrac{\Delta \rho}{\rho} = -\beta \Delta T = -(57 \times 10^{-6}\ °C^{-1})(-10.0°C - 32°C) = \boxed{2.4 \times 10^{-3}}$

13. $\Delta L = \alpha L_0 \Delta T = (12 \times 10^{-6}\text{ K}^{-1})(1.6 \times 10^3\text{ m})[105°F - (-15°F)]\left(\dfrac{1\text{ K}}{1.8°F}\right) = \boxed{1.3\text{ m}}$

15. $\dfrac{\Delta V}{V_0} = \dfrac{V - V_0}{V_0}$

$\qquad = \dfrac{(s_0 + \Delta s)^3 - s_0^3}{s_0^3}$

$\qquad = \dfrac{s_0^3 + 2s_0^2 \Delta s + s_0 (\Delta s)^2 + s_0^2 \Delta s + 2 s_0 (\Delta s)^2 + (\Delta s)^3 - s_0^3}{s_0^3}$

$\qquad = \dfrac{3 s_0^2 \Delta s + 3 s_0 (\Delta s)^2 + (\Delta s)^3}{s_0^3}$

$\qquad \approx \dfrac{3 s_0^2 \Delta s}{s_0^3} \quad [\Delta s \ll s_0,\ \text{so}\ 3 s_0^2 \Delta s \gg s_0 (\Delta s)^2\ \text{and}\ (\Delta s)^3]$

$\qquad = 3 \dfrac{\Delta s}{s_0}$

$\dfrac{\Delta V}{V_0} = 3 \alpha \Delta T$

since $\dfrac{\Delta s}{s_0} = \alpha \Delta T$.

17. Find the temperature at which the diameter of the hole is 1.0000 cm. The diameter of the hole expands as if it were a solid piece of copper.

$\dfrac{\Delta L}{L_0} = \alpha \Delta T$

$\dfrac{\Delta L}{\alpha L_0} = T - T_0$

$T = \dfrac{\Delta L}{\alpha L_0} + T_0$

$\quad = \dfrac{1.0000\ \text{cm} - 0.9980\ \text{cm}}{(16 \times 10^{-6}\ {}^{\circ}\text{C}^{-1})(0.9980\ \text{cm})} + 20.0\,{}^{\circ}\text{C}$

$\quad = \boxed{150\,{}^{\circ}\text{C}}$

21. mass of CO_2 in kg $= \dfrac{m_C + 2m_O}{N_A} = \dfrac{\left[12.011\ \frac{\text{g}}{\text{mol}} + 2\left(15.9994\ \frac{\text{g}}{\text{mol}} \right) \right] \left(\frac{1\ \text{kg}}{1000\ \text{g}} \right)}{6.02 \times 10^{23}\ \text{mol}^{-1}} = \boxed{7.31 \times 10^{-26}\ \text{kg}}$

25. The number of SiO_2 atoms N is roughly equal to the volume of a sand grain V_g divided by the volume of a SiO_2 atom V_a.

$N = \dfrac{V_g}{V_a} = \dfrac{\frac{4}{3} \pi r_g^3}{\frac{4}{3} \pi r_a^3} = \left(\dfrac{d_g}{d_a} \right)^3 = \left(\dfrac{0.5 \times 10^{-3}\ \text{m}}{0.5 \times 10^{-9}\ \text{m}} \right)^3 = \boxed{10^{18}\ \text{atoms}}$

27. $m_{C_{12}H_{22}O_{11}} = 12(12.011\ \text{u}) + 22(1.00794\ \text{u}) + 11(15.9994\ \text{u}) = 342.30\ \text{u}$

There are 342.30 grams of sucrose per mole.

Find the number of moles of sucrose.

$\dfrac{684.6\ \text{g}}{342.30\ \frac{\text{g}}{\text{mol}}} = 2.000\ \text{mol}$

There are $2.000(22) = 44.00$ moles of hydrogen. Find the number of hydrogen atoms.

$N = n N_A = (44.00\ \text{mol})(6.02 \times 10^{23}\ \text{mol}^{-1}) = \boxed{2.65 \times 10^{25}\ \text{atoms}}$

29. $n_{CH_4} = \dfrac{\text{mass of CH}_4}{\text{molecular mass of CH}_4} = \dfrac{144.36 \text{ g}}{12.011 \frac{g}{mol} + 4\left(1.00794 \frac{g}{mol}\right)} = \boxed{8.9985 \text{ mol}}$

33. PV has SI units $\text{Pa} \cdot \text{m}^3 = \dfrac{N}{m^2} \cdot m^3 = N \cdot m = J.$

37. The volume and moles of the gas are constant.

$\dfrac{P_f}{P_i} = \dfrac{T_f}{T_i} = \dfrac{273.15 \text{ K} + 100.0 \text{ K}}{273.15 \text{ K} - 33 \text{ K}} = \boxed{1.55}$

39. The number of moles of the gas is constant.

$\dfrac{P_f V_f}{T_f} = \dfrac{P_i V_i}{T_i}$

$V_f = \dfrac{(P_f + \rho g h) V_i T_f}{P_f T_i}$

$= \dfrac{\left(1 + \frac{\rho g h}{P_f}\right) V_i T_f}{T_i}$

$= \dfrac{\left[1 + \dfrac{\left(1.0 \times 10^3 \frac{kg}{m^3}\right)\left(9.8 \frac{m}{s^2}\right)(20.0 \text{ m})}{1.013 \times 10^5 \text{ Pa}}\right](1.00 \text{ cm}^3)(273.15 \text{ K} + 25.0 \text{ K})}{273.15 \text{ K} + 10.0 \text{ K}}$

$= \boxed{3.1 \text{ cm}^3}$

41. The number of moles of the gas is constant.

$\dfrac{P_f V_f}{T_f} = \dfrac{P_i V_i}{T_i}$

$P_f = \dfrac{P_i V_i T_f}{V_f T_i}$

$= \dfrac{(1.0 \times 10^5 \text{ Pa})(1.2 \text{ m}^3)(273.15 \text{ K} + 227 \text{ K})}{(0.60 \text{ m}^3)(273.15 \text{ K} + 27 \text{ K})}$

$= \boxed{3.3 \times 10^5 \text{ Pa}}$

43. (a) The temperature and the number of moles of the gas are constant.

$V_f = \dfrac{P_i V_i}{P_f} = \dfrac{\left(2200 \frac{lb}{in^2}\right)(0.60 \text{ ft}^3)}{14.7 \frac{lb}{in^2}} = \boxed{90 \text{ ft}^3}$

(b) $t = \dfrac{V}{\frac{\Delta V}{\Delta t}} = \dfrac{9.0 \times 10^1 \text{ ft}^3}{8 \frac{L}{min}}\left(\dfrac{1 \text{ L}}{0.0353 \text{ ft}^3}\right)\left(\dfrac{1 \text{ h}}{60 \text{ min}}\right) = \boxed{5.3 \text{ h}}$

45. Use the microscopic form of the ideal gas law.

$P = \dfrac{NkT}{V} = \left(1 \dfrac{\text{atom}}{cm^3}\right)\left(\dfrac{10^6 \text{ cm}^3}{1 \text{ m}^3}\right)\left(1.38 \times 10^{-23} \dfrac{J}{K}\right)(3 \text{ K}) = \boxed{4 \times 10^{-17} \text{ Pa}}$

49. From Table 13.2, $\beta_{air} = 3340 \times 10^{-6}$ K^{-1} and the range for liquids is 182×10^{-6} K^{-1} for mercury to 1240×10^{-6} K^{-1} for benzene.

So, $\beta_{ideal} \approx \beta_{air}$ and β_{ideal} is 3 to 19 times larger than that for liquids.

$\langle K_{tr} \rangle = \dfrac{3}{2} kT$ for an ideal gas.

$$T = \frac{2\langle K_{tr} \rangle}{3k} = \frac{2(3.20 \times 10^{-20} \text{ J})}{3\left(1.38 \times 10^{-23} \frac{\text{J}}{\text{K}}\right)} = \boxed{1550 \text{ K}}$$

51. (a) $\dfrac{K_{total}}{V} = \dfrac{N\langle K_{tr} \rangle}{V} = \dfrac{N\langle \frac{3}{2} kT \rangle}{V} = \dfrac{3}{2} P = \dfrac{3}{2}(1.00 \text{ atm})\left(1.013 \times 10^5 \dfrac{\text{Pa}}{\text{atm}}\right) = \boxed{1.52 \times 10^5 \text{ J/m}^3}$

(b) $\dfrac{K_{total}}{V} = \dfrac{3}{2}(300.0 \text{ atm})\left(1.013 \times 10^5 \dfrac{\text{Pa}}{\text{atm}}\right) = \boxed{4.559 \times 10^7 \text{ J/m}^3}$

53. The speed of sound at $0.0°$C and 1.00 atm is 331 m/s.

According to Figure 13.13, approximately $\boxed{50\%}$ of the O_2 molecules are moving faster than the speed of sound.

57. (a) $v_{rms} = \sqrt{\dfrac{3kT}{m}} = \sqrt{\dfrac{3\left(1.38 \times 10^{-23} \frac{\text{J}}{\text{K}}\right)(273.15 \text{ K} + 0.0 \text{ K})}{2(14.00674 \text{ u})\left(1.66 \times 10^{-27} \frac{\text{kg}}{\text{u}}\right)}} = \boxed{493 \text{ m/s}}$

(b) $v_{rms} = \sqrt{\dfrac{3\left(1.38 \times 10^{-23} \frac{\text{J}}{\text{K}}\right)(273.15 \text{ K} + 0.0 \text{ K})}{2(15.9994 \text{ u})\left(1.66 \times 10^{-27} \frac{\text{kg}}{\text{u}}\right)}} = \boxed{461 \text{ m/s}}$

(c) $v_{rms} = \sqrt{\dfrac{3\left(1.38 \times 10^{-23} \frac{\text{J}}{\text{K}}\right)(273.15 \text{ K} + 0.0 \text{ K})}{[12.011 \text{ u} + 2(15.9994 \text{ u})]\left(1.66 \times 10^{-27} \frac{\text{kg}}{\text{u}}\right)}} = \boxed{393 \text{ m/s}}$

61. $\langle K_{tr} \rangle = \dfrac{1}{2} mv_{rms}^2 = \dfrac{1}{2} m\left(\sqrt{\dfrac{3kT}{m}}\right)^2 = \dfrac{1}{2} m\left(\dfrac{3kT}{m}\right) = \dfrac{3kT}{2}$, so $T = \dfrac{2\langle K_{tr} \rangle}{3k} = \dfrac{2(3.20 \times 10^{-20} \text{ J})}{3\left(1.38 \times 10^{-23} \frac{\text{J}}{\text{K}}\right)} = \boxed{1550 \text{ K}}$.

63. The average translational energy of a molecule in an ideal gas is $\langle K_{tr} \rangle = \dfrac{1}{2} m\langle v^2 \rangle$. The rms speed is $v_{rms} = \sqrt{\langle v^2 \rangle}$, so $\dfrac{1}{2} mv_{rms}^2 = \langle K_{tr} \rangle$. From Equation (13–19), we know that $\langle K_{tr} \rangle = \dfrac{3PV}{2N}$, and using the ideal gas law, $PV = nRT$, we have

$$\frac{1}{2} mv_{rms}^2 = \frac{3}{2}\left(\frac{PV}{N}\right)$$

$$= \frac{3}{2}\left(\frac{nRT}{N}\right)$$

$$v_{rms}^2 = 3\left(\frac{n}{mN}\right)RT$$

$$= \frac{3RT}{M}$$

$$v_{rms} = \sqrt{\frac{3RT}{M}}$$

65. Form a proportion with the two reaction rates and solve for the increase in temperature.

$$\frac{1.035}{1} = \frac{e^{-\frac{E_a}{kT_2}}}{e^{-\frac{E_a}{kT_1}}}$$

$$1.035 = e^{\frac{E_a}{k}\left(\frac{1}{T_1} - \frac{1}{T_2}\right)}$$

$$\ln 1.035 = \frac{E_a}{k}\left(\frac{1}{T_1} - \frac{1}{T_2}\right)$$

$$\frac{k\ln 1.035}{E_a} = \frac{1}{T_1} - \frac{1}{T_2}$$

$$\frac{1}{T_2} = \frac{1}{T_1} - \frac{k\ln 1.035}{E_a}$$

$$T_2 = \left(\frac{1}{T_1} - \frac{k\ln 1.035}{E_a}\right)^{-1}$$

$$\Delta T = \left(\frac{1}{T_1} - \frac{k\ln 1.035}{E_a}\right)^{-1} - T_1$$

$$= \left[\frac{1}{273.15\ \text{K} + 10.00\ \text{K}} - \frac{\left(1.38\times 10^{-23}\ \frac{\text{J}}{\text{K}}\right)\ln 1.035}{2.81\times 10^{-19}\ \text{J}}\right]^{-1} - (273.15\ \text{K} + 10.00\ \text{K})$$

$$= 0.14\ \text{K}$$

$$= \boxed{0.14°\text{C}}$$

69. $x_{\text{rms}} = \sqrt{2Dt}$, so $t = \dfrac{x_{\text{rms}}^2}{2D} = \dfrac{(5.00\times 10^{-3}\ \text{m})^2}{2\left(5.0\times 10^{-10}\ \frac{\text{m}^2}{\text{s}}\right)} = \boxed{2.5\times 10^4\ \text{s}}$.

73. The increase in volume of the mercury minus the increase in volume of the glass bulb equals the volume of mercury that moves up the tube, taking into account the expansion of the glass tube.

$$\Delta V_{\text{Hg}} - \Delta V_g = A_{\text{tube}}h$$

$$V_0\beta_{\text{Hg}}\Delta T - V_0\beta_g\Delta T = (A_0 + 2\alpha_g A_0\Delta T)h$$

$$h = \frac{V_0(\beta_{\text{Hg}} - \beta_g)\Delta T}{A_0(1 + 2\alpha_g\Delta T)}$$

$$= \frac{(0.200\times 10^{-6}\ \text{m}^3)[(182 - 9.75)\times 10^{-6}\ \text{K}^{-1}](1.00\ \text{K})}{\frac{1}{4}\pi(0.120\times 10^{-3}\ \text{m})^2[1 + 2(3.25\times 10^{-6}\ \text{K}^{-1})(1.00\ \text{K})]}$$

$$= \boxed{3.05\ \text{mm}}$$

77. (a) Find the distance between N_2 molecules and multiply by the scale factor $\dfrac{0.0375 \text{ m}}{0.30\times10^{-9} \text{ m}} = 1.25\times10^8$ to get the distance between ping pong balls. Let each N_2 molecule be at the center of a sphere with diameter d. Then the average distance between N_2 molecules is approximately d. The volume of each sphere is V/N with

$V = 0.0224 \text{ m}^3$ for

$N = 6.02\times10^{23}$ molecules, $P = 1.00$ atm, and $T = 0.0°C$.

$$\frac{V}{N} = \frac{1}{6}\pi d^3$$

$$d = \sqrt[3]{\frac{6V}{\pi N}}$$

So, the distance between ping pong balls is $(1.25\times10^8)\sqrt[3]{\dfrac{6(0.0224 \text{ m}^3)}{\pi(6.02\times10^{23})}} = \boxed{52 \text{ cm}}$.

(b) Find the mean free path for an N_2 molecule and multiply by the scale factor to find the average distance between ping pong ball collisions.

$$\Lambda = \frac{1}{\sqrt{2}\pi d^2 (N/V)} = \frac{kT}{\sqrt{2}\pi d^2 P}$$

So, the average distance between ping pong ball collisions is

$$\frac{(1.25\times10^8)\left(1.38\times10^{-23} \frac{\text{J}}{\text{K}}\right)(273.15 \text{ K} + 0.0 \text{ K})}{\sqrt{2}\pi(0.30\times10^{-9} \text{ m})^2(1.00 \text{ atm})\left(1.013\times10^5 \frac{\text{Pa}}{\text{atm}}\right)} = \boxed{12 \text{ m}}.$$

80. (a) $18\left(12.011 \frac{\text{g}}{\text{mol}}\right) + 34\left(1.00794 \frac{\text{g}}{\text{mol}}\right) + 2\left(15.9994 \frac{\text{g}}{\text{mol}}\right) = \boxed{282.47 \text{ g/mol}}$

(b) $\dfrac{2.3\times10^{-5} \text{ g}}{282.47 \frac{\text{g}}{\text{mol}}} = \boxed{8.1\times10^{-8} \text{ mol}}$

(c) $V = Ah$

$h = \dfrac{V}{A}$

$7d =$

$d = \dfrac{V}{7A}$

$= \dfrac{2.6\times10^{-5} \text{ cm}^3}{7(70.0 \text{ cm}^2)}$

$= \boxed{5.3\times10^{-8} \text{ cm}}$

(d) $\dfrac{\text{total area}}{\text{area of one molecule}} = \dfrac{70.0 \text{ cm}^2}{(5.3\times10^{-8} \text{ cm})^2} = \boxed{2.5\times10^{16} \text{ molecules}}$

(e) $\dfrac{2.5\times10^{16}}{8.1\times10^{-8} \text{ mol}} = \boxed{3.1\times10^{23} \text{ mol}^{-1}}$

84. Use the ideal gas law with the number of moles constant to find V_a, the volume of air at standard temperature and pressure.

$$\frac{P_a V_a}{T_a} = \frac{P_L V_L}{T_L}$$

$$V_a = \frac{P_L T_a V_L}{P_a T_L}$$

$$\frac{\text{volume per day}}{\text{volume per breath}} = \frac{\text{volume per day}}{V_a}$$

$$= \frac{(\text{volume per day}) P_a T_L}{P_L T_a V_L}$$

$$= \frac{\left(210\ \frac{L}{day}\right)\left(\frac{10^3\ \text{cm}^3}{L}\right)(1\ \text{atm})\left(1.013\times10^5\ \frac{Pa}{atm}\right)(39\ K + 273.15\ K)}{(450\ \text{mm Hg})\left(133.3\ \frac{Pa}{\text{mm Hg}}\right)(0\ K + 273.15\ K)(100\ \text{cm}^3)}$$

$$= \boxed{4000\ \text{breaths}}$$

88. (a) If $V = 10.0$ L and N is the number of N_2 molecules, V/N is approximately the volume of a sphere centered on one molecule with diameter d. d is approximately the nearest-neighbor distance.

$$\frac{1}{6}\pi d^3 = \frac{V}{N}$$

$$d^3 = \frac{6V}{\pi N}$$

$$d = \left(\frac{6V}{\pi N}\right)^{1/3}$$

$$= \left[\frac{6(10.0\ L)\left(\frac{10^{-3}\ \text{m}^3}{L}\right)}{\pi(12\ g)(6.02\times10^{23}\ \text{mol}^{-1})\over 2\left(14.00674\ \frac{g}{\text{mol}}\right)}\right]^{1/3}$$

$$= \boxed{4.2\ \text{nm}}$$

(b) Since the nearest neighbor distance is significantly larger than the diameter of an N_2 molecule (4.2 nm/0.3 nm = 14), $\boxed{\text{the gas is dilute}}$.

Chapter 14

HEAT

Problems

1. (a) The gravitational potential energy of the 1.4 kg of water is converted to internal energy in the 6.4-kg system.

$$U = mgh = (1.4 \text{ kg})\left(9.8 \ \frac{\text{m}}{\text{s}^2}\right)(2.5 \text{ m}) = \boxed{34 \text{ J}}$$

(b) | Yes; the increase in internal energy increases the average kinetic energy of the water molecules, thus the temperature is increased. |

3. The amount of internal energy generated is equal to the decrease in kinetic energy of the bullet.

$$|\Delta K| = \frac{1}{2}mv_i^2 = \frac{1}{2}(0.0200 \text{ kg})\left(7.00 \times 10^2 \ \frac{\text{m}}{\text{s}}\right)^2 = \boxed{4.90 \text{ kJ}}$$

5. (a) The decrease in gravitational potential energy of the child is equal to the amount of internal energy generated.

$$U = mgh = (15 \text{ kg})\left(9.8 \ \frac{\text{m}}{\text{s}^2}\right)(1.7 \text{ m}) = \boxed{250 \text{ J}}$$

(b) Friction warms the slide and the child, and the air molecules are deflected by the child's body. The energy goes into $\boxed{\text{all three}}$.

9. $(1.00 \text{ kcal})\left(\dfrac{4.186 \text{ J}}{\text{cal}}\right)\left(\dfrac{1 \text{ W}}{1 \ \frac{\text{J}}{\text{s}}}\right)\left(\dfrac{1 \text{ h}}{3600 \text{ s}}\right) = \boxed{1.16 \times 10^{-3} \text{ kWh}}$

11. heat capacity $= mc = (0.00500 \text{ kg})\left(0.0306 \ \dfrac{\text{kcal}}{\text{kg} \cdot \text{K}}\right) = \boxed{0.153 \text{ cal/K}}$

13. $Q = mc\Delta T = (2.0 \times 10^{-3} \text{ m}^3)\left(1.0 \times 10^3 \ \dfrac{\text{kg}}{\text{m}^3}\right)\left(4186 \ \dfrac{\text{J}}{\text{kg} \cdot \text{K}}\right)(80.0 \text{ K} - 20.0 \text{ K}) = \boxed{0.50 \text{ MJ}}$

15. The 3.3% of the energy from the food is converted to gravitational potential energy of the high jumper.

$$mgh = U$$

$$h = \frac{U}{mg}$$

$$= \frac{(3.00 \times 10^3 \text{ cal})\left(10^3 \ \frac{\text{cal}}{\text{Cal}}\right)\left(4.186 \ \frac{\text{J}}{\text{cal}}\right)(0.033)}{(60.0 \text{ kg})\left(9.8 \ \frac{\text{m}}{\text{s}^2}\right)}$$

$$= \boxed{700 \text{ m}}$$

17. (a)   heat capacity $= mc = \rho Vc = \left(2702 \ \dfrac{\text{kg}}{\text{m}^3}\right)(1.00 \text{ m}^3)\left(0.215 \ \dfrac{\text{kcal}}{\text{kg}\cdot\text{K}}\right) = \boxed{581 \text{ kcal/K}}$

(b)   heat capacity $= mc = \rho Vc = \left(7860 \ \dfrac{\text{kg}}{\text{m}^3}\right)(1.00 \text{ m}^3)\left(0.11 \ \dfrac{\text{kcal}}{\text{kg}\cdot\text{K}}\right) = \boxed{860 \text{ kcal/K}}$

19. The heat capacity of the system is $m_{\text{Al}}c_{\text{Al}} + m_{\text{w}}c_{\text{w}}$.

$$Q = mc\Delta T = \left[(0.400 \text{ kg})\left(0.215 \ \dfrac{\text{kcal}}{\text{kg}\cdot\text{K}}\right) + (2.00 \text{ kg})\left(1.000 \ \dfrac{\text{kcal}}{\text{kg}\cdot\text{K}}\right)\right](100.0°\text{C} - 15.0°\text{C}) = \boxed{177 \text{ kcal}}$$

21. $c = \dfrac{Q}{m\Delta T} = \dfrac{210 \text{ cal}}{(0.35 \text{ kg})(20.0 \text{ K})} = \boxed{0.030 \text{ kcal/(kg}\cdot\text{K)}}$

25. The change in internal energy of the water is equal to the work done on the water by the mixer plus the heat that flows into the water: $Q + W = \Delta U = mc\Delta T$. So,

$$Q = mc\Delta T - W = (2.00 \text{ kg})\left(4.186 \ \dfrac{\text{kJ}}{\text{kg}\cdot\text{K}}\right)(4.00 \text{ K}) - 6.0 \text{ kJ} = \boxed{27.5 \text{ kJ}}.$$

29. The gas is monatomic, so the molar specific is $\dfrac{3}{2}R = \dfrac{3Nk}{2n}$, so $Q = \dfrac{3}{2}Nk\Delta T$. Find N.

$$\dfrac{3}{2}Nk\Delta T = Q$$

$$N = \dfrac{2Q}{3k\Delta T}$$

$$= \dfrac{2(10.0 \text{ J})}{3\left(1.38\times10^{-23} \ \frac{\text{J}}{\text{K}}\right)(1.00\times10^2 \text{ K})}$$

$$= \boxed{4.83\times10^{21} \text{ molecules}}$$

33. The sum of the heat flows is zero. Find the heat of vaporization of water.

$$0 = Q_{\text{s}} + Q_{\text{w}} + Q_{\text{c}}$$
$$= -m_{\text{s}}L_{\text{v}} + m_{\text{s}}c_{\text{w}}\Delta T_{\text{s}} + m_{\text{w}}c_{\text{w}}\Delta T_{\text{w}} + m_{\text{c}}c_{\text{c}}\Delta T_{\text{c}}$$
$$m_{\text{s}}L_{\text{v}} = c_{\text{w}}(m_{\text{s}}\Delta T_{\text{s}} + m_{\text{w}}\Delta T_{\text{w}}) + m_{\text{c}}c_{\text{c}}\Delta T_{\text{c}}$$
$$L_{\text{v}} = \dfrac{c_{\text{w}}(m_{\text{s}}\Delta T_{\text{s}} + m_{\text{w}}\Delta T_{\text{w}}) + m_{\text{c}}c_{\text{c}}\Delta T_{\text{c}}}{m_{\text{s}}}$$
$$= \dfrac{\left(1.000 \ \frac{\text{cal}}{\text{g}\cdot\text{K}}\right)[(18.5 \text{ g})(-38.0 \text{ K}) + (2.00\times10^2 \text{ g})(47.0 \text{ K})] + (3.00\times10^2 \text{ g})\left(0.090 \ \frac{\text{cal}}{\text{g}\cdot\text{K}}\right)(47.0 \text{ K})}{18.5 \text{ g}}$$
$$= \boxed{539 \text{ cal/g}}$$

35. Find the sum of the heats required to raise the temperature of the ice to 0.0°C, melt the ice, raise the resulting water to 100.0°C, evaporate the water, and raise the temperature of the resulting steam to 110.0°C.

$$Q = Q_{ice} + Q_w + Q_s$$
$$= mL_f + mc_{ice}\Delta T_{ice} + mc_w \Delta T_w + mL_v + mc_s \Delta T_s$$
$$= (1.0 \text{ kg}) \left[79.7 \frac{\text{kcal}}{\text{kg}} + \left(0.50 \frac{\text{kcal}}{\text{kg} \cdot \text{K}} \right)(20.0 \text{ K}) + \left(1.000 \frac{\text{kcal}}{\text{kg} \cdot \text{K}} \right)(100.0 \text{ K}) + 539 \frac{\text{kcal}}{\text{kg}} + \left(0.480 \frac{\text{kcal}}{\text{kg} \cdot \text{K}} \right)(10.0 \text{ K}) \right]$$
$$= \boxed{730 \text{ kcal}}$$

37. (a)

Segment	Pressure	Temperature	Phase Change
AB	Decreases	Constant	Liquid to solid
BC	Constant	Increases	Solid to liquid
CD	Decreases	Constant	Liquid to vapor
DE	Constant	Decreases	Vapor to solid

(b) $\boxed{a \text{ is the critical point}}$: If the path for changing a liquid to a gas goes around the critical point without crossing the vapor pressure curve, no phase change occurs. At temperatures above the critical temperature or pressures above the critical pressure, it is impossible to make a clear distinction between the liquid and gas phases. $\boxed{b \text{ is the triple point}}$: The three states—solid, liquid, and vapor—can coexist in equilibrium.

39. The heat required to melt the ice is 1.20 kcal − 0.40 kcal = 0.80 kcal.

$$m = \frac{Q}{L_f} = \frac{0.80 \text{ kcal}}{79.7 \frac{\text{kcal}}{\text{kg}}} = \boxed{10 \text{ g}}$$

41. Heat flows from the aluminum into the ice. Find the mass of aluminum required to melt 10.0 g of ice.

$$Q_{Al} + Q_{ice} = 0$$
$$m_{Al}c_{Al}\Delta T_{Al} + m_{ice}L_f = 0$$
$$m_{Al} = -\frac{m_{ice}L_f}{c_{Al}\Delta T_{Al}}$$
$$= -\frac{(10.0 \text{ g})\left(333.7 \frac{\text{J}}{\text{g}}\right)}{\left(0.900 \frac{\text{J}}{\text{g} \cdot \text{K}}\right)(0.0°\text{C} - 80.0°\text{C})}$$
$$= \boxed{46.3 \text{ g}}$$

45. The rate of heat loss is $\frac{\Delta Q}{\Delta t} = \frac{L_v \Delta m}{\Delta t}$ since $Q = mL_v$ for evaporation and where Δm represents the mass of water evaporated.

$$\frac{\Delta Q}{\Delta t} = (670 \text{ min}^{-1})(0.010 \text{ g})\left(2256 \frac{\text{J}}{\text{g}} \right)\left(\frac{1 \text{ min}}{60 \text{ s}} \right) = \boxed{250 \text{ W}}$$

49. From the given information, $\Delta T = I_1 R_1 = I_2 R_2 = I(R_1 + R_2)$.

So, $\frac{R_1}{R_2} = \frac{I_2}{I_1}$ and $I = \frac{I_2 R_2}{R_1 + R_2}$. Thus, $I = \frac{I_2}{\frac{R_1}{R_2} + 1} = \frac{I_2}{\frac{I_2}{I_1} + 1} = \frac{20.0 \frac{\text{W}}{\text{m}^2}}{\frac{20.0}{10.0} + 1} = \boxed{6.67 \text{ W/m}^2}$.

53. $I_{cd} = \kappa A \dfrac{\Delta T}{d}$

$\dfrac{dI_{cd}}{\kappa A} = T_i - T_o$

$T_o = 38°C - \dfrac{(0.050\ \text{m})(51\ \text{W})}{\left(0.026\ \frac{\text{W}}{\text{m·K}}\right)(1.31\ \text{m}^2)}$

$= \boxed{-37°C}$

57. $I_{cv} = hA\Delta T = \left(21.0\ \dfrac{\text{W}}{\text{m}^2 \cdot °C}\right)(0.500\ \text{m}^2)(25.0°C - 35.0°C) = -105\ \text{W}$

The child loses heat at a rate of $\boxed{105\ \text{W}}$ due to convection.

61. $A = \dfrac{I_{em}}{e\sigma T^4} = \dfrac{40.0\ \text{W}}{0.32\left(5.670 \times 10^{-8}\ \frac{\text{W}}{\text{m}^2 \cdot \text{K}^4}\right)(2.6 \times 10^3\ \text{K})^4} = \boxed{4.8 \times 10^{-5}\ \text{m}^2}$

65. ΔT and t are related to I, A, m, and c by $P = \dfrac{Q}{t} = \dfrac{mc\Delta T}{t} = IA.$

Calculate the rate of temperature rise of the leaf, $\Delta T/t$.

$\dfrac{\Delta T}{t} = \dfrac{IA}{mc} = \dfrac{0.700\left(9.00 \times 10^2\ \frac{\text{W}}{\text{m}^2}\right)(5.00 \times 10^{-3}\ \text{m}^2)}{(0.500\ \text{g})\left(3.70\ \frac{\text{J}}{\text{g·°C}}\right)} = \boxed{1.70°C/s}$

67. (a) Set $I_{st} = I_{Cu}$.

$\kappa_{st}A\dfrac{\Delta T_{st}}{d_{st}} = \kappa_{Cu}A\dfrac{\Delta T_{Cu}}{d_{Cu}}$

$\Delta T_{st} = \dfrac{\kappa_{Cu}d_{st}}{\kappa_{st}d_{Cu}}\Delta T_{Cu}$

$= \dfrac{(401)(0.350)}{(46.0)(0.150)}\Delta T_{Cu}$

$= 20.3\Delta T_{Cu} \quad (20.3406\Delta T_{Cu})$

Since $\Delta T_{st} + \Delta T_{Cu} = \Delta T = 4.00°C,\ \Delta T_{Cu}(20.3406 + 1) = 4.00°C,$ or $\Delta T_{Cu} = 0.187°C\ (0.1874°C).$

Thus, $T = 104.00°C - 0.1874°C = \boxed{103.81°C}.$

(b) The rate at which the water evaporates is $\dfrac{\Delta m}{\Delta t}$. The rate at which heat enters the water is $\dfrac{\Delta Q}{\Delta t} = I_{cd} = \kappa A\dfrac{\Delta T}{d},$

and $\dfrac{\Delta Q}{\Delta t} = \dfrac{\Delta m L_v}{\Delta t} = L_v\left(\dfrac{\Delta m}{\Delta t}\right).$ So, $\dfrac{\Delta m}{\Delta t} = \dfrac{\kappa A \Delta T}{d L_v}.$ Use the values for steel.

$\dfrac{\Delta m}{\Delta t} = \dfrac{\left(46.0\ \frac{\text{W}}{\text{m·K}}\right)\pi\left(\frac{0.180\ \text{m}}{2}\right)^2(3.8126°C)}{(0.00350\ \text{m})\left(2256\ \frac{\text{J}}{\text{g}}\right)} = \boxed{0.565\ \text{g/s}}$

69. The person must lose heat at the same rate as it is produced and absorbed to maintain a constant body temperature.
Produced: 90 W

Absorbed: $P = IA = \left(7.00 \times 10^2 \; \frac{W}{m^2}\right)(0.57)(1.80 \; m^2)(0.42) = 300 \; W$

Rate of heat loss: 90 W + 300 W = 390 W
So, heat must be carried away from the body by perspiration at a rate of 390 W.

$Q = mL_v$

$\dfrac{Q}{t} = \dfrac{mL_v}{t}$

$P =$

$\dfrac{m}{t} = \dfrac{P}{L_v}$

$= \dfrac{390 \; \frac{J}{s}}{580 \; \frac{cal}{g}} \left(\dfrac{1 \; cal}{4.186 \; J}\right)\left(\dfrac{3600 \; s}{1 \; h}\right)\left(\dfrac{1}{1.0 \; \frac{g}{cm^3}}\right)\left(\dfrac{1 \; L}{10^3 \; cm^3}\right)$

$= \boxed{0.58 \; L/h}$

73. Gravitational potential energy is converted into internal energy.

$Q = 0.75U$

$m_m L_f = 0.75mgh$

$m_m = \dfrac{0.75mgh}{L_f}$

$= \dfrac{0.75(75 \; kg)\left(9.8 \; \frac{m}{s^2}\right)(2.43 \; m)}{333{,}700 \; \frac{J}{kg}}$

$= \boxed{4.0 \; g}$

75. **(a)** $Q = -mc_w \Delta T + mL_v = (4.0 \; g)\left[-\left(1.00 \; \dfrac{cal}{g \cdot K}\right)(45.0°C - 100.0°C) + 539 \; \dfrac{cal}{g}\right] = \boxed{2.4 \; kcal}$

   (b) $mc\Delta T = Q$

$m = \dfrac{Q}{c\Delta T}$

$= \dfrac{2376 \; cal}{\left(0.84 \; \frac{cal}{g \cdot K}\right)(45.0°C - 37.0°C)}$

$= \boxed{350 \; g}$

77. $Q = mc\Delta T$

$\Delta T = \dfrac{Q}{mc}$

$= \dfrac{0.13 \times 10^{-3} \; cal + \left(0.35 \times 10^{-3} \; \frac{cal}{cm}\right)(1.5 \; cm)}{(0.10 \; g)\left(1.0 \; \frac{cal}{g \cdot °C}\right)}$

$= \boxed{6.6 \times 10^{-3} °C}$

81.

Animal	(a) BMR/kg	(b) BMR/m^2
Mouse	210	1200
Dog	51	1000
Human	32	1000
Pig	18	1000
Horse	11	960

(a) According to the table, since BMR/kg is larger for smaller animals, $\boxed{\text{it is true}}$ that smaller animals must consume more food per kilogram of body mass.

(c) When an animal is resting, the food energy metabolized must be shed as heat (no work). Since $\boxed{\text{radiative loss depends upon surface area}}$, BMR/m^2 must be approximately the same for different-sized animals.

85. Heat flows from the bullet to the ice. Assume that all the kinetic energy goes into heating the bullet and ice. Find the mass of ice that melts.

$$0 = Q_{ice} + Q_{bullet}$$

$$Q_{ice} = -Q_{bullet}$$

$$m_{ice}L_f = -m_{Pb}c_{Pb}\Delta T - \frac{1}{2}m_{Pb}(v_f^2 - v_i^2)$$

$$m_{ice} = \frac{m_{Pb}}{L_f}\left(\frac{v_i^2}{2} - c_{Pb}\Delta T\right)$$

$$= \frac{0.0200 \text{ kg}}{333{,}700 \frac{J}{kg}}\left[\frac{\left(5.00\times10^2 \frac{m}{s}\right)^2}{2} - \left(130 \frac{J}{kg\cdot K}\right)(0°C - 47.0°C)\right]$$

$$= \boxed{7.86 \text{ g}}$$

89. Heat flows from the gold to the water and copper pot. Find the final temperature of the system.

$$0 = Q_w + Q_{Au} + Q_{Cu}$$

$$= m_w c_w(T - T_0) + m_{Au}c_{Au}(T - T_{Au}) + m_{Cu}c_{Cu}(T - T_0)$$

$$= T(m_w c_w + m_{Au}c_{Au} + m_{Cu}c_{Cu}) - m_{Au}c_{Au}T_{Au} - (m_w c_w + m_{Cu}c_{Cu})T_0$$

$$T = \frac{m_{Au}c_{Au}T_{Au} + (m_w c_w + m_{Cu}c_{Cu})T_0}{m_w c_w + m_{Au}c_{Au} + m_{Cu}c_{Cu}}$$

$$= \frac{(0.250 \text{ kg})\left(128 \frac{J}{kg\cdot K}\right)(75.0°C) + \left[(0.500 \text{ L})\left(1.00 \frac{kg}{L}\right)\left(4186 \frac{J}{kg\cdot K}\right) + (1.500 \text{ kg})\left(385 \frac{J}{kg\cdot K}\right)\right](22.0°C)}{(0.500 \text{ L})\left(1.00 \frac{kg}{L}\right)\left(4186 \frac{J}{kg\cdot K}\right) + (0.250 \text{ kg})\left(128 \frac{J}{kg\cdot K}\right) + (1.500 \text{ kg})\left(385 \frac{J}{kg\cdot K}\right)}$$

$$= \boxed{22.6°C}$$

Chapter 15

THERMODYNAMICS

Problems

1. Find the change in internal energy using the first law of thermodynamics. $Q > 0$ and $W > 0$.
$$\Delta U = Q - W = 550 \text{ J} - 840 \text{ J} = \boxed{-290 \text{ J}}$$

5. No work is done during the constant volume process, but during the constant pressure process:
$$W = P\Delta V = (1.000 \text{ atm})\left(1.013 \times 10^5 \ \frac{\text{Pa}}{\text{atm}}\right)(2.000 \text{ L} - 1.000 \text{ L})\left(10^{-3} \ \frac{\text{m}^3}{\text{L}}\right) = \boxed{101.3 \text{ J}}.$$

7. (a) For $A - C$ (constant temperature), $W = nRT \ln \dfrac{V_f}{V_i}$, and for $C - D$ (constant pressure), $W = P\Delta V$. Use the ideal gas law to find T.
$$
\begin{aligned}
W_{\text{total}} &= nRT \ln \frac{V_f}{V_i} + P\Delta V \\
&= nR\left(\frac{P_A V_A}{nR}\right) \ln \frac{V_C}{V_A} + P\Delta V \\
&= \left[(2.000 \text{ atm})(4.000 \text{ L}) \ln \frac{8.000 \text{ L}}{4.000 \text{ L}} + (1.000 \text{ atm})(16.000 \text{ L} - 8.000 \text{ L})\right]\left(1.013 \times 10^5 \ \frac{\text{Pa}}{\text{atm}}\right)\left(10^{-3} \ \frac{\text{m}^3}{\text{L}}\right) \\
&= \boxed{1372 \text{ J}}
\end{aligned}
$$

(b) For constant temperature, $\Delta U = 0$. For constant pressure,
$$\Delta U = Q - W = nC_p\Delta T - P\Delta V = \frac{5}{2}nR\left(\frac{P\Delta V}{nR}\right) - P\Delta V = \frac{3}{2}P\Delta V.$$

So, $\Delta U = \dfrac{3}{2}(1.000 \text{ atm})(16.000 \text{ L} - 8.000 \text{ L})\left(1.013 \times 10^5 \ \dfrac{\text{Pa}}{\text{atm}}\right)\left(10^{-3} \ \dfrac{\text{m}^3}{\text{L}}\right) = \boxed{1216 \text{ J}}.$

The total heat flow is $Q = \Delta U + W = 1216 \text{ J} + 1372 \text{ J} = \boxed{2588 \text{ J}}$.

9. For an isothermal process, $\Delta U = 0$. 5.00 kJ of work is done on the gas, so $W < 0$. By the first law of thermodynamics, $Q = \Delta U + W = 0 + W = \boxed{-5.00 \text{ kJ}}$

Since $Q < 0$, $\boxed{\text{the heat flows out of the gas and into the reservoir}}$.

11. (a) $Q_{\text{in}} = \dfrac{W}{e} = \dfrac{1.00 \times 10^3 \text{ J}}{0.333} = \boxed{3.00 \text{ kJ}}$

(b) $Q_{\text{out}} = W - Q_{\text{in}} = 1.00 \text{ kJ} - 3.00 \text{ kJ} = -2.00 \text{ kJ}$
$\boxed{2.00 \text{ kJ}}$ of heat is exhausted.

13. **(a)** Since 5.0×10^{16} J of electric energy is generated by power plants with an average efficiency of 0.30, Q_{in} for

the power plants is $\frac{5.0}{0.30} \times 10^{16}$ J. The heat dumped into the environment daily is $|Q_{out}|$.

$$Q_{out} = W - Q_{in} = eQ_{in} - Q_{in} = Q_{in}(e-1) = \left(\frac{5.0}{0.30} \times 10^{16} \text{ J}\right)(0.30-1) = -1.2 \times 10^{17} \text{ J}$$

So, $\boxed{1.2 \times 10^{17} \text{ J}}$ of heat is dumped into the environment daily.

(b) $m = \frac{Q}{c\Delta T} = \frac{1.2 \times 10^{17} \text{ J}}{\left(4186 \frac{\text{J}}{\text{kg·K}}\right)(2.0°C)} = \boxed{1.4 \times 10^{13} \text{ kg}}$

15. $e = \frac{W}{Q_{in}} = \frac{W}{W - Q_{out}} = \frac{1}{1 - \frac{Q_{out}}{W}} = \frac{1}{1 - \frac{(-0.450 \text{ kJ})}{0.100 \text{ kJ}}} = \boxed{0.182}$

17. $Q_H = \frac{W}{e} = \frac{1.00 \times 10^3 \text{ J}}{0.333} = \boxed{3.00 \text{ kJ}}$

19. The minimum amount of heat is discharged when the steam engine is reversible.

$e_r = 1 - \frac{T_C}{T_H} = 1 - \frac{273.15 \text{ K} + 27 \text{ K}}{273.15 \text{ K} + 127 \text{ K}} = 0.250$

$Q_C = W - Q_H = W - \frac{W}{e} = W\left(1 - \frac{1}{e}\right) = (2.0 \text{ kcal})\left(1 - \frac{1}{0.250}\right) = -6.0 \text{ kcal}$

$\boxed{6.0 \text{ kcal}}$ of heat is discharged at minimum.

21. Assuming constant rates and reversibility, find the power used.

$e_r = 1 - \frac{T_C}{T_H} = 1 - \frac{273.15 \text{ K} + 2.0 \text{ K}}{273.15 \text{ K} + 40.0 \text{ K}} = 0.1213$

$Q_C = W - Q_H = W - \frac{W}{e} = W\left(1 - \frac{1}{e}\right)$, so $\frac{Q_C}{\Delta t} = \frac{W}{\Delta t}\left(1 - \frac{1}{e}\right)$, and $P = \frac{\frac{Q_C}{\Delta t}}{1 - \frac{1}{e}} = \frac{-0.10 \times 10^3 \text{ W}}{1 - \frac{1}{0.1213}} = \boxed{14 \text{ W}}$.

25. **(a)** $e_r = 1 - \frac{T_C}{T_H}$

$\frac{T_C}{T_H} = 1 - e_r$

$T_H = \frac{T_C}{1 - e_r}$

$= \frac{310.0 \text{ K}}{1 - 0.300}$

$= \boxed{433 \text{ K}}$

(b) $Q_C = W - Q_H = W - \frac{W}{e} = W\left(1 - \frac{1}{e}\right) = (0.100 \times 10^3 \text{ J})\left(1 - \frac{1}{0.300}\right) = -233 \text{ J}$

$\boxed{233 \text{ J}}$ of heat is exhausted.

29. $e_r = 1 - \dfrac{T_C}{T_H} = 1 - \dfrac{273.15\text{ K} - 4\text{ K}}{273.15\text{ K} + 21\text{ K}} = 0.085$

$Q_H = \dfrac{W}{e} = \dfrac{1.0\text{ kJ}}{0.085} = \boxed{12\text{ kJ}}$

33. $Q_C = W - Q_H = W - \dfrac{W}{e} = W\left(1 - \dfrac{1}{e}\right)$, and since the water is initially at 0°C, $Q_C = mL_f$ is the amount of heat that must be removed from the water to freeze it.

$W = \dfrac{Q_C}{\frac{1}{e} - 1} = \dfrac{mL_f}{\frac{1}{e} - 1} = \dfrac{(1.0\text{ kg})\left(333.7\,\frac{\text{kJ}}{\text{kg}}\right)}{\frac{1}{0.25} - 1} = \boxed{110\text{ kJ}}$

37. The number of moles is the same for each case. For an equal number of moles, gas has more entropy than liquid, and the more diffuse the gas, the greater the entropy, so the order is $\boxed{\text{(c), (a), (b)}}$.

39. The temperature is constant and the heat entering the system is $Q = mL_v$.

$\Delta S = \dfrac{Q}{T} = \dfrac{mL_v}{T} = \dfrac{(1.0\text{ kg})\left(540\,\frac{\text{kcal}}{\text{kg}}\right)}{273.15\text{ K} + 100.0\text{ K}} = \boxed{+1.4\text{ kcal/K}}$

Gas is more disordered than liquid, so the entropy increases.

41. $\Delta S = -\dfrac{Q}{T_H} + \dfrac{Q}{T_C} = Q\left(\dfrac{1}{T_C} - \dfrac{1}{T_H}\right) = (10.0 \times 10^3\text{ cal})\left(\dfrac{1}{273.15\text{ K} + 0.0\text{ K}} - \dfrac{1}{273.15\text{ K} + 100.0\text{ K}}\right) = \boxed{9.81\text{ cal/K}}$

45. (a) $P = \left(2{,}000{,}000\,\dfrac{\text{cal}}{\text{day}}\right)\left(4.186\,\dfrac{\text{J}}{\text{cal}}\right)\left(\dfrac{1\text{ day}}{86{,}400\text{ s}}\right) = \boxed{100\text{ W}}$

(b) $\dfrac{\Delta S}{\Delta t} = \dfrac{\Delta Q / \Delta t}{T} = \dfrac{P}{T} = \dfrac{96.9\text{ W}}{273.15 + 20\text{ K}} = \boxed{0.3\text{ W/K}}$

47. A sum of 7 is the most likely macrostate, and can occur 6 different ways (microstates: 1 and 6, 6 and 1, 2 and 5, 5 and 2, 3 and 4, 4 and 3). So, the maximum entropy is $S = k_B \ln W = k_B \ln 6 = \boxed{1.79 k_B}$.

49. (a) The most probable outcome is half heads and half tails, so the most probable macrostate is $\boxed{\text{3 heads and 3 tails}}$.

(b) The least probable outcomes are all heads or all tails, so the least probable macrostates are $\boxed{\text{6 heads or 6 tails}}$.

(c) The number of ways to have N coins arranged so that N_1 are in one group (heads) and the remainder, $N - N_1 = N_2$, are in the other group (tails) is $\dfrac{N!}{N_1! N_2!}$. This divided by the total number of possibilities gives the probability of obtaining a particular macrostate.

$\dfrac{\frac{6!}{3!3!}}{2^6} = \boxed{\dfrac{20}{64} = \dfrac{5}{16} = 0.3125}$

53. Calculate the efficiency.

$$e_r = 1 - \frac{T_C}{T_H} = 1 - \frac{273.15 \text{ K} - 5.0 \text{ K}}{273.15 \text{ K} + 20.0 \text{ K}} = 0.0853$$

$$Q_C = W - Q_H = W - \frac{W}{e} = W\left(1 - \frac{1}{e}\right) \text{ where } W = P\Delta t. \ Q_C \text{ is equal to the heat removed from the water,}$$

$$-mL_f + mc\Delta T.$$

$$Q_C = P\Delta t\left(1 - \frac{1}{e}\right)$$

$$-mL_f + mc\Delta T = P\Delta t\left(1 - \frac{1}{e}\right)$$

$$m = \frac{P\Delta t\left(\frac{1}{e} - 1\right)}{L_f - c\Delta T}$$

$$= \frac{(148 \text{ W})(2.0 \text{ h})\left(\frac{3600 \text{ s}}{h}\right)\left(\frac{1}{0.0853} - 1\right)}{333,700 \ \frac{J}{kg} - \left(4186 \ \frac{J}{kg \cdot K}\right)(-8.0°C)}$$

$$= \boxed{31 \text{ kg}}$$

57. $e_r = 1 - \frac{T_C}{T_H}$ is the efficiency of a reversible engine.

$$\frac{\text{decrease low } T}{\text{increase high } T} = \frac{1 - \frac{T_C - \Delta T}{T_H}}{1 - \frac{T_C}{T_H + \Delta T}}$$

$$f = \frac{\frac{T_H - T_C + \Delta T}{T_H}}{\frac{T_H + \Delta T - T_C}{T_H + \Delta T}}$$

$$= \frac{T_H + \Delta T}{T_H}$$

$$= 1 + \frac{\Delta T}{T_H}$$

$$f > 1$$

$\boxed{\text{Decreasing the low temperature reservoir}}$ by ΔT will result in a greater efficiency than increasing the high temperature reservoir by ΔT.

61. $W = nRT \ln \frac{V_f}{V_i}$ is the work done by an ideal gas during isothermal expansion or contraction. Here work is done by the bladder on the gas, so $W = -nRT \ln \frac{V_f}{V_i}$.

$$W = -nRT \ln \frac{V_f}{V_i}$$

$$= -P_i V_i \ln \frac{V_f}{V_i}$$

$$= -(1.1 \text{ atm})\left(1.013 \times 10^5 \ \frac{\text{Pa}}{\text{atm}}\right)(8.16 \times 10^{-3} \text{ L})\left(10^{-3} \ \frac{m^3}{L}\right) \ln \frac{7.48 \text{ mL}}{8.16 \text{ mL}}$$

$$= \boxed{0.079 \text{ J}}$$

65. $W = mgh$ and $e = \dfrac{W}{W + \Delta U} = \dfrac{1}{1 + \frac{\Delta U}{W}} = \dfrac{1}{1 + \frac{\Delta U}{mgh}}$ $(g = 9.80 \text{ m/s}^2)$.

m (g)	h (cm)	ΔU (J)	W (J)	e (%)
16.4	0.577	1.39×10^{-3}	9.27×10^{-4}	40.0
8.09	0.745	1.64×10^{-3}	5.91×10^{-4}	26.5
1.05	0.880	1.85×10^{-3}	9.06×10^{-5}	4.67

69. (a) $\Delta S_{\text{universe}} = \Delta S_1 + \Delta S_2$

$$\approx \frac{Q_1}{T_{1\text{av}}} + \frac{Q_2}{T_{2\text{av}}}$$

$$= \frac{m_1 c \Delta T_1}{T_{1\text{av}}} + \frac{m_2 c \Delta T_2}{T_{2\text{av}}}$$

$$= (0.500 \text{ kg}) \left(110 \ \frac{\text{cal}}{\text{kg} \cdot \text{K}} \right) \left(\frac{40.0°\text{C} - 20.0°\text{C}}{273.15 \text{ K} + \frac{20.0 \text{ K} + 40.0 \text{ K}}{2}} + \frac{40.0°\text{C} - 60.0°\text{C}}{273.15 \text{ K} + \frac{60.0 \text{ K} + 40.0 \text{ K}}{2}} \right)$$

$$= \boxed{0.22 \text{ cal/K}}$$

(b) $\Delta S_{\text{universe}} = (0.500 \text{ kg}) \left(110 \ \dfrac{\text{cal}}{\text{kg} \cdot \text{K}} \right) \left(\dfrac{0.0°\text{C} - 20.0°\text{C}}{273.15 \text{ K} + \frac{20.0 \text{ K} + 0.0 \text{ K}}{2}} + \dfrac{80.0°\text{C} - 60.0°\text{C}}{273.15 \text{ K} + \frac{60.0 \text{ K} + 80.0 \text{ K}}{2}} \right) = \boxed{-0.68 \text{ cal/K}}$

73. (a) Stage B:

$W = 0$ and $\Delta U = Q$ for a constant volume process.

$\Delta U = Q = \dfrac{5}{2} nR \Delta T$ for an ideal diatomic gas, and $Q_{\text{cold}} = -Q$.

Calculate the change in entropy.

$$\Delta S = \frac{Q_{\text{cold}}}{T} = \frac{-\frac{5}{2} nR \Delta T}{T} = -\frac{5(1.000 \text{ mol}) \left(8.31 \ \frac{\text{J}}{\text{mol} \cdot \text{K}} \right)(273 \text{ K} - 373 \text{ K})}{2(273 \text{ K})} = \boxed{7.61 \text{ J/K}}$$

(b) Stage D:

$W = 0$ and $\Delta U = Q$ for a constant volume process.

$\Delta U = Q = \dfrac{5}{2} nR \Delta T$ for an ideal diatomic gas, and $Q_{\text{hot}} = -Q$.

Calculate the change in entropy.

$$\Delta S = \frac{Q_{\text{hot}}}{T} = \frac{-\frac{5}{2} nR \Delta T}{T} = -\frac{5(1.000 \text{ mol}) \left(8.31 \ \frac{\text{J}}{\text{mol} \cdot \text{K}} \right)(373 \text{ K} - 273 \text{ K})}{2(373 \text{ K})} = \boxed{-5.57 \text{ J/K}}$$

(c) $\Delta S_{\text{system+reservoirs}} = 7.61 \ \dfrac{\text{J}}{\text{K}} + \left(-5.57 \ \dfrac{\text{J}}{\text{K}} \right) = \boxed{2.04 \text{ J/K}}$

Chapter 16

ELECTRIC FORCES AND FIELDS

Problems

1. There are 10 protons in each water molecule.

$$10(1.0 \text{ mol})(6.02 \times 10^{23} \text{ mol}^{-1})(1.602 \times 10^{-19} \text{ C}) = \boxed{9.6 \times 10^5 \text{ C}}$$

3. **(a)** Since electrons have negative charge, and since the balloon acquired a negative net charge, electrons were $\boxed{\text{added}}$ to the balloon.

   (b) $\dfrac{-0.60 \times 10^{-9} \text{ C}}{-1.602 \times 10^{-19} \text{ C}} = \boxed{3.7 \times 10^9}$

5. **(a)** When the rod is brought near sphere A, negative charge flows from sphere B to sphere A. The spheres are then moved apart and the rod is removed, so A is left with a net $\boxed{\text{negative charge}}$.

   (b) Sphere B has $\boxed{\text{an equal magnitude of positive charge}}$, since the two spheres were initially uncharged.

7. Solve for q using Coulomb's law.

$$\frac{kq^2}{r^2} = F$$

$$q = \sqrt{\frac{Fr^2}{k}}$$

$$= \sqrt{\frac{(0.036 \text{ N})(0.250 \text{ m})^2}{8.99 \times 10^9 \ \frac{\text{N} \cdot \text{m}^2}{\text{C}^2}}}$$

$$= 5.0 \times 10^{-7} \text{ C}$$

Each sphere has $\boxed{-5.0 \times 10^{-7} \text{ C}}$ of charge on it.

9. $\dfrac{F_q}{F_g} = \dfrac{\frac{kq^2}{r^2}}{\frac{Gm_p m_e}{r^2}} = \dfrac{kq^2}{Gm_p m_e} = \dfrac{\left(8.988 \times 10^9 \ \frac{\text{N} \cdot \text{m}^2}{\text{C}^2}\right)(1.602 \times 10^{-19} \text{ C})^2}{\left(6.673 \times 10^{-11} \ \frac{\text{N} \cdot \text{m}^2}{\text{kg}^2}\right)(1.673 \times 10^{-27} \text{ kg})(9.109 \times 10^{-31} \text{ kg})} = \boxed{2.268 \times 10^{39}}$

11. Use Coulomb's law, $F = \dfrac{k|q_1||q_2|}{r^2}$.

The force due to the 0.60-μC charge is to the left and that due to the 0.80-μC charge is radially away.

$$F_x = -\frac{\left(8.988\times10^9\ \frac{\text{N·m}^2}{\text{C}^2}\right)(0.60\times10^{-6}\ \text{C})(1.0\times10^{-6}\ \text{C})}{\left(\sqrt{(0.100\ \text{m})^2 - (0.080\ \text{m})^2}\right)^2}$$

$$+ \frac{\left(8.988\times10^9\ \frac{\text{N·m}^2}{\text{C}^2}\right)(0.80\times10^{-6}\ \text{C})(1.0\times10^{-6}\ \text{C})}{(0.100\ \text{m})^2}\left(\frac{\sqrt{(0.100\ \text{m})^2 - (0.080\ \text{m})^2}}{0.100\ \text{m}}\right)$$

$$= -1.1\ \text{N}$$

$$F_y = -\frac{\left(8.988\times10^9\ \frac{\text{N·m}^2}{\text{C}^2}\right)(0.80\times10^{-6}\ \text{C})(1.0\times10^{-6}\ \text{C})}{(0.100\ \text{m})^2}\left(\frac{0.080\ \text{m}}{0.100\ \text{m}}\right) = -0.58\ \text{N}$$

Calculate the magnitude of the force.

$$F = \sqrt{F_x^2 + F_y^2} = \sqrt{(-1.067\ \text{m})^2 + (-0.575\ \text{m})^2} = 1.2\ \text{N}$$

Calculate the direction.

$$\theta = \tan^{-1}\frac{F_y}{F_x} = \tan^{-1}\frac{-0.575}{-1.067} = 28°$$

So, $\bar{\mathbf{F}} = \boxed{1.2\ \text{N at } 28° \text{ below the negative } x\text{-axis}}$.

13. Use Newton's second law to find the force of one ball on the other, then use Coulomb's law to find Q.

$$\Sigma F_x = T\sin\frac{\theta}{2} - F = 0$$

$$F = T\sin\frac{\theta}{2} = T\frac{\frac{d}{2}}{L} = \frac{Td}{2L}$$

$$\Sigma F_y = T\cos\frac{\theta}{2} - mg = 0$$

$$T = \frac{mg}{\cos\frac{\theta}{2}} = \frac{mg}{\frac{\sqrt{L^2 - \left(\frac{d}{2}\right)^2}}{L}} = \frac{mg}{\sqrt{1 - \left(\frac{d}{2L}\right)^2}}$$

Solve for Q.

$$F = \frac{Td}{2L}$$

$$\frac{kQ^2}{r^2} = \frac{mgd}{2L\sqrt{1-\left(\frac{d}{2L}\right)^2}}$$

$$\frac{kQ^2}{d^2} = \frac{mgd}{\sqrt{4L^2 - d^2}}$$

$$Q^2 = \frac{mgd^3}{k\sqrt{4L^2 - d^2}}$$

$$Q = \sqrt{\frac{mgd^3}{k\sqrt{4L^2 - d^2}}}$$

$$= \sqrt{\frac{(9.0\times10^{-8} \text{ kg})\left(9.8 \text{ } \frac{m}{s^2}\right)(0.020 \text{ m})^3}{\left(8.988\times10^9 \text{ } \frac{N\cdot m^2}{C^2}\right)\sqrt{4(0.98 \text{ m})^2 - (0.020 \text{ m})^2}}}$$

$$= \boxed{0.020 \text{ nC}}$$

17. $F = \dfrac{kq^2}{r^2}$, according to Coulomb's law.

So, $F_{0.25} = \dfrac{kq^2}{(0.25r)^2} = 16\left(\dfrac{kq^2}{r^2}\right) = \boxed{16F}$.

21. **(a)** Since positive charges move along the direction of electric field lines, the sodium ions flow $\boxed{\text{into the cell}}$.

(b) $F = eE = (1.602\times10^{-19} \text{ C})\left(1.0\times10^7 \text{ } \dfrac{N}{C}\right) = \boxed{1.6\times10^{-12} \text{ N}}$

23.

25. Use Newton's second law and $\vec{F} = q\vec{E} = e\vec{E}$ for a proton.

$$m\vec{a} = e\vec{E}$$

$$\vec{a} = \frac{e\vec{E}}{m}$$

$$= \frac{(1.602\times10^{-19} \text{ C})\left(33\times10^3 \text{ } \frac{N}{C} \text{ up}\right)}{1.673\times10^{-27} \text{ kg}}$$

$$= \boxed{3.2\times10^{12} \text{ m/s}^2 \text{ up}}$$

27. $E = E_q + E_{2q} = \dfrac{kq}{d^2} - \dfrac{k(2q)}{(2d)^2} = \dfrac{kq}{d^2}\left(1 - \dfrac{1}{2}\right) = \dfrac{kq}{2d^2}$

So, $\bar{E} = \boxed{\dfrac{kq}{2d^2} \text{ in the } +x\text{-direction}}$.

29. If r is the distance to $(x, y) = (0.50 \text{ m}, 0.50 \text{ m})$ from each charge, then $\cos\theta = \dfrac{x}{r}$ and $\sin\theta = \dfrac{y}{r}$. Find E.

$$E = \sqrt{E_x^2 + E_y^2}$$

$$= \sqrt{\left[\dfrac{kq_1}{r^2}\left(\dfrac{x}{r}\right) - \dfrac{kq_2}{r^2}\left(\dfrac{x}{r}\right)\right]^2 + \left[\dfrac{kq_1}{r^2}\left(\dfrac{y}{r}\right) + \dfrac{kq_2}{r^2}\left(\dfrac{y}{r}\right)\right]^2}$$

$$= \dfrac{k}{r^3}\sqrt{[(q_1 - q_2)x]^2 + [(q_1 + q_2)y]^2}$$

$$= \dfrac{8.988\times10^9 \ \frac{\text{N·m}^2}{\text{C}^2}}{\left(\sqrt{(0.50 \text{ m})^2 + (0.50 \text{ m})^2}\right)^3}\sqrt{\begin{array}{l}[(20.0\times10^{-9} \text{ C} - 10.0\times10^{-9} \text{ C})(0.50 \text{ m})]^2 \\ +[(20.0\times10^{-9} \text{ C} + 10.0\times10^{-9} \text{ C})(0.50 \text{ m})]^2\end{array}}$$

$$= \boxed{400 \text{ N/C}}$$

33.

35. (a) Since electrons travel opposite electric field lines and the electrons are deflected upward, $\boxed{\text{the electric field is directed from the top plate to the bottom plate}}$.

(b) $\dfrac{Q}{A} = \varepsilon_0 E = \left(8.854\times10^{-12} \ \dfrac{\text{C}^2}{\text{N·m}^2}\right)\left(2.00\times10^4 \ \dfrac{\text{N}}{\text{C}}\right) = \boxed{1.77\times10^{-7} \text{ C/m}^2}$

(c) $\Delta y = \dfrac{1}{2}a_y t^2 = d$

Find t.

$t = \dfrac{\Delta x}{v_i}$

Find a_y using Newton's second law.

$ma_y = eE$

$a_y = \dfrac{eE}{m}$

Substitute.

$d = \dfrac{1}{2}\left(\dfrac{eE}{m}\right)\left(\dfrac{\Delta x}{v_i}\right)^2 = \dfrac{(1.602\times10^{-19} \text{ C})\left(2.00\times10^4 \ \frac{\text{N}}{\text{C}}\right)(0.020 \text{ m})^2}{2(9.109\times10^{-31} \text{ kg})\left(4.0\times10^7 \ \frac{\text{m}}{\text{s}}\right)^2} = \boxed{0.44 \text{ mm}}$

37. (a) Electrons have negative charge, so the field must be oriented $\boxed{\text{vertically downward}}$ for them to be deflected upward.

(b) The acceleration of the electrons is related to their deflection by $d = \Delta y = \frac{1}{2} a_y t^2$ where $t = \frac{\Delta x}{v_i}$. According to Newton's second law, $F_y = ma_y$, so $ma_y = eE$, or $E = ma_y/e$. Solve for a_y.

$$a_y = \frac{2d}{t^2} = \frac{2dv_i^2}{(\Delta x)^2}$$

Calculate E.

$$E = \frac{m}{e}\left[\frac{2dv_i^2}{(\Delta x)^2}\right] = \frac{2(9.109 \times 10^{-31} \text{ kg})(0.0020 \text{ m})\left(8.4 \times 10^6 \ \frac{\text{m}}{\text{s}}\right)^2}{(1.602 \times 10^{-19} \text{ C})(0.0250 \text{ m})^2} = \boxed{2600 \text{ N/C}}$$

(c) $d = \frac{1}{2}gt^2 = \frac{1}{2}g\left(\frac{\Delta x}{v_i}\right)^2 = \frac{\left(9.8 \ \frac{\text{m}}{\text{s}^2}\right)(0.0250 \text{ m})^2}{2\left(8.4 \times 10^6 \ \frac{\text{m}}{\text{s}}\right)^2} = \boxed{4.3 \times 10^{-17} \text{ m}}$

39. The -6 μC of charge on the conducting sphere induces a positive charge of 6 μC on the inner surface of the conducting shell. This, in turn, induces a negative charge on the outer surface of the shell. The conducting shell has a net 1 μC charge, so -6 μC $+1$ μC $= \boxed{-5 \text{ μC}}$ is the charge on the outer surface.

41. **(a)** $q_1 + q_2 = 5$ μC $+ (-12$ μC$) = -7$ μC is the net charge contained within the cavity. So, the charge on the inner surface is $\boxed{7 \text{ μC}}$.

    (b) The conductor has a net charge of -4 μC, so the outer surface has a charge of -7 μC -4 μC $= \boxed{-11 \text{ μC}}$.

45. $\vec{\mathbf{E}}$ is at $60.0°$ with respect to A, so it is at $30.0°$ with respect to the normal of A.
    $$\Phi_E = EA \cos\theta = EA \cos 30.0° = \boxed{0.866EA}$$

47. **(a)** Since both surfaces of the sheet have charge q, the electric fields due to the surfaces are equal in magnitude and opposite in direction, and thus, they cancel. The electric field inside is $\boxed{0}$.

    (b) The Gaussian surface is a "pill box." It is a cylinder with its top and bottom circular surfaces parallel to the surface of the sheet, which bisects the cylinder. The electric field lines are approximately parallel to the side of the cylinder, so $\Phi_{E \text{ side}} = E_\perp A_{\text{side}} = 0$, or $E_\perp = 0$.

    $$\Phi_{\text{net}} = E_{\text{top}} A_{\text{top}} + E_{\text{bottom}} A_{\text{bottom}} = \frac{q}{\varepsilon_0}$$ where the top is outside the sheet and the bottom is inside the sheet.

    $E_{\text{bottom}} = 0$, and let $A_{\text{top}} = A_{\text{bottom}} = A$ and $E_{\text{top}} = E$, the field just outside the sheet. Find E.

    $$EA + (0)A = \frac{q}{\varepsilon_0}$$
    $$EA = \frac{q}{\varepsilon_0}$$
    $$E = \frac{1}{\varepsilon_0}\left(\frac{q}{A}\right)$$
    $$E = \frac{\sigma}{\varepsilon_0}$$

(c) No, the results do not contradict each other. Applying the superposition principle to two parallel sheets of charge gives the same result.

49. (a) $\Phi_E = E_\perp A = 4\pi kq$

The electric field outside a spherically symmetric charge distribution (with total charge q) is directed radially away from its center, and is parallel at any point to the normal of a spherical Gaussian surface outside the distribution and concentric with it.

So, $E_\perp = E$ and

$$EA = 4\pi kq$$

$$E(4\pi r^2) =$$

$$E = \frac{kq}{r^2}$$

which is the same as the electric field due to a point charge q.

(b) If a spherical Gaussian surface is placed within the charge distribution, $q = 0$ (no enclosed charge), and Gauss's law gives

$$E_\perp A = 4\pi kq$$

$$E = \frac{4\pi kq}{A}$$

$$= \frac{4\pi k(0)}{A}$$

$$= 0$$

53. (a) Let the Gaussian surface be a cylinder coaxial with and between the two charged cylinders. The ends of the Gaussian cylinder do not contribute to the flux, since $\Phi_E = E_\perp A = EA\cos\theta = EA\cos 90° = 0$. (The radially directed field is parallel to the ends.) Find the flux through the side.

$$E_\perp A = 4\pi kq_1$$

$$E(2\pi rL) = 4\pi k[\sigma_1(2\pi r_1 L)]$$

$$E = 4\pi k\left(\frac{\sigma_1 r_1}{r}\right)$$

$$\boxed{E(r_1 < r < r_2) = \frac{\sigma_1}{\varepsilon_0}\left(\frac{r_1}{r}\right)}$$

(b) $E_{max} = \frac{\sigma_1}{\varepsilon_0}\left(\frac{r_1}{r_1}\right) = \frac{\sigma_1}{\varepsilon_0}$

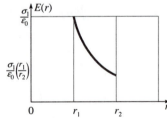

It is assumed that $\sigma_2 = 2\sigma_1 > 0$. For $r_1 < r < r_2$, $E = \frac{\sigma_1}{\varepsilon_0}\left(\frac{r_1}{r}\right)$ [from part (a)].

57. Since the semicircle is positively charged, the field lines point toward the center of curvature. Let the semicircle be oriented such that its ends are on the x-axis and its midpoint is on the negative y-axis. The x-components of $\vec{E}$ all cancel due to symmetry, and the y-components all add and point in the positive y-direction. So, the electric field at the center points away from the midpoint of the semicircle.

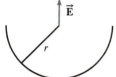

61. Set the centripetal force equal to the electric force.

$$\frac{mv^2}{r} = \frac{ke^2}{r^2}$$

$$v^2 = \frac{ke^2}{mr}$$

$$v = \sqrt{\frac{\left(8.988\times10^9 \ \frac{\text{N·m}^2}{\text{C}^2}\right)(1.602\times10^{-19} \ \text{C})^2}{(9.109\times10^{-31} \ \text{kg})(5.3\times10^{-11} \ \text{m})}}$$

$$= \boxed{2.2\times10^6 \ \text{m/s}}$$

65. (a) Let θ_+ / θ_- be the angle between r_+ / r_- and the x-axis. By symmetry, $E_{x, \text{ net}} = 0$ on the x-axis, and the y-components of $\vec{E}$ due to each charge are directed downward. Use the binomial approximation $(1\pm x)^n \approx 1+nx$ for $x \ll 1$.

If $x \gg d$, then

$$E_y(x>0, 0) = -\frac{kq}{r_+^2}\sin\theta_+ - \frac{kq}{r_-^2}\sin\theta_-$$

$$= -\frac{kq}{r_+^2}\left(\frac{\frac{d}{2}}{r_+}\right) - \frac{kq}{r_-^2}\left(\frac{\frac{d}{2}}{r_-}\right)$$

$$= -\frac{kq}{x^2+\frac{d^2}{4}}\left(\frac{\frac{d}{2}}{\sqrt{x^2+\frac{d^2}{4}}}\right) - \frac{kq}{x^2+\frac{d^2}{4}}\left(\frac{\frac{d}{2}}{\sqrt{x^2+\frac{d^2}{4}}}\right)$$

$$= -\frac{kqd}{\left(x^2+\frac{d^2}{4}\right)^{3/2}}$$

$$= -\frac{kqd}{x^3\left(1+\frac{d^2}{4x^2}\right)^{3/2}}$$

$$E_y(x\gg d, 0) \approx -\frac{kqd}{x^3}\left(1-\frac{3d^2}{8x^2}\right) \qquad \text{(binomial approximation)}$$

$$\approx -\frac{kqd}{x^3} \qquad [3d^2/(8x^2) \ll 1]$$

So, $\left|E_y\right| = E = \boxed{\dfrac{kqd}{x^3}}$.

(b) E_{+y} and E_{-y} are both directed downward, so

$\boxed{\vec{E}(x, 0) \text{ is directed in the negative } y\text{-direction for all } x.}$

69. $Q_{net} = 5.0 \ \mu C - 1.0 \ \mu C = 4.0 \ \mu C$

After the spheres are brought into contact, each will have a charge $Q_{net}/2 = 2.0 \ \mu C = Q$.

$$\frac{F_{after}}{F_{before}} = \frac{\frac{kQ^2}{L^2}}{\frac{k|Q_1||Q_2|}{L^2}} = \frac{Q^2}{|Q_1||Q_2|} = \frac{(2.0 \ \mu C)^2}{(5.0 \ \mu C)(1.0 \ \mu C)} = \boxed{0.80}$$

73. (a) Use Newton's second law.

$\Sigma F_x = 0$

$\Sigma F_y = F_D + F_b - W = 0$

Find R, the radius of a droplet.

$0 = 6\pi\eta R v_t + m_{air}g - m_{oil}g$

$6\pi\eta R v_t = m_{oil}g - m_{air}g$

$\qquad\qquad = \rho_{oil}Vg - \rho_{air}Vg$

$\qquad\qquad = (\rho_{oil} - \rho_{air})g\left(\frac{4}{3}\pi R^3\right)$

$9\eta v_t = 2(\rho_{oil} - \rho_{air})gR^2$

$R^2 = \dfrac{9\eta v_t}{2(\rho_{oil} - \rho_{air})g}$

$\boxed{R = \sqrt{\dfrac{9\eta v_t}{2(\rho_{oil} - \rho_{air})g}}}$

(b) Use Newton's second law.

$\Sigma F_x = 0$

$\Sigma F_y = F_E + F_b - W = 0$

Find q, the charge of a droplet.

$0 = qE + \rho_{air}Vg - \rho_{oil}Vg$

$qE = (\rho_{oil} - \rho_{air})g\dfrac{4}{3}\pi R^3$

$\boxed{q = \dfrac{4\pi R^3(\rho_{oil} - \rho_{air})g}{3E}}$

Chapter 17

ELECTRIC POTENTIAL

Problems

1. $U_E = k\dfrac{q_1 q_2}{r} = \dfrac{\left(8.988\times10^9 \ \frac{\text{N·m}^2}{\text{C}^2}\right)(5.0\times10^{-6} \ \text{C})(-2.0\times10^{-6} \ \text{C})}{5.0 \ \text{m}} = \boxed{-18 \ \text{mJ}}$

5. $U_E = k\left(\dfrac{q_1 q_2}{r_{12}} + \dfrac{q_1 q_3}{r_{13}} + \dfrac{q_2 q_3}{r_{23}}\right)$

$= \left(8.988\times10^9 \ \dfrac{\text{N·m}^2}{\text{C}^2}\right)\left[(4.0\times10^{-6} \ \text{C})\left(\dfrac{3.0\times10^{-6} \ \text{C}}{\sqrt{(4.0 \ \text{m})^2 + (3.0 \ \text{m})^2}} + \dfrac{-1.0\times10^{-6} \ \text{C}}{3.0 \ \text{m}}\right) + \dfrac{(3.0\times10^{-6} \ \text{C})(-1.0\times10^{-6} \ \text{C})}{4.0 \ \text{m}}\right]$

$= \boxed{2.8 \ \text{mJ}}$

7. Sum the electric fields at the center due to each charge.

$\vec{\mathbf{E}} = \vec{\mathbf{E}}_a + \vec{\mathbf{E}}_b + \vec{\mathbf{E}}_c + \vec{\mathbf{E}}_d = \vec{\mathbf{E}}_a + \vec{\mathbf{E}}_b - \vec{\mathbf{E}}_a - \vec{\mathbf{E}}_b = \boxed{0}$

Do the same for the potential at the center.

$V = \Sigma\dfrac{kQ_i}{r_i} = \dfrac{4kQ}{r} = \dfrac{4\left(8.988\times10^9 \ \frac{\text{N·m}^2}{\text{C}^2}\right)(9.0\times10^{-6} \ \text{C})}{\dfrac{\sqrt{(0.020 \ \text{m})^2 + (0.020 \ \text{m})^2}}{2}} = \boxed{2.3\times10^7 \ \text{V}}$

9. **(a)** $V = \dfrac{kQ}{r} = \dfrac{\left(8.988\times10^9 \ \frac{\text{N·m}^2}{\text{C}^2}\right)(-50.0\times10^{-9} \ \text{C})}{0.30 \ \text{m}} = \boxed{-1.5 \ \text{kV}}$

(b) $V = \dfrac{\left(8.988\times10^9 \ \frac{\text{N·m}^2}{\text{C}^2}\right)(-50.0\times10^{-9} \ \text{C})}{0.50 \ \text{m}} = \boxed{-900 \ \text{V}}$

(c) $\Delta V = kQ\left(\dfrac{1}{r_B} - \dfrac{1}{r_A}\right) = \left(8.988\times10^9 \ \dfrac{\text{N·m}^2}{\text{C}^2}\right)(-50.0\times10^{-9} \ \text{C})\left(\dfrac{1}{0.50 \ \text{m}} - \dfrac{1}{0.30 \ \text{m}}\right) = \boxed{600 \ \text{V}}$

$\Delta V > 0$, so the potential $\boxed{\text{increases}}$.

(d) $\Delta U_E = q\Delta V = (-1.0\times10^{-9} \ \text{C})(6.0\times10^2 \ \text{V}) = \boxed{-6.0\times10^{-7} \ \text{J}}$

$\Delta U_E < 0$, so the potential energy $\boxed{\text{decreases}}$.

(e) $W_{\text{field}} = -\Delta U_E = \boxed{6.0\times10^{-7} \ \text{J}}$

11. **(a)** Since V is positive, q is $\boxed{\text{positive}}$.

(b) $V \propto \dfrac{1}{r}$, so since the potential is doubled, the distance is halved, or $\boxed{10.0 \text{ cm}}$.

13. **(a)** $E_0 = \dfrac{kQ_0}{R_0^2} = \dfrac{k(3Q_0)}{R_E^2} = E$

    Solve for R_E.

    $$\dfrac{kQ_0}{R_0^2} = \dfrac{3kQ_0}{R_E^2}$$

    $$R_E^2 = 3R_0^2$$

    $$R_E = \boxed{\sqrt{3}R_0}$$

    (b) $V_0 = \dfrac{kQ_0}{R_0} = \dfrac{k(3Q_0)}{R_V} = V$

    Solve for R_V.

    $$\dfrac{kQ_0}{R_0} = \dfrac{3kQ_0}{R_V}$$

    $$R_V = \boxed{3R_0}$$

17. **(a)** Use the principle of superposition.
    Let $d = 4.00$ cm, $r = 12.0$ cm, and $q = 8.00$ nC.

    $$V_a = \dfrac{kq_1}{r_1} + \dfrac{kq_2}{r_2} = \dfrac{kq}{d} + \dfrac{k(-q)}{4d} = \dfrac{3kq}{4d} = \dfrac{3\left(8.988 \times 10^9 \ \frac{\text{N} \cdot \text{m}^2}{\text{C}^2}\right)(8.00 \times 10^{-9} \text{ C})}{4(0.0400 \text{ m})} = \boxed{1350 \text{ V}}$$

    $$V_b = \dfrac{kq}{2d} + \dfrac{k(-q)}{d} = -\dfrac{kq}{2d} = -\dfrac{\left(8.988 \times 10^9 \ \frac{\text{N} \cdot \text{m}^2}{\text{C}^2}\right)(8.00 \times 10^{-9} \text{ C})}{2(0.0400 \text{ m})} = \boxed{-899 \text{ V}}$$

    $$V_c = \dfrac{kq}{r} + \dfrac{k(-q)}{r} = \boxed{0}$$

    (b) The work done by an external agent is equal to ΔU_E.

    $$W_{a \text{ to } b} = \Delta U_E = q\Delta V = (2.00 \times 10^{-9} \text{ C})(-899 \text{ V} - 1348 \text{ V}) = \boxed{-4.49 \ \mu\text{J}}$$

    $$W_{b \text{ to } c} = (2.00 \times 10^{-9} \text{ C})(0 + 899 \text{ V}) = \boxed{1.80 \ \mu\text{J}}$$

21. $\Delta V = Ed$ for a uniform electric field.

    $$d = \dfrac{\Delta V}{E} = \dfrac{1.0 \text{ V}}{100.0 \ \frac{\text{N}}{\text{C}}} = \boxed{1.0 \text{ cm}}$$

23. Outside the cylinder, $\bar{E}$ is radially directed away from the axis of the cylinder. The equipotential surfaces are perpendicular to $\bar{E}$ at any point, so they are ⎡cylinders⎤.

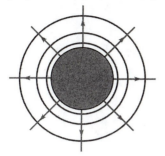

25. (a)

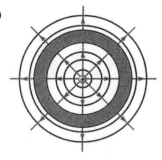

(b) For $r < r_1$, E is that due to the point charge, $E = \dfrac{kq}{r^2}$. For $r_1 < r < r_2$, $E = 0$, since this is inside a conductor.

For $r > r_2$, E once again is that due to the point charge, $\dfrac{kq}{r^2}$. For $r < r_1$, $V = \dfrac{kq}{r}$ (point charge). For

$r_1 < r < r_2$, $V = \dfrac{kq}{r_1}$, since V is continuous, and it is constant in a conductor. For $r > r_2$, $V = \dfrac{kq}{r_1} + \left(\dfrac{kq}{r} - \dfrac{kq}{r_2} \right)$

(to preserve continuity).

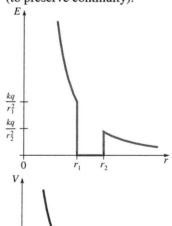

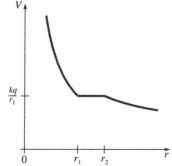

27. Set the weight of the oil drop equal to the electric force.

$$qE = mg$$

$$q = \frac{mg}{E}$$

$$= \frac{(1.0\times10^{-15} \text{ kg})\left(9.8 \ \frac{\text{m}}{\text{s}^2}\right)}{6.1\times10^4 \ \frac{\text{N}}{\text{C}}}$$

$$= \boxed{1.6\times10^{-19} \text{ C} \approx e}$$

29. Use energy conservation.

$$\Delta U = -\Delta K$$

$$-e\Delta V = -\frac{1}{2}mv^2$$

$$\Delta V = \frac{mv^2}{2e}$$

$$= \frac{(9.109\times10^{-31} \text{ kg})\left(7.26\times10^6 \ \frac{\text{m}}{\text{s}}\right)^2}{2(1.602\times10^{-19} \text{ C})}$$

$$= \boxed{150 \text{ V}}$$

31. Since positive charges move through decreases in potential, and since the potential and potential energy are greatest at A, the proton will spontaneously travel from point A to point E. So, $K_A = \boxed{0}$.

33. **(a)** Electrons travel opposite the direction of the electric field, so $\bar{\text{E}}$ is directed $\boxed{\text{upward}}$.

(b) For a uniform electric field, $F_y = eE = \dfrac{e\Delta V}{d} = ma_y$, so $a_y = \dfrac{e\Delta V}{md}$. Thus, $t = \dfrac{v_y}{a_y} = \boxed{\dfrac{v_y md}{e\Delta V}}$.

(c) Since the electron gains kinetic energy, its potential energy $\boxed{\text{decreases}}$.

37. **(a)** Since $\bar{\text{E}}$ does not depend upon the separation of the plates $(E = \sigma/\varepsilon_0)$, it $\boxed{\text{stays the same}}$.

(b) Since $\Delta V \propto d$, ΔV $\boxed{\text{increases}}$ if d increases.

41. Assuming the field is uniform, $d = \dfrac{\Delta V}{E} = \dfrac{1.00\times10^8 \text{ V}}{3.33\times10^5 \ \frac{\text{V}}{\text{m}}} = \boxed{300 \text{ m}}$.

45. $C = \kappa\dfrac{\varepsilon_0 A}{d} = \dfrac{2.5\left(8.854\times10^{-12} \ \frac{\text{C}^2}{\text{N·m}^2}\right)(0.30 \text{ m})(0.40 \text{ m})}{0.030\times10^{-3} \text{ m}} = \boxed{89 \text{ nF}}$

49. **(a)** $Q = C\Delta V = \dfrac{\varepsilon_0 A}{d}\Delta V = \dfrac{\left(8.854\times10^{-12} \ \frac{\text{C}^2}{\text{N·m}^2}\right)(0.100 \text{ m})^2(150 \text{ V})}{0.75\times10^{-3} \text{ m}} = \boxed{18 \text{ nC}}$

(b) $U = \frac{1}{2}Q\Delta V = \frac{1}{2}(17.7\times10^{-9} \text{ C})(150 \text{ V}) = \boxed{1.3 \text{ μJ}}$

53. $W = \Delta U = \frac{Q^2}{2C_f} - \frac{Q^2}{2C_i}$ since $U = \frac{Q^2}{2C}$; $C \propto \frac{1}{d}$.

$W = \frac{Q^2}{2C_i}\left(\frac{C_i}{C_f} - 1\right) = \frac{Q^2}{2C_i}\left(\frac{d_f}{d_i} - 1\right) = \frac{(0.80\times10^{-6} \text{ C})^2}{2(1.20\times10^{-9} \text{ F})}(2-1) = \boxed{0.27 \text{ mJ}}$

55. (a) $Q = C\Delta V = (15\times10^{-6} \text{ F})(9.0\times10^3 \text{ V}) = \boxed{0.14 \text{ C}}$

(b) $P_{av} = \frac{U}{t} = \frac{C(\Delta V)^2}{2t} = \frac{(15\times10^{-6} \text{ F})(9.0\times10^3 \text{ V})^2}{2(2.0\times10^{-3} \text{ s})} = \boxed{0.30 \text{ MW}}$

57. (a) $U = \frac{1}{2}Q\Delta V = \frac{1}{2}(20.0 \text{ C})(1.00\times10^9 \text{ V}) = \boxed{10.0 \text{ GJ}}$

(b) $Q = $ energy absorbed

$mL_V = 0.100(10.0\times10^9 \text{ J})$

$m = \frac{1.00\times10^9 \text{ J}}{2,256,000 \frac{\text{J}}{\text{kg}}}$

$= \boxed{443 \text{ kg}}$

(c) $\dfrac{0.100(10.0\times10^9 \text{ J})}{\left(400.0\times10^3 \frac{\text{W·h}}{\text{month}}\right)\left(\frac{3600 \text{ s}}{\text{h}}\right)\left(\frac{12 \text{ months}}{365 \text{ days}}\right)} = \boxed{0.694 \text{ month}}$

61. For a conducting sphere, $V = Er = \left(3.0\times10^6 \frac{\text{N}}{\text{C}}\right)(0.15 \text{ m}) = \boxed{450 \text{ kV}}$.

65.

69. (a) $Q = C\Delta V = \left(\frac{C}{A}\right)A\Delta V = \left(1\times10^{-6} \frac{\text{F}}{\text{cm}^2}\right)(0.05 \text{ cm}^2)[20\times10^{-3} \text{ V} - (-90\times10^{-3} \text{ V})] = \boxed{6 \text{ nC}}$

(b) $\frac{Q}{e} = \frac{5.5\times10^{-9} \text{ C}}{1.602\times10^{-19} \frac{\text{C}}{\text{ion}}} = \boxed{3\times10^{10} \text{ ions}}$

73. Let $E_0 = 20.0$ V/m, E_1 be the field outside of the dielectric after it is inserted, and E_2 be the field inside the dielectric. Use the principle of superposition for the potential after the dielectric is inserted and the fact that

    $E_2 = \dfrac{E_1}{\kappa}$.

    Initially:
    $\Delta V = E_0 d$

    Finally:

    $$\Delta V = E_1 \frac{d}{2} + E_2 \frac{d}{2} = E_1 \frac{d}{2} + \left(\frac{E_1}{\kappa}\right)\frac{d}{2} = \frac{E_1 d}{2}\left(1 + \frac{1}{\kappa}\right)$$

    Solve for E_1 in terms of E_0.

    $$\frac{E_1 d}{2}\left(1 + \frac{1}{\kappa}\right) = E_0 d$$

    $$E_1 = \frac{2E_0}{1 + \frac{1}{\kappa}}$$

    Calculate E_2.

    $$E_2 = \frac{E_1}{\kappa} = \frac{2E_0}{\kappa + 1} = \frac{2\left(20.0 \frac{\text{V}}{\text{m}}\right)}{4.0 + 1} = \boxed{8.0 \text{ V/m}}$$

77. Use $U = \dfrac{1}{2}C(\Delta V)^2$, $C = \dfrac{\kappa \varepsilon_0 A}{d}$, and the fact that ΔV is constant to find out what happens to the energy stored in the capacitor.

    Calculate $\dfrac{\Delta U}{U_0}$ by forming a proportion.

    $$\frac{\Delta U}{U_0} = \frac{\Delta C}{C_0} = \frac{\kappa \varepsilon_0 A\left(\frac{1}{d_f} - \frac{1}{d_i}\right)}{\frac{\kappa \varepsilon_0 A}{d_i}} = \frac{d_i}{d_f} - 1 = \frac{1}{1.25} - 1 = -0.200$$

    $\boxed{\text{The energy is reduced by 20.0\%.}}$

81. **(a)** Calculate the initial potential energy stored in the capacitor (without the dielectric).

    $$U_i = \frac{1}{2}C_i(\Delta V_i)^2 = \frac{1}{2}(4.00 \times 10^{-6} \text{ F})(100.0 \text{ V})^2 = \boxed{20.0 \text{ mJ}}$$

    $C_f = \kappa C_i$ and $Q = C_i \Delta V_i = C_f \Delta V_f$. So, $\Delta V_f = \dfrac{C_i}{C_f} \Delta V_i = \dfrac{\Delta V_i}{\kappa}$.

    Calculate the final potential energy.

    $$U_f = \frac{1}{2}C_f(\Delta V_f)^2 = \frac{1}{2}\kappa C_i\left(\frac{\Delta V_i}{\kappa}\right)^2 = \frac{1}{\kappa}\left[\frac{1}{2}C_i(\Delta V_i)^2\right] = \frac{1}{\kappa}U_i = \frac{20.0 \text{ mJ}}{6.0} = \boxed{3.3 \text{ mJ}}$$

    (b) Since the energy of the capacitor increases when the dielectric is removed, an external agent has to do $\boxed{\text{positive work to remove the dielectric}}$.

Chapter 18

ELECTRIC CURRENT AND CIRCUITS

Problems

1. **(a)** By the definition of electric current, $\Delta q = I \Delta t = (0.500 \text{ A})(10.0 \text{ s}) = \boxed{5.00 \text{ C}}$.

   (b) $N = \dfrac{\Delta q}{e} = \dfrac{5.00 \text{ C}}{1.602 \times 10^{-19} \frac{\text{C}}{\text{electron}}} = \boxed{3.12 \times 10^{19} \text{ electrons}}$

5. Since the negatively-charged electrons and positive ions move in opposite directions, they both contribute to the current in the same direction.

   $I = \dfrac{\Delta q}{\Delta t} = \dfrac{(3.8 \times 10^{16} + 1.2 \times 10^{16})(1.602 \times 10^{-19} \text{ C})}{1.0 \text{ s}} = \boxed{8.0 \text{ mA}}$

7. The energy delivered by each battery is equal to the total work done by them.
   Scooter:

   $W = \mathcal{E}q = (12 \text{ V})(4.0 \text{ kC}) = \boxed{48 \text{ kJ}}$

   Automobile:

   $W = (12 \text{ V})(30.0 \text{ kC}) = \boxed{360 \text{ kJ}}$

9. **(a)** $(180.0 \text{ A} \cdot \text{h}) \left(\dfrac{3600 \text{ s}}{\text{h}} \right) = \boxed{6.480 \times 10^5 \text{ C}}$

   (b) The total energy stored in a battery is equal to the total work the battery is able to do.

   $W = \mathcal{E}q = (12.0 \text{ V})(6.480 \times 10^5) = \boxed{7.78 \text{ MJ}}$

   (c) By the definition of electric current, $\Delta t = \dfrac{\Delta q}{I} = \dfrac{6.480 \times 10^5 \text{ C}}{3.30 \text{ A}} \left(\dfrac{1 \text{ h}}{3600 \text{ s}} \right) = \boxed{54.5 \text{ h}}$.

13. Let h be the thickness of the strip so that the cross-sectional area $A = hw$, where w is the width.

    $$I = neAv_D$$
    $$= ne(hw)v_D$$
    $$\frac{I}{newv_D} = h$$

    $$h = \frac{130 \times 10^{-6} \text{ A}}{(8.8 \times 10^{22} \text{ m}^{-3})(1.602 \times 10^{-19} \text{ C})(260 \times 10^{-6} \text{ m}) \left(0.44 \frac{\text{m}}{\text{s}} \right)}$$
    $$= \boxed{81 \text{ μm}}$$

15. Find t using $d = v_D t$, $I = neAv_D$, and $n = \dfrac{3.5\rho N_A}{M}$.

$$t = \frac{d}{v_D} = \frac{neAd}{I} = \frac{3.5\rho N_A eAd}{MI}$$

$$= \frac{3.5\left(2.7\times10^6 \ \frac{g}{m^3}\right)(6.022\times10^{23}\ \text{mol}^{-1})(1.602\times10^{-19}\ \text{C})\frac{1}{4}\pi(0.0026\ \text{m})^2(12\ \text{m})}{\left(27\ \frac{g}{\text{mol}}\right)(12\ \text{A})\left(\frac{3600\ \text{s}}{1\ \text{h}}\right)} = \boxed{50\ \text{h}}$$

17. Use the definition of resistance and the relationship between resistance, length, cross-sectional area, and resistivity to find ΔV.

$$\Delta V = IR = \frac{I\rho L}{A} = \frac{(150\ \text{A})(2.65\times10^{-8}\ \Omega\cdot\text{m})(0.020\ \text{m})}{\frac{1}{4}\pi(0.020\ \text{m})^2} = \boxed{0.25\ \text{mV}}$$

21. Find the diameter using the relationship between resistance, length, cross-sectional area, and resistivity.

$$R = \rho\frac{L}{A}$$

$$A = \frac{\rho L}{R}$$

$$\frac{1}{4}\pi d^2 =$$

$$d = 2\sqrt{\frac{\rho L}{\pi R}}$$

$$= 2\sqrt{\frac{(108\times10^{-8}\ \Omega\cdot\text{m})(46\ \text{m})}{\pi(10.0\ \Omega)}}$$

$$= \boxed{2.5\ \text{mm}}$$

25. The terminal voltage is $V = \mathscr{E} - Ir$. Solve for I.

$$I = \frac{\mathscr{E} - V}{r} = \frac{1.5\ \text{V} - 1.0\ \text{V}}{0.10\ \Omega} = \boxed{5\ \text{A}}$$

27. Let D = mass density. Use the relationship between resistance, length, cross-sectional area, and resistivity.

$$D = \frac{m}{V} = \frac{m}{AL}, \text{ so } A = \frac{m}{DL}. \text{ Thus, } \frac{R_1}{R_2} = \frac{\rho_1 L/A_1}{\rho_2 L/A_2} = \frac{\rho_1 A_2}{\rho_2 A_1} = \frac{\rho_1\left(\frac{m}{D_2 L}\right)}{\rho_2\left(\frac{m}{D_1 L}\right)} = \frac{\rho_1 D_1}{\rho_2 D_2}.$$

(a) $\dfrac{R_{Ag}}{R_{Cu}} = \dfrac{(1.59\times10^{-8})(10.1\times10^3)}{(1.67\times10^{-8})(8.9\times10^3)} = \boxed{1.1}$

(b) $\dfrac{R_{Al}}{R_{Cu}} = \dfrac{(2.65\times10^{-8})(2.7\times10^3)}{(1.67\times10^{-8})(8.9\times10^3)} = \boxed{0.48}$

(c) Since $0.48 < 1.1$, $\boxed{\text{aluminum}}$ is the best conductor for wires of equal length and equal mass.

29. $L_{Al} = 3L_{Cu}$, $r_{Al} = 2r_{Cu}$, $\rho_{Cu} = 0.6\rho_{Al}$, and $\alpha_{Cu} = \alpha_{Al}$. Form a proportion using the relationship between resistance, length, cross-sectional area, and resistivity.

(a)
$$\frac{R_{Al}}{R_{Cu}} = \frac{\rho_{Al}\frac{L_{Al}}{A_{Al}}}{\rho_{Cu}\frac{L_{Cu}}{A_{Cu}}}$$

$$= \frac{\rho_{Al}L_{Al}A_{Cu}}{\rho_{Cu}L_{Cu}A_{Al}}$$

$$R_{Al} = \frac{\rho_{Al}(3L_{Cu})\pi r_{Cu}^2}{(0.6\rho_{Al})L_{Cu}\pi(2r_{Cu})^2}R_{Cu}$$

$$= \frac{3}{0.6(2)^2}(24\ \Omega)$$

$$= \boxed{30\ \Omega}$$

(b) At $I = 10$ A, $V = 300$ V, so $R = \dfrac{V}{I} = \dfrac{300\text{ V}}{10\text{ A}} = \boxed{30\ \Omega}$.

(c) As found in Example 18.4, $\dfrac{R}{R_0} = 1 + \alpha\Delta T$. Find T.

$$1 + \alpha\Delta T = \frac{R}{R_0}$$

$$\alpha\Delta T = \frac{R}{R_0} - 1$$

$$T = \frac{1}{\alpha}\left(\frac{R}{R_0} - 1\right) + T_0$$

$$= \frac{1}{0.004°C^{-1}}\left(\frac{30\ \Omega}{24\ \Omega} - 1\right) + 20°C$$

$$= \boxed{80°C}$$

(d) E does not depend upon T, but ρ is directly proportional to T, and $v_D \propto I$. So,

$\boxed{\text{the electric field stays the same, the resistivity decreases, and the drift speed increases}}$.

31. Sum the individual emfs with those with their left terminal at the higher potential being positive.
$$\mathcal{E}_{eq} = 3.0\text{ V} + 3.0\text{ V} + 2.5\text{ V} - 1.5\text{ V} = \boxed{7.0\text{ V}}$$

33. $C_{eq} = \Sigma C_i$ for capacitors in parallel.
$$C_{eq} = 4\ \mu F + 2\ \mu F + 3\ \mu F + 9\ \mu F + 5\ \mu F = \boxed{23\ \mu F}$$

35. $R_{eq} = \left(\dfrac{1}{2\ \Omega} + \dfrac{1}{1\ \Omega + 1\ \Omega}\right)^{-1} + 4\ \Omega = \boxed{5\ \Omega}$

37. $R_{eq} = 1\ \Omega + \left[\dfrac{1}{2\ \Omega + 1\ \Omega} + \dfrac{1}{\frac{10}{3}\ \Omega + \left(\frac{1}{4\ \Omega} + \frac{1}{8\ \Omega}\right)^{-1}}\right]^{-1} = \boxed{3\ \Omega}$

41. $C_{eq} = \left(\dfrac{1}{12\ \mu F} + \dfrac{1}{12\ \mu F + 12\ \mu F} \right)^{-1} = \boxed{8.0\ \mu F}$

43. Let I_1 be the top branch, I_2 be the middle branch, and I_3 be the bottom branch. Assume that each current flows right to left.

(1)　$I_1 = -I_2 - I_3$

(2)　$0 = 5.00\ \text{V} + (56\ \Omega)I_2 - (22\ \Omega)I_1$

(3)　$0 = 1.00\ \text{V} + (56\ \Omega)I_2 - (75\ \Omega)I_3$

Substitute (1) into (2).

(4)　$0 = 5.00\ \text{V} + (56\ \Omega)I_2 - (22\ \Omega)(-I_2 - I_3) = 5.00\ \text{V} + (78\ \Omega)I_2 + (22\ \Omega)I_3$

Solve (3) for I_2 and substitute into (4). Then solve for I_3.

$(56\ \Omega)I_2 = (75\ \Omega)I_3 - 1.00\ \text{V}$

$$I_2 = \frac{75}{56}I_3 - \frac{1}{56}\ \text{A}$$

$$0 = 5.00\ \text{V} + (78\ \Omega)\left(\frac{75}{56}I_3 - \frac{1}{56}\ \text{A} \right) + (22\ \Omega)I_3$$

$$= \frac{5}{22}\ \text{A} + \frac{39}{616}(75I_3 - 1\ \text{A}) + I_3$$

$$= 0.164\ \text{A} + 5.75I_3$$

$I_3 = -0.0285\ \text{A}$

Calculate I_2.

$$I_2 = \frac{75}{56}(-0.0285\ \text{A}) - \frac{1}{56}\ \text{A} = -0.0560\ \text{A}$$

Calculate I_1.

$I_1 = -I_2 - I_3 = 0.0560\ \text{A} + 0.0285\ \text{A} = 0.0845\ \text{A}$

To two significant figures, the currents are:

Branch	I (mA)	Direction
Top	85	right to left
Middle	56	left to right
Bottom	29	left to right

45. Let I be the current flowing up through the 5.00-Ω resistor, and I_1 be the current flowing to the left through the 4.00-Ω resistor.

(1) $I = I_1 - 0.0500$ A

$0 = \mathcal{E} - (1.00\ \Omega)I_1 + 1.20$ V $- (4.00\ \Omega)I_1 - (2.00\ \Omega)(50.0$ mA$)$
(2) $0 = \mathcal{E} + 1.10$ V $- (5.00\ \Omega)I_1$

$0 = \mathcal{E} + (5.00\ \Omega)I - 1.00$ V $- (2.00\ \Omega)(50.0$ mA$)$
(3) $0 = \mathcal{E} - 1.10$ V $+ (5.00\ \Omega)I$

Subtract (3) from (2).
$0 = 2.20$ V $- (5.00\ \Omega)(I + I_1)$
$I + I_1 = \dfrac{2.20\text{ V}}{5.00\ \Omega}$
$I = 0.440$ A $- I_1$

Solve the result above for I_1 and set the result equal to (1).

0.440 A $- I_1 = I_1 - 0.0500$ A
$I_1 = \dfrac{0.490\text{ A}}{2}$
$= 0.245$ A

Solve for I.
$I = I_1 - 0.0500$ A $= 0.245$ A $- 0.0500$ A $= 0.195$ A

Solve for $\mathcal{E}$.
$0 = \mathcal{E} - 1.10$ V $+ (5.00\ \Omega)I$
$\mathcal{E} = 1.10$ V $- (5.00\ \Omega)(0.195$ A$)$
$= 0.13$ V

The current through the 5.00-Ω resistor flows upward and is 0.195 A. The current through the 4.00-Ω resistor flows right to left and is 0.245 A. The emf is 0.13 V.

49. $P = I^2 R = (2.0$ A$)^2 (5.00\ \Omega) = \boxed{20\text{ W}}$

53. $V = 1.50$ V $+ 1.50$ V $+ 1.50$ V $= 4.50$ V since the batteries are in series.
$P = IV = (0.2500$ A$)(4.50$ V$) = \boxed{1.13\text{ W}}$

57.

Currents	
Branch	I; direction of flow
AB	I_1; left
CD	I_2; left
EF	I_3; right

Use Kirchhoff's rules.
(1) $I_1 + I_2 = I_3$

$0 = 9.00$ V $- 2.00$ V $+ I_2(5.00\ \Omega) - I_1(4.00\ \Omega)$
(2) $0 = 7.00$ V $+ I_2(5.00\ \Omega) - I_1(4.00\ \Omega)$

(3) $0 = 9.00$ V $- I_3(8.00\ \Omega) - I_1(4.00\ \Omega)$

Subtract (2) from (3).

$$0 = 2.00 \text{ V} - I_3(8.00 \text{ } \Omega) - I_2(5.00 \text{ } \Omega)$$

(4) $I_2 = 0.400 \text{ A} - 1.60I_3$

Substitute (1) into (2).

$$0 = 7.00 \text{ V} + I_2(5.00 \text{ } \Omega) - (I_3 - I_2)(4.00 \text{ } \Omega)$$

(5) $0 = 7.00 \text{ V} + I_2(9.00 \text{ } \Omega) - I_3(4.00 \text{ } \Omega)$

Substitute (4) into (5).

$$0 = 7.00 \text{ V} + (0.400 \text{ A} - 1.60I_3)(9.00 \text{ } \Omega) - I_3(4.00 \text{ } \Omega)$$

$$0 = 7.00 \text{ V} + 3.60 \text{ V} - I_3(18.4 \text{ } \Omega)$$

$$I_3 = 0.576 \text{ A}$$

$$I_2 = 0.400 \text{ A} - 1.60(0.576 \text{ A}) = -0.522 \text{ A}$$

$$I_1 = I_3 - I_2 = 0.576 \text{ A} - (-0.522 \text{ A}) = 1.098 \text{ A}$$

Calculate the rate at which electrical energy is converted to internal energy in the chosen resistors; this is the same as the power dissipated.

$$P_4 = I_1^2(4.00 \text{ } \Omega) = (1.098 \text{ A})^2(4.00 \text{ } \Omega) = \boxed{4.82 \text{ W}}$$

$$P_5 = I_2^2(5.00 \text{ } \Omega) = (-0.522 \text{ A})^2(5.00 \text{ } \Omega) = \boxed{1.36 \text{ W}}$$

61. The resistances are in series, so $V = IR_{eq}$.

$$(0.120 \times 10^{-3} \text{ A})(R_S + 34.0 \text{ } \Omega) = 100.0 \text{ V}$$

$$R_S = \frac{100.0 \text{ V} - (0.120 \times 10^{-3} \text{ A})(34.0 \text{ } \Omega)}{0.120 \times 10^{-3} \text{ A}}$$

$$= \boxed{833 \text{ k}\Omega}$$

63. The resistances are in series, so $V = IR_{eq}$.

(a) $(2.0 \times 10^{-3} \text{ A})(R_S + 75 \text{ } \Omega) = 50.0 \text{ V}$

$$R_S = \frac{50.0 \text{ V} - (2.0 \times 10^{-3} \text{ A})(75 \text{ } \Omega)}{2.0 \times 10^{-3} \text{ A}}$$

$$= \boxed{25 \text{ k}\Omega}$$

(b) $R_S = \dfrac{500.0 \text{ V} - (2.0 \times 10^{-3} \text{ A})(75 \text{ } \Omega)}{2.0 \times 10^{-3} \text{ A}} = \boxed{250 \text{ k}\Omega}$

65.

Currents	
Branch	I; direction of flow
left	I_1; down
middle	I_2; up
right	I_3; up

(a) Use Kirchhoff's rules.

(1) $I_1 = I_2 + I_3$

(2) $0 = 9.00 \text{ V} - I_1(35 \ \Omega) - I_2(1.40 \times 10^3 \ \Omega)$

$$0 = I_2(1.40 \times 10^3 \ \Omega) - I_3(16.0 \times 10^3 \ \Omega + 83.0 \times 10^3 \ \Omega)$$

$$I_2 = \frac{99.0 \times 10^3 \ \Omega}{1.40 \times 10^3 \ \Omega} I_3$$

(3) $I_2 = 70.7 I_3$

Substitute (3) into (1).

$$I_1 = I_2 + \frac{1}{70.7} I_2$$

(4) $I_1 = \dfrac{71.7}{70.7} I_2$

Substitute (4) into (2).

$$0 = 9.00 \text{ V} - \frac{71.7}{70.7} I_2(35 \ \Omega) - I_2(1.40 \times 10^3 \ \Omega)$$

$$I_2 = \frac{9.00 \text{ V}}{\frac{71.7}{70.7}(35 \ \Omega) + 1.40 \times 10^3 \ \Omega}$$

$$= \boxed{6.27 \text{ mA}}$$

(b) Use Kirchhoff's rules.

(1) $I_1 = I_2 + I_3$

(2) $0 = 9.00 \text{ V} - I_1(35 \ \Omega) - I_2(1.40 \times 10^3 \ \Omega + 240 \ \Omega)$

$$0 = I_2(1.40 \times 10^3 \ \Omega + 240 \ \Omega) - I_3(99.0 \times 10^3 \ \Omega)$$

$$I_3 = \frac{1.40 \times 10^3 \ \Omega + 240 \ \Omega}{99.0 \times 10^3 \ \Omega} I_2$$

(3) $I_3 = 0.0166 I_2$

Substitute (3) into (1).

$$I_1 = I_2 + 0.0166 I_2$$

(4) $I_1 = 1.0166 I_2$

Substitute (4) into (2).

$$0 = 9.00 \text{ V} - 1.0166 I_2(35 \ \Omega) - I_2(1.40 \times 10^3 \ \Omega + 240 \ \Omega)$$

$$I_2 = \frac{9.00 \text{ V}}{1.0166(35 \ \Omega) + 1.40 \times 10^3 \ \Omega + 240 \ \Omega}$$

$$= \boxed{5.37 \text{ mA}}$$

67. (a) $I(t = \tau) = Ie^{-1} \approx 0.368I_0 = 0.368(100.0 \text{ mA}) = 36.8 \text{ mA}$, so $\tau \approx 12.8 \text{ ms} = RC$.

$$R = \frac{V_0}{I_0} = \frac{9.0 \text{ V}}{100.0 \times 10^{-3} \text{ A}} = \boxed{90 \ \Omega}$$

$$C = \frac{\tau}{R} = \frac{0.0128 \text{ s}}{90 \ \Omega} = \boxed{140 \ \mu\text{F}}$$

$$U = \frac{1}{2}CV_0^2 = \frac{1}{2}(142 \times 10^{-6} \text{ F})(9.0 \text{ V})^2 = \boxed{5.8 \text{ mJ}}$$

(b) The energy is half its initial value when $V_C^2 = \frac{1}{2}V_0^2 = \left(\frac{V_0}{\sqrt{2}}\right)^2$, or $V_C = \frac{V_0}{\sqrt{2}}$.

$$V_C = V_0 e^{-t/\tau} = \frac{V_0}{\sqrt{2}}, \text{ so}$$

$$e^{-t/\tau} = \frac{1}{\sqrt{2}}$$

$$-\frac{t}{\tau} = \ln\frac{1}{\sqrt{2}}$$

$$t = \frac{1}{2}\tau\ln 2$$

$$= \frac{1}{2}(12.8 \text{ ms})(0.693)$$

$$= \boxed{4.4 \text{ ms}}$$

(c) $V_C(t) = V_0 e^{-t/\tau} = (9.0 \text{ V})e^{-t/12.8 \text{ ms}}$

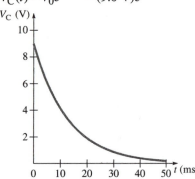

69. (a) Using the relationship between C, ΔV, and U for a capacitor, find ΔV.

$$\frac{1}{2}C(\Delta V)^2 = U$$

$$\Delta V = \sqrt{\frac{2U}{C}}$$

$$= \sqrt{\frac{2(20.0 \text{ J})}{100.0 \times 10^{-6} \text{ F}}}$$

$$= \boxed{632 \text{ V}}$$

(b) $Q = C(\Delta V) = (100.0 \times 10^{-6} \text{ F})(632 \text{ V}) = \boxed{63.2 \text{ mC}}$

(c) Solve for R using $I = I_0 e^{-t/\tau}$ where $\tau = RC$.

$$I = I_0 e^{-t/\tau}$$

$$0.050 = e^{-t/\tau}$$

$$\ln 0.050 = -\frac{t}{RC}$$

$$R = -\frac{t}{C \ln 0.050}$$

$$= -\frac{0.0020 \text{ s}}{(100.0 \times 10^{-6} \text{ F}) \ln 0.050}$$

$$= \boxed{6.7 \ \Omega}$$

73. (a) $\tau = RC = (0.40 \times 10^3 \ \Omega)(0.50 \text{ F}) = 0.20 \times 10^3 \text{ s}$

Find V_0.

$$U_0 = \frac{1}{2} C V_0^2$$

$$V_0 = \sqrt{\frac{2 U_0}{C}}$$

$$= \sqrt{\frac{2(25 \text{ J})}{0.50 \text{ F}}}$$

$$= 1.0 \times 10^1 \text{ V}$$

The voltage across the resistor is given by $V_R(t) = V_0 e^{-t/\tau} = (1.0 \times 10^1 \text{ V}) e^{-t/(0.20 \times 10^3 \text{ s})}$.

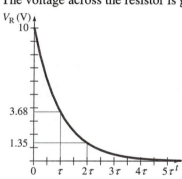

(b) $U = \frac{1}{2}CV^2$ and $V = V_0 e^{-t/\tau}$. Solve for t.

$$U = \frac{1}{2}CV^2$$
$$= \frac{1}{2}CV_0^2 e^{-2t/\tau}$$
$$= U_0 e^{-2t/\tau}$$
$$e^{2t/\tau} = \frac{U_0}{U}$$
$$\frac{2t}{\tau} = \ln\frac{U_0}{U}$$
$$t = \frac{\tau}{2}\ln\frac{U_0}{U}$$
$$= \frac{0.20\times10^3 \text{ s}}{2}\ln\frac{25 \text{ J}}{1.25 \text{ J}}$$
$$= \boxed{5.0 \text{ min}}$$

77. (a) $I = \frac{V}{R} = \frac{100.0 \text{ V}}{2.0\times10^3 \text{ }\Omega} = \boxed{50 \text{ mA}}$

(b) I_1 passes through the 15 Ω resistor, and I_2 passes through Oscar; they are in parallel, so the voltage across each is the same, 100.0 V. Use Kirchhoff's rules.
(1) $1.00 \text{ A} = I_1 + I_2$
$V = I_1 R_1 = I_2 R_2$, so
(2) $(15 \text{ }\Omega)I_1 = (2.0\times10^3 \text{ }\Omega)I_2$
Solve (2) for I_1 and substitute it into (1).
$$(15 \text{ }\Omega)I_1 = (2.0\times10^3 \text{ }\Omega)I_2$$
$$I_1 = \frac{2.0\times10^3}{15}I_2$$
Substitute.
$$1.00 \text{ A} = \frac{2.0\times10^3}{15}I_2 + I_2$$
$$I_2 = \frac{1.00 \text{ A}}{\frac{2.0\times10^3}{15}+1}$$
$$= \boxed{7.4 \text{ mA}}$$

81. Using $P = \frac{\Delta E}{\Delta t}$ and $P = IV$ gives $\Delta E = P\Delta t = IV\Delta t = (0.30 \text{ A})(1.5 \text{ V})(4.0 \text{ h})\left(\frac{3600 \text{ s}}{\text{h}}\right) = \boxed{6.5 \text{ kJ}}$.

85. (a) The current through A_1 is the same as that through the emf.
$$I = \frac{V}{R_{eq}} = \frac{10.0 \text{ V}}{2.00 \text{ }\Omega + 0.200 \text{ }\Omega + \left[\frac{1}{2.00 \text{ }\Omega} + \frac{1}{0.200 \text{ }\Omega + \left(\frac{1}{3.00 \text{ }\Omega}+\frac{1}{6.00 \text{ }\Omega}\right)^{-1}}\right]^{-1} + 2.00 \text{ }\Omega} = \boxed{1.91 \text{ A}} \quad (1.9056)$$

(b) The resistance due to A_2 is in series with the parallel combination of the 3.00-Ω and 6.00-Ω resistors. The combination of these resistors (R_R) is in parallel with the rightmost 2.00-Ω resistor (R_L).

$$R_R = 0.200\ \Omega + \left(\frac{1}{3.00\ \Omega} + \frac{1}{6.00\ \Omega}\right)^{-1} = 2.20\ \Omega$$

Since these resistances are in parallel, the voltage is the same across each, so $I_L R_L = I_R R_R$, where I_R is the current through A_2. Also, $I = I_L + I_R$.

$$I_L R_L = I_R R_R$$
$$(I - I_R)R_L =$$
$$IR_L = I_R(R_L + R_R)$$
$$I_R = \frac{R_L}{R_L + R_R}I$$
$$= \frac{2.00\ \Omega}{2.00\ \Omega + 2.20\ \Omega}(1.9056\ \text{A}) = \boxed{0.907\ \text{A}}$$

89. Since $P = IV$, we have $P_1 = (0.02\ \text{A})(0.3\ \text{V}) = \boxed{6\ \text{mW}}$ and $P_2 = (0.04\ \text{A})(0.4\ \text{V}) = \boxed{16\ \text{mW}}$.

93. (a) Oliver should use one of the 1.5 V batteries to oppose the 6.0 V battery; 6.0 V + (−1.5 V) = 4.5 V.

(b) The current will flow in the wrong direction through the 1.5 V-battery. This current may be too large for the battery to handle, since $\boxed{\text{the 1.5-V battery is not meant to be recharged}}$.

97. The current is related to the drift speed by $I = neAv_D$. Form a proportion.

$$\frac{I_{Al}}{I_{Au}} = \frac{n_{Al}eAv_{Al}}{n_{Au}eAv_{Au}}$$
$$1 = \frac{n_{Al}v_{Al}}{n_{Au}v_{Au}}$$
$$v_{Au} = \frac{3n_{Au}}{n_{Au}}v_{Al}$$
$$\boxed{v_{Au} = 3v_{Al}}$$

99. Since the resistances are equal and in series, the voltage is dropped by half by each resistor in Circuit 1. So, the

power is $P_1 = \dfrac{V^2}{R} = \dfrac{\left(\frac{\mathscr{E}}{2}\right)^2}{R} = \dfrac{\mathscr{E}^2}{4R} = 5.0\ \text{W}$.

Since the bulbs are connected in parallel in Circuit 2, the voltage across each is $\mathscr{E}$, and thus, the power dissipated by each is $P_2 = \dfrac{V^2}{R} = \dfrac{\mathscr{E}^2}{R} = 4P_1 = 4(5.0\ \text{W}) = \boxed{20\ \text{W}}$.

101. (a) $P = \dfrac{V^2}{R}$, or $R = \dfrac{V^2}{P}$.

$$R_{60} = \frac{(120 \text{ V})^2}{60.0 \text{ W}} = \boxed{240 \ \Omega}$$

$$R_{100} = \frac{(120 \text{ V})^2}{100.0 \text{ W}} = \boxed{140 \ \Omega}$$

(b) Since $P = I^2 R$, and I is the same through each bulb (connected in series), the bulb with the larger resistance dissipates more power, and thus, shines brighter. So, the $\boxed{60.0\text{-W bulb}}$ shines brighter ($240 \ \Omega > 140 \ \Omega$).

(c) When the bulbs are connected in parallel, the voltage across each is the same; and since $P = \dfrac{V^2}{R}$, the bulb with the smaller resistance dissipates the most power, therefore, the $\boxed{100.0\text{-W bulb}}$ shines brighter ($140 \ \Omega < 240 \ \Omega$).

105. (a) Since the diode and the resistor are in parallel, the voltage drop across each is $\mathscr{E} = 1.0 \text{ V} = V_D$. According to the figure, for $V_D = 1.0 \text{ V}$, $I_D = \boxed{2 \text{ mA}}$.

(b) The resistance of the diode is $R_D = \dfrac{V_D}{I_D} = \dfrac{1.0 \text{ V}}{0.002 \text{ A}} = 500 \ \Omega$.

The current through the battery is $I = \dfrac{\mathscr{E}}{R_{eq}} = \mathscr{E}\left(\dfrac{1}{R_D} + \dfrac{1}{R}\right) = (1.0 \text{ V})\left(\dfrac{1}{500 \ \Omega} + \dfrac{1}{1.0 \times 10^3 \ \Omega}\right) = \boxed{3 \text{ mA}}$.

(c) $P_{total} = \dfrac{\mathscr{E}^2}{R_{eq}} = (1.0 \text{ V})^2\left(\dfrac{1}{500 \ \Omega} + \dfrac{1}{1.0 \times 10^3 \ \Omega}\right) = \boxed{3 \text{ mW}}$

(d) The slope of the I_D vs. V_D graph is increasing. Since $I_D = \left(\dfrac{1}{R_D}\right)V_D$, the slope of the graph is the inverse of the resistance. Therefore, R_D decreases as V_D increases. Form a proportion using $P = \dfrac{V^2}{R}$.

$$\frac{P_R}{P_D} = \frac{\dfrac{V^2}{R}}{\dfrac{V^2}{R_D}} = \frac{R_D}{R}, \text{ or } P_D = \frac{R}{R_D}P_R.$$

Since R is fixed and R_D decreases, the ratio R/R_D increases. Thus, doubling the power dissipated in the resistor will more than double, or $\boxed{\text{increase by a factor greater than two}}$, that dissipated in the diode.

109. (a) S_1 closed, S_2 open:

Since no current flows through the galvanometer, the current flows only through R_1, R, and the 20.0-V battery. The voltage across R_1 is $\mathscr{E}_S = 2.00$ V. The voltage across R is $\mathscr{E} = 20.0$ V. The current is

$I = \dfrac{\mathscr{E}_S}{R_1} = \dfrac{\mathscr{E}}{R}$. Solve for R.

$R = \dfrac{\mathscr{E}}{\mathscr{E}_S} R_1 = \dfrac{20.0 \text{ V}}{2.00 \text{ V}} (20.0 \text{ } \Omega) = 2.00 \times 10^2 \text{ } \Omega$

S_1 open, S_2 closed:

Since no current flows through the galvonometer, the current flows only through R_2, R, and the 20.0-V battery. The voltage across R_2 is $\mathscr{E}_x$. The voltage across R is $\mathscr{E} = 20.0$ V. The current is $I = \dfrac{\mathscr{E}_x}{R_2} = \dfrac{\mathscr{E}}{R}$.

Solve for $\mathscr{E}_x$.

$\mathscr{E}_x = \dfrac{R_2}{R} \mathscr{E} = \dfrac{80.0 \text{ } \Omega}{2.00 \times 10^2 \text{ } \Omega} (20.0 \text{ V}) = \boxed{8.00 \text{ V}}$

(b) Since $\boxed{\text{no current passes through the source}}$, its internal resistance is irrelevant.

Chapter 19

MAGNETIC FORCES AND FIELDS

Problems

1. (a) The field lines are farthest apart (lowest density) at point $\boxed{F}$, so the magnetic field strength is smallest there.

(b) The field lines are closest together (highest density) at point $\boxed{A}$, so the magnetic field strength is largest there.

3.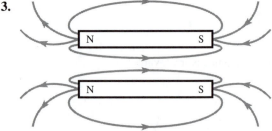

5.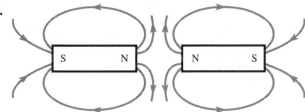

9. Determine the speed of the proton using its kinetic energy.

$$K = \frac{1}{2}mv^2$$

$$v = \sqrt{\frac{2K}{m}}$$

Calculate the force.

$$\bar{\mathbf{F}} = e\bar{\mathbf{v}} \times \bar{\mathbf{B}} = (1.602 \times 10^{-19}\ \text{C}) \left\{ \left[\sqrt{\frac{2(8.0 \times 10^{-13}\ \text{J})}{1.673 \times 10^{-27}\ \text{kg}}}\ \text{down} \right] \times (1.5\ \text{T north}) \right\} = \boxed{7.4 \times 10^{-12}\ \text{N east}}$$

13. Use Newton's second law and the magnetic force on a point charge.

$$m\bar{\mathbf{a}} = -e\bar{\mathbf{v}} \times \bar{\mathbf{B}}$$

$$\bar{\mathbf{a}} = -\frac{e}{m}[(v\ \text{right}) \times (B\ \text{up})]$$

$$= \frac{evB}{m}\ \text{into the page}$$

Let v_d be the deflection speed and $t_\mathrm{d} = \dfrac{d}{v}$ be the time of deflection where $d = 0.024$ m.

$$v_\mathrm{d} = at_\mathrm{d} = a\left(\frac{d}{v}\right) = \frac{eBd}{m}$$

Calculate the deflection with $L = 0.25$ m.

$$\text{deflection} = v_\mathrm{d}t = \frac{eBd}{m}\left(\frac{L}{v}\right) = \frac{(1.602\times10^{-19}\ \text{C})(0.20\times10^{-2}\ \text{T})(0.024\ \text{m})(0.25\ \text{m})}{(9.109\times10^{-31}\ \text{kg})\left(1.8\times10^{7}\ \frac{\text{m}}{\text{s}}\right)} = 12\ \text{cm}$$

The deflection is $\boxed{12 \text{ cm into the page}}$.

15. Since the (negatively charged) electron is moving due west and the magnetic force is upward, the component of the magnetic field perpendicular to the motion of the electron points north. Find the angle.

$$evB\sin\theta = F$$

$$\theta = \sin^{-1}\frac{F}{evB}$$

$$= \sin^{-1}\frac{3.2\times10^{-14}\ \text{N}}{(1.602\times10^{-19}\ \text{C})\left(2.0\times10^{5}\ \frac{\text{m}}{\text{s}}\right)(1.2\ \text{T})}$$

$$= 56°$$

$\boxed{\text{There are two possibilities: } 56° \text{ N of W and } 56° \text{ N of E.}}$

17. $\vec{\mathbf{B}}$ and $\vec{\mathbf{v}}$ are perpendicular, so $F = evB = (1.602\times10^{-19}\ \text{C})\left(1.0\times10^{7}\ \frac{\text{m}}{\text{s}}\right)(0.50\ \text{T}) = \boxed{8.0\times10^{-13}\ \text{N}}$.

21. Use energy conservation to find the speed of the accelerated isotopes.

$$\Delta K = -\Delta U$$

$$\frac{1}{2}mv^2 = |q|V$$

$$v = \sqrt{\frac{2|q|V}{m}}$$

Relate m to r using the centripetal force and the magnetic force.

$$m\frac{v^2}{r} = |q|vB$$

$$\frac{v^2}{r} = \frac{|q|vB}{m}$$

$$\frac{v}{r} = \frac{|q|B}{m}$$

$$\frac{1}{r}\sqrt{\frac{2|q|V}{m}} =$$

$$\frac{1}{r^2}\left(\frac{2|q|V}{m}\right) = \frac{q^2B^2}{m^2}$$

$$\frac{2V}{r^2} = \frac{|q|B^2}{m}$$

$$\frac{m}{r^2} = \frac{|q|B^2}{2V}$$

$$= \text{constant}$$

$\dfrac{m}{r^2}$ is the same for both isotopes. Find m_r, the mass of the rare isotope.

$$\frac{m_r}{r_r^2} = \frac{m_a}{r_a^2}$$

$$m_r = \left(\frac{r_r}{r_a}\right)^2 m_a$$

$$= \left(\frac{15.6 \text{ cm}}{15.0 \text{ cm}}\right)^2 (12.0000 \text{ u})$$

$$= \boxed{13.0 \text{ u}}$$

23. **(a)** Since the ions are accelerated through the same potential difference and they have the same charge, they have the same kinetic energy. Let m_u be the mass of the unknown element.

$$\frac{1}{2} m_C v_C^2 = \frac{1}{2} m_u v_u^2$$

$$\frac{v_C}{v_u} = \sqrt{\frac{m_u}{m_C}}$$

Since $r = \dfrac{mv}{|q|B}$,

$$\frac{r_C}{r_u} = \frac{m_C v_C}{m_u v_u} = \frac{m_C}{m_u}\sqrt{\frac{m_u}{m_C}} = \sqrt{\frac{m_C}{m_u}}, \text{ or } m_u = \left(\frac{r_u}{r_C}\right)^2 m_C = \left(\frac{r_C + 1.160 \text{ cm}}{r_C}\right)^2 m_C = \left(1 + \frac{1.160 \text{ cm}}{r_C}\right)^2 m_C.$$

Find r_C.

$$\frac{1}{2} m_O v_O^2 = \frac{1}{2} m_C v_C^2$$

$$\frac{v_O}{v_C} = \sqrt{\frac{m_C}{m_O}}$$

$$\frac{r_O}{r_C} = \frac{m_O v_O}{m_C v_C} = \frac{m_O}{m_C}\sqrt{\frac{m_C}{m_O}} = \sqrt{\frac{m_O}{m_C}}, \text{ or } r_O = r_C\sqrt{\frac{m_O}{m_C}}.$$

So,

$$r_O - r_C = r_C\left(\sqrt{\frac{m_O}{m_C}} - 1\right)$$

$$r_C = \frac{r_O - r_C}{\sqrt{\dfrac{m_O}{m_C}} - 1}$$

Thus, $m_u = \left(1 + \dfrac{1.160 \text{ cm}}{\dfrac{2.250 \text{ cm}}{\sqrt{\dfrac{16 \text{ u}}{12 \text{ u}}} - 1}}\right)^2 (12 \text{ u}) = \boxed{14 \text{ u}}$.

(b) According to the periodic table, the unknown element is $\boxed{\text{nitrogen}}$.

25. Form a proportion using the result for the radius of a charged particle's circular motion in a uniform magnetic field.

(a)

$$\frac{r_{14}}{r_{12}} = \frac{\frac{m_{14}v}{|q|B}}{\frac{m_{12}v}{|q|B}}$$

$$\frac{2r_{14}}{2r_{12}} = \frac{m_{14}}{m_{12}}$$

$$d_{14} = \frac{m_{14}}{m_{12}} d_{12}$$

$$= \frac{14}{12}(25 \text{ cm})$$

$$= \boxed{29 \text{ cm}}$$

(b) Find the frequency of revolution.

$$f = \frac{v}{\lambda} = \frac{v}{2\pi r}$$

Calculate f_{12}/f_{14}.

$$\frac{f_{12}}{f_{14}} = \frac{\frac{v}{2\pi r_{12}}}{\frac{v}{2\pi r_{14}}} = \frac{r_{14}}{r_{12}} = \frac{m_{14}}{m_{12}} = \frac{14.0 \text{ u}}{12.0 \text{ u}} = \boxed{1.17}$$

(c) Set the kinetic energies equal.

$$\frac{1}{2}m_{12}v_{12}^2 = \frac{1}{2}m_{14}v_{14}^2$$

$$\sqrt{\frac{m_{12}}{m_{14}}} = \frac{v_{14}}{v_{12}}$$

Relate r to m and v using $r = \frac{mv}{|q|B}$.

$$\frac{r_{12}}{r_{14}} = \frac{\frac{m_{12}v_{12}}{|q|B}}{\frac{m_{14}v_{14}}{|q|B}} = \frac{m_{12}v_{12}}{m_{14}v_{14}} = \frac{m_{12}}{m_{14}}\sqrt{\frac{m_{14}}{m_{12}}} = \sqrt{\frac{m_{12}}{m_{14}}}$$

So, $d_{14} = 2r_{14} = 2r_{12}\sqrt{\frac{m_{14}}{m_{12}}} = (25 \text{ cm})\sqrt{\frac{14}{12}} = \boxed{27 \text{ cm}}$.

Calculate f_{12}/f_{14}.

$$\frac{f_{12}}{f_{14}} = \frac{\frac{v_{12}}{2\pi r_{12}}}{\frac{v_{14}}{2\pi r_{14}}} = \frac{v_{12}r_{14}}{v_{14}r_{12}} = \sqrt{\frac{m_{14}}{m_{12}}}\sqrt{\frac{m_{14}}{m_{12}}} = \frac{m_{14}}{m_{12}} = \frac{14.0 \text{ u}}{12.0 \text{ u}} = \boxed{1.17}$$

29. The drift velocity is $v_d = \frac{E_H}{B}$ where $E_H = \frac{V_H}{w}$. So, $v_d = \frac{V_H}{wB} = \frac{7.2 \times 10^{-6} \text{ V}}{(0.035 \text{ m})(0.43 \text{ T})} = \boxed{0.48 \text{ mm/s}}$.

33. (a) The blood speed is equal to the Hall drift speed $v_d = \dfrac{E_H}{B} = \dfrac{V_H}{wB}$, where the width w is the diameter of the artery.

$$v_d = \frac{V_H}{wB} = \frac{0.35 \times 10^{-3} \text{ V}}{(0.25 \text{ T})(0.0040 \text{ m})} = \boxed{0.35 \text{ m/s}}$$

(b) flow rate $= v_d A = \left(0.35 \dfrac{\text{m}}{\text{s}}\right)\pi(0.0020 \text{ m})^2 = \boxed{4.4 \times 10^{-6} \text{ m}^3/\text{s}}$

(c) According to the RHR and $\vec{F} = q\vec{v} \times \vec{B}$, the positive ions are deflected east, so $\boxed{\text{the east lead}}$ is at the higher potential.

35. (a) The maximum force occurs when $\vec{L}$ and $\vec{B}$ are perpendicular.

$$F_{\text{max}} = ILB \sin 90° = (18.0 \text{ A})(0.60 \text{ m})(0.20 \text{ T})(1) = \boxed{2.2 \text{ N}}$$

(b) $\boxed{\begin{array}{l}\text{Only the maximum possible force can be calculated, since only the magnitudes, and not the directions of} \\ \vec{B} \text{ and } \vec{L} \text{ are given.}\end{array}}$

37. Since the east track is at the higher potential, the current flows east to west. According to the RHR and $\vec{F} = I\vec{L} \times \vec{B}$, the magnetic force points north.

$$\vec{F} = ILB \sin 90° \text{ north} = (3.0 \text{ A})(0.020 \text{ m})(1.2 \text{ T}) \text{ north} = \boxed{0.072 \text{ N north}}$$

39. (a) Calculate the force on each wire segment.

$$\vec{F}_{\text{top}} = I\vec{L}_{\text{top}} \times \vec{B} = (1.0 \text{ A})(0.300 \text{ m right}) \times (2.5 \text{ T out of the page}) = \boxed{0.75 \text{ N in the } -y\text{-direction}}$$

$$\vec{F}_{\text{bottom}} = I\vec{L}_{\text{bottom}} \times \vec{B} = -I\vec{L}_{\text{top}} \times \vec{B} = \boxed{0.75 \text{ N in the } +y\text{-direction}}$$

$$\vec{F}_{\text{left}} = I\vec{L}_{\text{left}} \times \vec{B} = (1.0 \text{ A})(0.200 \text{ m up}) \times (2.5 \text{ T out of the page}) = \boxed{0.50 \text{ N in the } +x\text{-direction}}$$

$$\vec{F}_{\text{right}} = I\vec{L}_{\text{right}} \times \vec{B} = -I\vec{L}_{\text{left}} \times \vec{B} = \boxed{0.50 \text{ N in the } -x\text{-direction}}$$

(b) $F_{\text{net}, x} = 0.50 \text{ N} - 0.50 \text{ N} = 0$

$F_{\text{net}, y} = 0.75 \text{ N} - 0.75 \text{ N} = 0$

So, $\vec{F}_{\text{net}} = \boxed{0}$.

43. The maximum torque occurs when $\theta = 90°$.

$$\tau = NIAB \sin \theta = 100(0.0500 \text{ A})\pi(0.020 \text{ cm})^2(0.20 \text{ T}) \sin 90° = \boxed{0.0013 \text{ N} \cdot \text{m}}$$

45. (a) $\tau = NIAB\sin\theta$ where θ is the angle between $\vec{B}$ and a line perpendicular to the plane of the loop. So, $\theta = 90° - 37° = 53°$.

$$\tau = NIAB\sin\theta = (1)(3.0\text{ A})(0.030\text{ m})^2(0.67\text{ T})\sin 53° = \boxed{0.0014\text{ N}\cdot\text{m}}$$

(b) $\vec{B}$ is the same at each side of the loop, and opposite sides of the loop have equal and opposite $\vec{L}$s, so the forces on opposite sides are equal and opposite.

$$\vec{F}_{net} = \vec{F}_{top} + \vec{F}_{bottom} + \vec{F}_{right} + \vec{F}_{left} = \vec{F}_{top} + (-\vec{F}_{top}) + \vec{F}_{right} + (-\vec{F}_{right}) = \boxed{0}$$

49. RHR 2 gives the direction of $\vec{B}$.

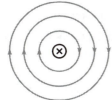

51. (a) Use the principle of superposition and the field for a long straight current-carrying wire. According to RHR 2, the field due to the bottom wire is out of the page and that due to the top wire is into the page. Since the bottom wire is closer to P, the net field is out of the page.

$$B = \frac{\mu_0 I}{2\pi}\left(\frac{1}{r_{bottom}} - \frac{1}{r_{top}}\right) = \frac{\left(4\pi\times10^{-7}\ \frac{\text{T}\cdot\text{m}}{\text{A}}\right)(10.0\text{ A})}{2\pi}\left(\frac{1}{0.25\text{ m}} - \frac{1}{0.25\text{ m} + 0.0030\text{ m}}\right) = 9\times10^{-8}\text{ T}$$

So, $\vec{B}(P) = \boxed{9\times10^{-8}\text{ T out of the page}}$.

(b) Both fields are now out of the page at P.

$$B = \frac{\mu_0 I}{2\pi}\left(\frac{1}{r_{bottom}} + \frac{1}{r_{top}}\right) = \frac{\left(4\pi\times10^{-7}\ \frac{\text{T}\cdot\text{m}}{\text{A}}\right)(10.0\text{ A})}{2\pi}\left(\frac{1}{0.25\text{ m}} + \frac{1}{0.25\text{ m} + 0.0030\text{ m}}\right) = 1.6\times10^{-5}\text{ T}$$

So, $\vec{B}(P) = \boxed{1.6\times10^{-5}\text{ T out of the page}}$.

53. $\vec{B}$ is down at the electron. $B = \dfrac{\mu_0 I}{2\pi r}$ for a long straight wire.

$$\vec{F} = q\vec{v}\times\vec{B}$$

$$= ev\left(\frac{\mu_0 I}{2\pi r}\right)\text{ parallel to the current}$$

$$= \frac{(1.602\times10^{-19}\text{ C})\left(1.0\times10^7\ \frac{\text{m}}{\text{s}}\right)\left(4\pi\times10^{-7}\ \frac{\text{T}\cdot\text{m}}{\text{A}}\right)(50.0\text{ A})}{2\pi(0.050\text{ m})}\text{ parallel to the current}$$

$$= \boxed{3.2\times10^{-16}\text{ N parallel to the current}}$$

57. **(a)** Sum the currents enclosed within loop 1. Currents out of the page are positive and into the page are negative.
$$I_{net} = 14I + (-6I) + (-3I) = 5I$$

So, the net current is $\boxed{5I \text{ out of the page}}$.

(b) $I_{net} = 14I + (-16I) = -2I$

So, the net current is $\boxed{2I \text{ into the page}}$.

61. Magnets must have both north and south poles. So, the new polarities are $\boxed{\text{(c) S and (d) N}}$.

65. **(a)** The best permanent magnet is obtained when $B_{final} / B_{0,\ max}$ is greatest. Figure 19.71a shows that B is a significant fraction of $B_{0,\ max}$ when B_0 is zero (turned off), so material $\boxed{(a)}$ would make the best permanent magnet.

(b) The core for an electromagnet should not be a permanent magnet. B is nearly zero when B_0 has returned to zero for case (c). So, material $\boxed{(c)}$ would make the best core.

69. The force on the particle is $F = qvB = ma_c = \dfrac{mv^2}{r}$. The period is $T = \dfrac{C}{v} = \dfrac{2\pi r}{v}$.

Solve for v in the force equation.
$$\frac{mv^2}{r} = qvB$$
$$v = \frac{qrB}{m}$$

Substitute for v in the equation for T.
$$T = \frac{2\pi r}{\frac{qrB}{m}} = \boxed{\frac{2\pi m}{qB}}, \text{ which is independent of the particle's speed.}$$

73. **(a)** According to RHR 1 and $\vec{\mathbf{F}} = q\vec{\mathbf{v}} \times \vec{\mathbf{B}}$, the ions must be $\boxed{\text{positive}}$; they are missing an electron.

(b) The east plate must be negatively charged to accelerate the ions to the right, so the $\boxed{\text{west}}$ plate must be positively charged.

(c) According to RHR 1 and $\vec{\mathbf{F}}_M = q\vec{\mathbf{v}} \times \vec{\mathbf{B}}$, the magnetic force on the positively-charged ions is upward between the plates, so $\vec{\mathbf{E}}$ must be downward to select the correct velocity ($\vec{\mathbf{F}}_E + \vec{\mathbf{F}}_M = 0$). Since $\vec{\mathbf{E}}$ is upward, the $\boxed{\text{north}}$ plate is positively charged.

(d) Using energy conservation, $\dfrac{1}{2}mv^2 = e\Delta V_1$.

For a parallel plate capacitor, $\Delta V_2 = Ed$.
Apply Newton's second law to the circular motion of an ion.
$$m\frac{v^2}{r} = evB$$
$$v = \frac{erB}{m}$$

For a velocity selector, $E = vB$, or $v = E/B$. So, $E = \dfrac{erB^2}{m}$ and

$$\Delta V_2 = \frac{erB^2 d}{m} = \frac{(1.602 \times 10^{-19} \text{ C})\left(\frac{0.20 \text{ m}}{2}\right)(0.20 \text{ T})^2 (0.010 \text{ m})}{12(1.66 \times 10^{-27} \text{ kg})} = \boxed{320 \text{ V}}$$

Find ΔV_1.

$$\Delta V_1 = \frac{mv^2}{2e} = \frac{m}{2e}\left(\frac{erB}{m}\right)^2 = \frac{er^2 B^2}{2m} = \frac{(1.602 \times 10^{-19} \text{ C})\left(\frac{0.20 \text{ m}}{2}\right)^2 (0.20 \text{ T})^2}{2(12)(1.66 \times 10^{-27} \text{ kg})} = \boxed{1.6 \text{ kV}}$$

(e) $\Delta V_1 = \dfrac{(1.602 \times 10^{-19} \text{ C})\left(\frac{0.20 \text{ m}}{2}\right)^2 (0.20 \text{ T})^2}{2(14)(1.66 \times 10^{-27} \text{ kg})} = \boxed{1.4 \text{ kV}}$

$$\Delta V_2 = \frac{(1.602 \times 10^{-19} \text{ C})\left(\frac{0.20 \text{ m}}{2}\right)(0.20 \text{ T})^2 (0.010 \text{ m})}{14(1.66 \times 10^{-27} \text{ kg})} = \boxed{280 \text{ V}}$$

77. $B = \dfrac{\mu_0 I}{2\pi r}$ for a long straight wire. Since the magnitude of the force is given by $F = ILB$ ($\vec{\mathbf{B}}$ is perpendicular to

$\vec{\mathbf{L}}$), the force on the lower coil (1) due to the upper coil (2) is $F = I_1 L_1 \dfrac{\mu_0 I_2}{2\pi r} = \dfrac{\mu_0 I_1 I_2 L_1}{2\pi r}$, where $r = 0.314$ cm,

$L_1 = 20[2\pi(12.5 \text{ cm})] = 500\pi$ cm, $I_1 = 4.0$ A, and $F = 1.0$ N. Calculate I_2.

$$I_2 = \frac{2\pi r F}{\mu_0 I_1 L_1} = \frac{2\pi(0.314 \text{ cm})(1.0 \text{ N})}{\left(4\pi \times 10^{-7}\ \frac{\text{T·m}}{\text{A}}\right)(4.0 \text{ A})(500\pi \text{ cm})} = 250 \text{ A}$$

To get the actual current in the wire of the upper coil, I_2 must be divided by the number of turns, 50, so the required current is $\boxed{5 \text{ A}}$.

81. Sum the electric and magnetic forces and use RHR 1.

$$\begin{aligned}
\vec{\mathbf{F}} &= \vec{\mathbf{F}}_E + \vec{\mathbf{F}}_M \\
&= q\vec{\mathbf{E}} + q\vec{\mathbf{v}} \times \vec{\mathbf{B}} \\
&= -e(E \text{ east}) - e[(v \text{ south}) \times (B \text{ east})] \\
&= eE \text{ west} - e(vB \text{ up}) \\
&= eE \text{ west} + evB \text{ down}
\end{aligned}$$

Calculate the magnitude.

$$\begin{aligned}
F &= \sqrt{e^2 E^2 + e^2 v^2 B^2} \\
&= e\sqrt{E^2 + v^2 B^2} \\
&= (1.602 \times 10^{-19} \text{ C})\sqrt{\left(3.0 \times 10^4\ \frac{\text{V}}{\text{m}}\right)^2 + \left(5.0 \times 10^6\ \frac{\text{m}}{\text{s}}\right)^2 (0.080 \text{ T})^2} \\
&= 6.4 \times 10^{-14} \text{ N}
\end{aligned}$$

Calculate the direction.

Let down be $+y$ and west be $+x$.

$$\theta = \tan^{-1}\frac{F_y}{F_x} = \tan^{-1}\frac{evB}{eE} = \tan^{-1}\frac{vB}{E} = \tan^{-1}\frac{\left(5.0 \times 10^6\ \frac{\text{m}}{\text{s}}\right)(0.080 \text{ T})}{3.0 \times 10^4\ \frac{\text{V}}{\text{m}}} = 86°$$

So, $\vec{\mathbf{F}} = \boxed{6.4 \times 10^{-14} \text{ N at } 86° \text{ below west}}$.

85. Since the ions are accelerated by the same potential difference, they have the same kinetic energy. So,

$$\frac{1}{2}m_{20}v_{20}^2 = \frac{1}{2}m_{22}v_{22}^2 \text{ or } \frac{v_{22}}{v_{20}} = \sqrt{\frac{m_{20}}{m_{22}}}. \text{ Apply Newton's second law to an ion moving in a circle.}$$

$$m\frac{v^2}{r} = evB$$

$$\frac{mv}{r} = eB$$

Since e and B are the same for both ions, mv/r is constant. Solve for $d_{22} = 2r_{22}$, the distance to the aperture.

$$\frac{m_{20}v_{20}}{r_{20}} = \frac{m_{22}v_{22}}{r_{22}}$$

$$d_{22} = \frac{m_{22}v_{22}}{m_{20}v_{20}}d_{20}$$

$$= \frac{m_{22}}{m_{20}}\sqrt{\frac{m_{20}}{m_{22}}}d_{20}$$

$$= d_{20}\sqrt{\frac{m_{22}}{m_{20}}}$$

$$= (50.0 \text{ cm})\sqrt{\frac{22.0 \text{ u}}{20.0 \text{ u}}}$$

$$= \boxed{52.4 \text{ cm}}$$

Chapter 20

ELECTROMAGNETIC INDUCTION

Problems

1. (a) The motional emf is $\mathscr{E} = vBL$, so $I = \dfrac{\mathscr{E}}{R} = \boxed{\dfrac{vBL}{R}}$.

(b) By the RHR and $\vec{\mathbf{F}} = -e\vec{\mathbf{v}} \times \vec{\mathbf{B}}$, the direction of the force on the electrons in the rod is down. So, the direction of the current is $\boxed{\text{CCW}}$.

(c) By the RHR and $\vec{\mathbf{F}} = I\vec{\mathbf{L}} \times \vec{\mathbf{B}}$, the direction of the force on the rod is $\boxed{\text{left}}$.

(d) $F = ILB = \dfrac{vBL}{R}LB = \boxed{\dfrac{vB^2L^2}{R}}$

3. (a) According to Problem 1d, the magnitude of the magnetic force on the rod is $\dfrac{vB^2L^2}{R}$. The net force must be zero for constant velocity. So, $F_{\text{ext}} = -F_{\text{B}} = \boxed{\dfrac{vB^2L^2}{R}}$.

(b) $\dfrac{\Delta W}{\Delta t} = P = Fv = \boxed{\dfrac{v^2B^2L^2}{R}}$

(c) $\mathscr{E} = vBL$, so $P = \dfrac{V^2}{R} = \boxed{\dfrac{v^2B^2L^2}{R}}$.

(d) $\boxed{\text{Energy is conserved since the rate that the external force does work is equal to the power dissipated in the resistor.}}$

5. (a) $\vec{\mathbf{v}}$ is directed down the rails. By $\vec{\mathbf{F}} = q\vec{\mathbf{v}} \times \vec{\mathbf{B}}$, the current flows $\boxed{\text{toward the left (front) end}}$ of the cylinder.

(b) By $\vec{\mathbf{F}} = I\vec{\mathbf{L}} \times \vec{\mathbf{B}}$, the magnetic force is directed $\boxed{\text{up the incline}}$.

(c) $\mathcal{E} = vLB$, so $I = \dfrac{\mathcal{E}}{R} = \dfrac{vLB}{R}$.

Use Newton's second law.

Set $F_{net} = 0$.

$-ma_0 + ILB = 0$

$$ma_0 = \left(\frac{v_t LB}{R}\right)LB$$

$$= \left(\frac{L^2 B^2}{R}\right)v_t$$

$$v_t = \boxed{\frac{ma_0 R}{L^2 B^2}}$$

9. The angle between $\vec{B}$ and the normal to the area is $\theta = 90° - 65° = 25°$.

$$\Phi_B = BA\cos\theta = (0.44\times10^{-3}\text{ T})(1.3\text{ m})(1.0\text{ m})\cos 25° = \boxed{5.2\times10^{-4}\text{ Wb}}$$

11. **(a)** According to the RHR, $\vec{B}$ is directed into the page at the loop. Since the current is decreasing and $B \propto I$ for a long straight wire, $\vec{B}$ is decreasing, thus a $\boxed{\text{CW}}$ current will flow in the loop to generate a magnetic field directed into the page.

    (b) At the uppermost point of the loop, the current in it is parallel to the current in the wire. Parallel currents attract and opposite currents repel, but since the half of the loop with the parallel components of current is closest to the long straight wire, the force on the circle is toward the wire. Thus, the external force must be $\boxed{\text{away from the long straight wire}}$.

    (c) By Faraday's law, $\left|\dfrac{\Delta\Phi_B}{\Delta t}\right| = |\mathcal{E}| = iR = (84\times10^{-3}\text{ A})(24\text{ }\Omega) = \boxed{2.0\text{ Wb/s}}$.

13. **(a)** $I = \dfrac{|\mathcal{E}|}{R} = \dfrac{1}{R}\left|\dfrac{\Delta\Phi_B}{\Delta t}\right| = \dfrac{1}{R}\left(\dfrac{NB_\perp A}{\Delta t}\right) = \dfrac{50(1.8\text{ T})\pi(0.050\text{ m})^2}{(2.8\text{ }\Omega)(3.6\text{ s})} = \boxed{0.070\text{ A}}$

    (b) The perpendicular component of $\vec{B}$ is away from the viewer and increasing, so the induced field is toward the viewer. Thus, the current must flow $\boxed{\text{CCW}}$ according to the RHR.

17. The fields due to the permanent magnet and the string are both directed to the left in the coil. As the string moves away from the coil, the magnetic field due to it in the coil decreases. To oppose this, a current flows $\boxed{\text{CCW as viewed from the left}}$ in the coil to generate a field directed to the left.

19. $\mathcal{E}_2 = \dfrac{N_2}{N_1}\mathcal{E}_1 = \dfrac{200}{4000}(2.2\times10^3\text{ V}) = \boxed{110\text{ V}}$

21. **(a)** $\dfrac{N_2}{N_1} = \dfrac{\mathcal{E}_2}{\mathcal{E}_1} = \dfrac{8.5\text{ V}}{170\text{ V}} = \boxed{\dfrac{1}{20}}$

    (b) $N_1 = \dfrac{\mathcal{E}_1}{\mathcal{E}_2}N_2 = \dfrac{170\text{ V}}{8.5\text{ V}}(50) = \boxed{1000}$

23. $\dfrac{N_2}{N_1} = \dfrac{\mathcal{E}_2}{\mathcal{E}_1} = \dfrac{10.0\ \text{V}}{5.00\ \text{V}} = \boxed{2.00}$

25. (a) $N_2 = \dfrac{\mathcal{E}_2}{\mathcal{E}_1} N_1 = \dfrac{7.8\ \text{V}}{170\ \text{V}}(300) = \boxed{14}$

(b) The maximum power is the same for both the primary and the secondary.

$I_1 = \dfrac{P}{\mathcal{E}_1} = \dfrac{5.0\ \text{W}}{170\ \text{V}} = \boxed{29\ \text{mA}}$

27. Assuming that the marble does not contact the sides of the pipe, the reading of the scale doesn't change and only reads the weight of the pipe, 12.0 N.

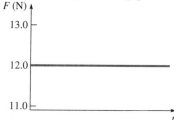

When the magnet reaches terminal velocity, the net force on it is zero. So, the scale supports both the weight of the pipe and the magnet, 12.0 N + 0.3 N = 12.3 N.

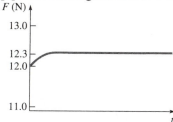

29. $E = \dfrac{1}{2} r \dfrac{\Delta B}{\Delta t}$ where $r = 5.4$ cm and $\dfrac{\Delta B}{\Delta t} = 0.30$ T/s. So, at the loop, $E = \dfrac{1}{2}(0.054\ \text{m})\left(0.30\ \dfrac{\text{T}}{\text{s}}\right) = 8.1\ \text{mN/C}$.

This field is parallel to the motion of a charge that goes around the loop, so $\vec{\mathbf{E}} = \boxed{8.1\ \text{mN/C tangent to the loop}}$.

33. (a) The emf through one winding is $\dfrac{|\mathcal{E}|}{N}$ where $\mathcal{E}$ is given by Faraday's law and $L = \dfrac{\mu_0 N^2 \pi r^2}{l}$ is the inductance of the solenoid.

$\dfrac{|\mathcal{E}|}{N} = \dfrac{1}{N}\left|-\dfrac{\Delta\Phi}{\Delta t}\right| = \dfrac{1}{N} L\left|\dfrac{\Delta I}{\Delta t}\right| = \dfrac{1}{N}\left[\dfrac{\mu_0 N^2 \pi \left(\frac{d}{2}\right)^2}{l}\right]\left|\dfrac{\Delta I}{\Delta t}\right| = \dfrac{1}{4}\mu_0 \pi n d^2 \left|\dfrac{\Delta I}{\Delta t}\right|$

$= \dfrac{1}{4}\left(4\pi\times10^{-7}\ \dfrac{\text{T}\cdot\text{m}}{\text{A}}\right)\pi(160\ \text{cm}^{-1})\left(\dfrac{100\ \text{cm}}{\text{m}}\right)(0.0075\ \text{m})^2\left(35.0\ \dfrac{\text{A}}{\text{s}}\right) = \boxed{3.1\times10^{-5}\ \text{V}}$

(b) $\mathcal{E} = N\left(\dfrac{\mathcal{E}}{N}\right) = nl\left(\dfrac{\mathcal{E}}{N}\right) = (160\ \text{cm}^{-1})(2.8\ \text{cm})(3.1\times10^{-5}\ \text{V}) = \boxed{14\ \text{mV}}$

37. (a) Start with $\Delta U = P\Delta t$ where $P = i\mathcal{E}$ and $\left|\mathcal{E}\right| = \left|\dfrac{\Delta\Phi}{\Delta t}\right|$ according to Faraday's law.

$$\Delta U = P\Delta t = i\left|\mathcal{E}\right|\Delta t = i\left|\dfrac{\Delta\Phi}{\Delta t}\right|\Delta t = i\left(L\left|\dfrac{\Delta i}{\Delta t}\right|\right)\Delta t = Li\Delta i \text{ assuming } \Delta i > 0.$$

(b) Although i may not be a linear function of t (increases at a constant rate), a graph of Li vs. i must be linear since L is constant. A qualitative graph is shown below.

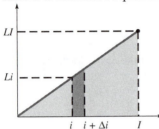

For a small current interval Δi, the area under the curve is $Li\Delta i = \Delta U$, where ΔU is the change in energy stored in the inductor due to a change in the current Δi.

(c) The total area under the curve is the area of a triangle with height LI and base I, and represents the total energy stored in the inductor.

$$\text{Area} = \dfrac{1}{2}\times\text{base}\times\text{height}$$

$$U = \dfrac{1}{2}(I)(LI)$$

$$= \dfrac{1}{2}LI^2$$

39. Since the inductors are in series, the current must be the same through both, as would an equivalent inductor. If the current is changing, each inductor has an induced emf. The induced emf of an equivalent inductor is the sum of the emfs of the individual inductors. The relation between induced emf and a changing current is given by Faraday's law.

So, $\dfrac{\Delta I_{eq}}{\Delta t} = \dfrac{\Delta I_1}{\Delta t} = \dfrac{\Delta I_2}{\Delta t}$, $\mathcal{E}_{eq} = \mathcal{E}_1 + \mathcal{E}_2$, and $\mathcal{E} = -L\dfrac{\Delta I}{\Delta t}$. Find L_{eq} in terms of L_1 and L_2.

$$\mathcal{E}_{eq} = \mathcal{E}_1 + \mathcal{E}_2 = -L_1\dfrac{\Delta I_1}{\Delta t} - L_2\dfrac{\Delta I_2}{\Delta t} = -L_1\dfrac{\Delta I_{eq}}{\Delta t} - L_2\dfrac{\Delta I_{eq}}{\Delta t} = -(L_1 + L_2)\dfrac{\Delta I_{eq}}{\Delta t} = -L_{eq}\dfrac{\Delta I_{eq}}{\Delta t}$$

So, $\boxed{L_{eq} = L_1 + L_2}$.

41. (a) Find the maximum current that flowed through the inductor.

$$I = \dfrac{\mathcal{E}}{12\ \Omega} = \dfrac{6.0\ \text{V}}{12\ \Omega} = 0.50\ \text{A}$$

Calculate the stored energy.

$$U = \dfrac{1}{2}LI^2 = \dfrac{1}{2}(0.30\ \text{H})(0.50\ \text{A})^2 = \boxed{38\ \text{mJ}}$$

(b) $P = I\mathcal{E}$ and $I = 0.50$ A (at $t = 0$).

$\left|\mathcal{E}\right|$ = the voltage drop across the resistors = $(0.50\ \text{A})(30\ \Omega) = 15$ V

So, $P = -(0.50\ \text{A})(15\ \text{V}) = \boxed{-7.5\ \text{W}}$, where $P < 0$ since the energy of the inductor is decreasing.

(c) Assume that $U_f \approx 0$.

$$P_{av} = \frac{\Delta U}{\Delta t} = \frac{0 - 38 \times 10^{-3} \text{ J}}{1.0 \text{ s}} = \boxed{-38 \text{ mW}}$$

(d) Solve for t when $I = 0.0010 I_0$.

$$I = I_0 e^{-t/\tau}$$

$$e^{t/\tau} = \frac{I_0}{I}$$

$$\ln e^{t/\tau} = \ln \frac{I_0}{I}$$

$$t = \tau \ln \frac{I_0}{I}$$

$$= \frac{L}{R_{eq}} \ln \frac{1}{0.0010}$$

$$= -\frac{0.30 \text{ H}}{18 \text{ } \Omega + 12 \text{ } \Omega} \ln 0.0010$$

$$= \boxed{69 \text{ ms}}$$

Since 69 ms $\ll$ 1.0 s, the assumption in part (c) is valid.

45. (a) When the current is no longer changing, the emf in the coil is zero.

$$I_0 = \frac{\mathscr{E}_b}{R} = \frac{6.0 \text{ V}}{33 \text{ } \Omega} = \boxed{180 \text{ mA}}$$

(b) Calculate the energy stored in the coil.

$$U = \frac{1}{2} L I_0^2 = \frac{1}{2} L \left(\frac{\mathscr{E}_b}{R} \right)^2 = \frac{(0.15 \text{ H})(6.0 \text{ V})^2}{2(33 \text{ } \Omega)^2} = \boxed{2.5 \text{ mJ}}$$

(c) Calculate the rate at which energy is dissipated as heat.

$$P = I_0^2 R = \left(\frac{\mathscr{E}_b}{R} \right)^2 R = \frac{\mathscr{E}_b^2}{R} = \frac{(6.0 \text{ V})^2}{33 \text{ } \Omega} = \boxed{1.1 \text{ W}}$$

(d) $\frac{\Delta I}{\Delta t} = 0$, so the induced emf is $\boxed{\text{zero}}$.

49. (a) L has units $H = \Omega \cdot s = \boxed{\dfrac{V \cdot s}{A}}$. R has units $\Omega = \boxed{\dfrac{V}{A}}$. $\mathscr{E}$ has units $\boxed{V}$.

(b) Only L has seconds, and only R has amperes, so the only combination with units of seconds is

$$\frac{L}{R} \text{ with } \frac{\frac{V \cdot s}{A}}{\frac{V}{A}} = s.$$

53. As the bar magnet travels from 1 to 2, $\vec{B}$ is increasing and to the left at the coil. As viewed from the left, a CW current is induced in the coil that generates a magnetic field to the right to oppose the increasing magnetic field due to the bar magnet. Thus, the current is negative and increasing in magnitude. As the bar magnet travels from 2 to 3, $\vec{B}$ is decreasing and to the left at the coil. The induced current flows CCW to oppose the decreasing field. Thus, the current is positive and decreasing in magnitude.

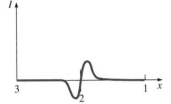

55. Since $a \ll R$, the field inside the toroid can be considered uniform and perpendicular to the cross-sectional area a^2. So, we can consider the toroid to be a square solenoid with length $2\pi R$. The self-inductance of a solenoid is given by $L = \dfrac{\mu_0 N^2 A}{l}$. So, $\boxed{L = \dfrac{\mu_0 N^2 a^2}{2\pi R}}$.

57. (a) The magnetic field of a solenoid with N turns is given by $B = \dfrac{\mu_0 NI}{L}$; $B_1 = \dfrac{\mu_0 N_1 I_1}{L}$ and $B_2 = \dfrac{\mu_0 N_2 I_2}{L}$.

The flux through N turns, each with cross-sectional area $A = \pi r^2$, is $\Phi = NBA = NB\pi r^2$. By the definition of mutual inductance, $M = \dfrac{\Phi_{21}}{I_1} = \dfrac{\Phi_{12}}{I_2}$. Now, $\Phi_{21} = N_2 B_1 \pi r^2$, so

$$M = \frac{N_2 B_1 \pi r^2}{I_1} = \frac{N_2 \pi r^2}{I_1}\left(\frac{\mu_0 N_1 I_1}{L}\right) = \boxed{\frac{\mu_0 N_1 N_2 \pi r^2}{L}}.$$

(b) $\Phi_{21} = MI_1 = \boxed{\dfrac{\mu_0 N_1 N_2 \pi r^2 I_m \sin \omega t}{L}}$

(c) If $\Phi(t) = \Phi_0 \sin \omega t$, then $\dfrac{\Delta \Phi}{\Delta t} = \omega \Phi_0 \cos \omega t$ (for small Δt).

So, by Faraday's law, $\mathscr{E}_{max} = \left|-\dfrac{\Delta \Phi_{21}}{\Delta t}\right| = M \dfrac{\Delta I_1}{\Delta t} = \boxed{\dfrac{\mu_0 N_1 N_2 \pi r^2 \omega I_m \cos \omega t}{L}}$.

61. The magnetic field in the solenoid is $B = \dfrac{\mu_0 NI}{L}$. The magnetic flux through one turn is $\Phi_M = BA = B\left(\dfrac{1}{4}\pi d^2\right)$.

So, $\Phi_M = \dfrac{\mu_0 NI}{L}\left(\dfrac{1}{4}\pi d^2\right) = \dfrac{\pi \mu_0 NI d^2}{4L} = \dfrac{\pi\left(4\pi \times 10^{-7}\ \frac{\text{T·m}}{\text{A}}\right)(350)(0.065\ \text{A})(0.016\ \text{m})^2}{4(0.085\ \text{m})} = \boxed{68\ \text{nWb}}$.

63. (a) We can model the airplane as a metal rod moving through a magnetic field. Then the potential difference is $\Delta V = vBL$, where B is the component of the field perpendicular to the motion of the plane and to the wing. Therefore, only the upwardly directed component of the magnetic field contributes to the potential difference,

$$\Delta V = vBL = \left(180\ \frac{\text{m}}{\text{s}}\right)(0.38 \times 10^{-3}\ \text{T})(46\ \text{m}) = \boxed{3.1\ \text{V}}.$$

(b) The force on an electron in the wing is $\vec{F} = -e\vec{v} \times \vec{B}$. So, according to the RHR, the electrons are forced along the southernmost wing. Negative charge builds up on the southernmost wing and positive on the northernmost. Thus, the northernmost wing is at the higher potential.

65. (a) The magnetic energy density is $u_B = \dfrac{1}{2\mu_0} B^2$.

$$u_B = \frac{(40\text{ T})^2}{2\left(4\pi \times 10^{-7}\ \frac{\text{T}\cdot\text{m}}{\text{A}}\right)} = \boxed{0.6\text{ GJ/m}^3}$$

(b) The electric energy density is $u_E = \dfrac{1}{2}\varepsilon_0 E^2$. Set $u_E = u_B$.

$$\frac{1}{2}\varepsilon_0 E^2 = \frac{1}{2\mu_0} B^2$$

$$E^2 = \frac{1}{\mu_0 \varepsilon_0} B^2$$

$$E = \frac{B}{\sqrt{\mu_0 \varepsilon_0}}$$

$$= \frac{40\text{ T}}{\sqrt{\left(4\pi \times 10^{-7}\ \frac{\text{T}\cdot\text{m}}{\text{A}}\right)\left(8.854 \times 10^{-12}\ \frac{\text{C}^2}{\text{N}\cdot\text{m}^2}\right)}}$$

$$= \boxed{1 \times 10^{10}\ \text{V/m}}$$

69. (a) By the definition of mutual inductance, $M = \dfrac{\Phi_{21}}{I_1} = \dfrac{\Phi_{12}}{I_2}$.

The magnetic field inside the solenoid is $B_1 = \mu_0 \dfrac{N_1}{l} I_1$.

So, $M = \dfrac{\Phi_{21}}{I_1} = \dfrac{N_2 B_1 A}{I_1} = \boxed{\dfrac{\mu_0 N_1 N_2 \pi r^2}{l}}$, where Φ_{21} is the flux through the coil of wire due to the solenoid.

(b) By Faraday's law, the magnitude of the induced emf is $\mathscr{E}_2 = \dfrac{\Delta\Phi_{21}}{\Delta t} = M\dfrac{\Delta I_1}{\Delta t} = \boxed{\dfrac{\mu_0 N_1 N_2 \pi r^2}{l}\dfrac{\Delta I_1}{\Delta t}}$.

Chapter 21

ALTERNATING CURRENT

Problems

1. The current reverses direction twice per cycle, and there are 60 cycles per second, so the current reverses direction $\boxed{120 \text{ times per second}}$.

3. 1500 W is the average power dissipated by the heater and $P_{av} = I_{rms}V_{rms}$. Calculate I, the peak current.

$$I = \sqrt{2}I_{rms} = \sqrt{2}\left(\frac{P_{av}}{V_{rms}}\right) = \sqrt{2}\left(\frac{1500 \text{ W}}{120 \text{ V}}\right) = \boxed{18 \text{ A}}$$

5. The *average* power dissipated by the heater is 4.0 kW when connected to a 120-V rms source. If connected to a 120 V dc source, the heater would dissipate a constant $\boxed{4.0 \text{ kW}}$ since rms values can be treated like dc values.

9. (a) $P_{av} = 1200 \text{ W}$ and $V_{rms} = 120 \text{ V}$. Calculate R.

$$R = \frac{V_{rms}^2}{P_{av}} = \frac{(120 \text{ V})^2}{1200 \text{ W}} = \boxed{12 \text{ }\Omega}$$

(b) Use Ohm's law.

$$I_{rms} = \frac{V_{rms}}{R} = \frac{120 \text{ V}}{12 \text{ }\Omega} = \boxed{10 \text{ A}}$$

(c) The average power is half the maximum power.

$$P_{max} = 2P_{av} = 2(1200 \text{ W}) = \boxed{2.4 \text{ kW}}$$

13. (a) The reactance is $X_C = \dfrac{1}{\omega C}$ where $\omega = 2\pi f$. Solve for f.

$$X_C = \frac{1}{\omega C}$$
$$\omega = \frac{1}{X_C C}$$
$$2\pi f =$$
$$f = \frac{1}{2\pi(6.63\times10^3 \text{ }\Omega)(0.400\times10^{-6} \text{ F})}$$
$$= \boxed{60.0 \text{ Hz}}$$

(b) $X_C = \dfrac{1}{\omega C} = \dfrac{1}{2\pi(30.0 \text{ Hz})(0.400\times10^{-6} \text{ F})} = \boxed{13.3 \text{ k}\Omega}$

15. $V_{rms} = I_{rms}X_C$ where $X_C = \dfrac{1}{\omega C}$. Solve for the capacitance, C.

$$V_{rms} = I_{rms}X_C$$
$$= \frac{I_{rms}}{\omega C}$$
$$C = \frac{I_{rms}}{2\pi f\, V_{rms}}$$
$$= \frac{2.3\times10^{-3}\ \text{A}}{2\pi(60.0\ \text{Hz})(115\ \text{V})}$$
$$= \boxed{53\ \text{nF}}$$

17. (a) $\Delta t = T = \dfrac{1}{4f}$ and $\Delta Q = Q = CV$. Find i_{av}.

$$i_{av} = \frac{\Delta Q}{\Delta t} = \left(\frac{1}{\Delta t}\right)\Delta Q = (4f)(CV) = \boxed{\frac{2\omega CV}{\pi}}$$

(b) $V_{rms} = I_{rms}X_C = V/\sqrt{2}$. Solve for I_{rms}.

$$I_{rms} = \frac{V_{rms}}{X_C} = \frac{\frac{V}{\sqrt{2}}}{\frac{1}{\omega C}} = \boxed{\frac{\omega CV}{\sqrt{2}}}$$

(c) | The rms current is the square root of the average of the *square* of the AC current. Squaring tends to emphasize higher values of current, so they contribute more to the resulting average than lower current values.

21. The inductive reactance is given by $X_L = \omega L$ and the inductance of a solenoid is given by $L = \dfrac{\mu_0 N^2 \pi r^2}{l}$.

$$X_L = \omega L = 2\pi f\left(\frac{\mu_0 N^2 \pi r^2}{l}\right) = \frac{2\pi^2(15.0\times10^3\ \text{Hz})\left(4\pi\times10^{-7}\ \frac{\text{T·m}}{\text{A}}\right)(240)^2(0.010\ \text{m})^2}{0.080\ \text{m}} = \boxed{27\ \Omega}$$

23. (a) $V = IX_L = I\omega L = 2\pi fIL$, so $\dfrac{V_i}{V} = \dfrac{2\pi fIL_i}{2\pi fIL_{eq}} = \dfrac{L_i}{L_{eq}} = \dfrac{L_i}{L_1+L_2}$. Thus,

$$V_i = \frac{L_i}{L_1+L_2}V = \frac{L_i}{0.10\ \text{H}+0.50\ \text{H}}(5.0\ \text{V}) = \left(\frac{25\ \text{V}}{3.0\ \text{H}}\right)L_i$$ is the peak voltage across inductor i.

The peak voltages are given in the table below.

L (H)	V (V)
0.10	0.83
0.50	4.2

(b) $I = \dfrac{V}{X_L} = \dfrac{V}{\omega L_{eq}} = \dfrac{V}{2\pi f(L_1+L_2)} = \dfrac{5.0\ \text{V}}{2\pi(126\ \text{Hz})(0.10\ \text{H}+0.50\ \text{H})} = \boxed{11\ \text{mA}}$

25. (a) If $\Phi(t) = \Phi_0 \sin \omega t$, then $\dfrac{\Delta \Phi}{\Delta t} = \omega \Phi_0 \cos \omega t$ (for small Δt). So, $v_L(t) = L \dfrac{\Delta i}{\Delta t} = L \dfrac{\Delta (I \sin \omega t)}{\Delta t} = \boxed{\omega L I \cos \omega t}$.

(b) $v_L(t) = V \cos \omega t$, so $V = \omega L I$. Calculate the reactance.

$$X_L = \frac{V}{I} = \frac{\omega L I}{I} = \omega L$$

(c) $\cos \omega t$ leads $\sin \omega t$ by $\dfrac{\pi}{2}$, so $\boxed{v_L(t) \text{ leads } i(t) \text{ by } \dfrac{\pi}{2}}$.

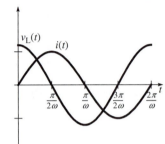

29. $Z = \sqrt{R^2 + X_L^2} = 30.0\ \Omega$ where $X_L = \omega L = 2\pi f L$.

Find L.

$$R^2 + X_L^2 = Z^2$$
$$\omega^2 L^2 = Z^2 - R^2$$
$$L = \frac{\sqrt{Z^2 - R^2}}{2\pi f}$$
$$= \frac{\sqrt{(30.0\ \Omega)^2 - (20.0\ \Omega)^2}}{2\pi(50.0\ \text{Hz})}$$
$$= \boxed{71.2\ \text{mH}}$$

31. (a) Find I using $\mathcal{E} = IZ$ where $Z = \sqrt{R^2 + X_L^2}$.

$$I = \frac{\mathcal{E}}{Z} = \frac{\mathcal{E}}{\sqrt{R^2 + X_L^2}} = \frac{\mathcal{E}}{\sqrt{R^2 + \omega^2 L^2}} = \frac{1.20 \times 10^3\ \text{V}}{\sqrt{(145.0\ \Omega)^2 + 4\pi^2(1250\ \text{Hz})^2(22.0 \times 10^{-3}\ \text{H})^2}} = 5.32\ \text{A}$$

Calculate the voltage amplitudes.

$$V_L = IX_L = I\omega L = 2\pi(5.32\ \text{A})(1250\ \text{Hz})(22.0 \times 10^{-3}\ \text{H}) = \boxed{919\ \text{V}}$$

$$V_R = IR = (5.32\ \text{A})(145.0\ \Omega) = \boxed{771\ \text{V}}$$

(b) $\boxed{\text{No}}$, the voltage amplitudes do not add to give the amplitude of the source voltage; the voltages across the resistor and the inductor are 90° out of phase. Similar to the impedance, the source voltage is the square root of the sum of squares, $\boxed{\mathcal{E} = \sqrt{V_C^2 + V_R^2}}$, as can be seen in a phasor diagram.

(c)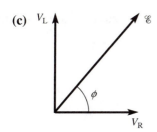

33. $X_L = 0,$ so the impedance is

$$Z = \sqrt{R^2 + X_C^2} = \sqrt{R^2 + \frac{1}{\omega^2 C^2}} = \sqrt{(300.0 \ \Omega)^2 + \frac{1}{4\pi^2 (159 \ \text{Hz})^2 (2.5 \times 10^{-6} \ \text{F})^2}} = \boxed{500 \ \Omega}.$$

35. (a) Set $V_R = IR$ equal to $V_L = IX_L = I\omega L = 2\pi fIL$ and solve for the frequency.

$$V_R = V_L$$
$$IR = IX_L$$
$$R = 2\pi fL$$
$$f = \frac{R}{2\pi L}$$
$$= \frac{150 \ \Omega}{2\pi(0.75 \ \text{H})}$$
$$= \boxed{32 \ \text{Hz}}$$

(b) In a phasor diagram, the source is the hypotenuse of a right triangle and V_R and V_C are the legs, so

$\mathcal{E} = \sqrt{V_R^2 + V_L^2}$ according to the Pythagorean theorem. Find $V_L / \mathcal{E} = V_R / \mathcal{E}.$

$$\mathcal{E} = \sqrt{V_R^2 + V_L^2}$$
$$\mathcal{E}^2 = V_R^2 + X_L^2$$
$$= V_R^2 + V_R^2$$
$$= 2V_R^2$$
$$\frac{\mathcal{E}^2}{2} = V_R^2$$
$$\frac{V_R^2}{\mathcal{E}^2} = \frac{1}{2}$$
$$\frac{V_R}{\mathcal{E}} = \frac{1}{\sqrt{2}}$$
$$\frac{V_L}{\mathcal{E}} =$$

So, the rms voltages across the components are not half of the rms voltage of the source: $\boxed{\dfrac{V_R}{\mathcal{E}} = \dfrac{V_L}{\mathcal{E}} = \dfrac{1}{\sqrt{2}}}.$

(c) The voltage across the inductor leads the current through it, so the source voltage leads the current. Use the power factor to find ϕ.

$$\cos\phi = \frac{R}{Z}$$

$$\phi = \cos^{-1}\frac{R}{Z}$$

$$= \cos^{-1}\frac{R}{\sqrt{R^2 + X_L^2}}$$

$$= \cos^{-1}\frac{IR}{\sqrt{(IR)^2 + (IX_L)^2}}$$

$$= \cos^{-1}\frac{V_R}{\sqrt{V_R^2 + V_L^2}}$$

$$= \cos^{-1}\frac{V_R}{\mathscr{E}}$$

$$= \cos^{-1}\frac{1}{\sqrt{2}}$$

$$= \frac{\pi}{4}$$

So, $\boxed{\mathscr{E} \text{ leads } I \text{ by } \dfrac{\pi}{4} \text{ rad} = 45°.}$

(d) Use the power factor to find Z.

$$\cos\phi = \frac{R}{Z}$$

$$Z = \frac{R}{\cos\phi}$$

$$= \frac{150\ \Omega}{\cos\frac{\pi}{4}}$$

$$= \boxed{210\ \Omega}$$

37. (a) $P_{av} = I_{rms}\mathscr{E}_{rms}\cos\phi$ is the average power. Solve for $\cos\phi$, the power factor.

$$P_{av} = I_{rms}\mathscr{E}_{rms}\cos\phi$$

$$\cos\phi = \frac{P_{av}}{I_{rms}\mathscr{E}_{rms}}$$

$$= \frac{240\ \text{W}}{(2.80\ \text{A})(120\ \text{V})}$$

$$= \boxed{0.71}$$

(b) $\phi = \cos^{-1}\dfrac{P_{av}}{I_{rms}\mathscr{E}_{rms}} = \cos^{-1}\dfrac{240\ \text{W}}{(2.80\ \text{A})(120\ \text{V})} = \boxed{44°}$

41. (a) Let $t = 0$.

$$V_1 \sin \omega t + V_2 \sin(\omega t + \phi_2) = V \sin(\omega t + \phi)$$
$$V_1 \sin \omega(0) + V_2 \sin[\omega(0) + \phi_2] = V \sin[\omega(0) + \phi]$$

$$\boxed{V_2 \sin \phi_2 = V \sin \phi}$$

The result indicates that the y-component of V_2 is equal to the y-component of V. This can be seen in the diagram.

(b) Let $t = \dfrac{\pi}{2\omega}$.

$$V_1 \sin \omega \left(\frac{\pi}{2\omega} \right) + V_2 \sin \left[\omega \left(\frac{\pi}{2\omega} \right) + \phi_2 \right] = V \sin \left[\omega \left(\frac{\pi}{2\omega} \right) + \phi \right]$$

$$V_1 \sin \frac{\pi}{2} + V_2 \sin \left(\frac{\pi}{2} + \phi_2 \right) = V \sin \left(\frac{\pi}{2} + \phi \right)$$

$$\boxed{V_1 + V_2 \cos \phi_2 = V \cos \phi}$$

The result indicates that the sum of the x-components of V_1 and V_2 is equal to the x-component of V. This can be seen in the diagram.

43. (a) $\omega_0 = \sqrt{\dfrac{1}{LC}} = \sqrt{\dfrac{1}{(0.300 \times 10^{-3} \text{ H})(33.0 \times 10^{-9} \text{ F})}} = \boxed{3.18 \times 10^5 \text{ rad/s}}$, or $f_0 = \dfrac{\omega_0}{2\pi} = \boxed{50.6 \text{ kHz}}$.

(b) Find the peak current in terms of the capacitance.

$$I = \frac{V_C}{X_C} = \omega C V_C$$

At resonance, $Z = R$. Find the maximum source voltage amplitude.

$$\mathscr{E} = IZ = IR = \omega C V_C R = \left(3.18 \times 10^5 \ \frac{\text{rad}}{\text{s}} \right)(33.0 \times 10^{-9} \text{ F})(7.0 \times 10^2 \text{ V})(325 \ \Omega) = \boxed{2.4 \text{ kV}}$$

45. At resonance, the reactances are equal, so $Z = \sqrt{R^2 + (X_L - X_C)^2} = \sqrt{R^2 + 0} = R = \boxed{500.0 \ \Omega}$.

49. If the currents are equal in amplitude, the impedances of the woofer and tweeter branches are equal. Solve for the capacitance.

$$Z_{\text{woofer}} = Z_{\text{tweeter}}$$

$$\sqrt{R^2 + \omega^2 L^2} = \sqrt{R^2 + \frac{1}{\omega^2 C^2}}$$

$$\omega L = \frac{1}{\omega C}$$

$$C = \frac{1}{\omega^2 L}$$

$$= \frac{1}{4\pi^2 (180 \text{ Hz})^2 (1.20 \times 10^{-3} \text{ H})}$$

$$= \boxed{650 \ \mu\text{F}}$$

53. (a) P_{av} is the average power for one cable, so $2P_{av}$ is the total average power for the line. $P_{av} = \dfrac{V_{rms}^2}{R}$, so

$$2P_{av} = 2\frac{V_{rms}^2}{R} = \frac{2V_{rms}^2}{\rho\frac{L}{A}} = \frac{2V_{rms}^2 A}{\rho L} = \frac{2V_{rms}^2\pi\left(\frac{d}{2}\right)^2}{\rho L} = \frac{\pi d^2 V_{rms}^2}{2\rho L} = \frac{\pi(0.092\text{ m})^2\left(\frac{22,000\text{ V}}{\sqrt{2}}\right)^2}{2(2.8\times10^{-8}\ \Omega\cdot\text{m})(10.0\times10^3\text{ m})}$$

$$= \boxed{1.1\times10^{10}\text{ W}}.$$

(b) Aluminum is both $\boxed{\text{cheaper and less dense}}$ than copper and silver, thus it is used for economic and engineering reasons.

57. $I_{rms} = \dfrac{\mathscr{E}_{rms}}{X_C} = \omega C\mathscr{E}_{rms} = 2\pi(60.0\text{ Hz})(0.025\times10^{-6}\text{ F})(110\text{ V}) = \boxed{1.0\text{ mA}}$

61. The maximum current flows at the resonance frequency, ω_0.

$$\omega_0 = \frac{1}{\sqrt{LC}}$$

$$f_0 = \frac{1}{2\pi\sqrt{LC}}$$

$$= \frac{1}{2\pi\sqrt{(0.44\text{ H})(520\times10^{-12}\text{ F})}}$$

$$= \boxed{11\text{ kHz}}$$

65. Find C such that the resonance frequency $\omega_0 = 2\pi f_0 = 2\pi(0.52\text{ MHz})$.

$$\omega_0 = \frac{1}{\sqrt{LC}}$$

$$\omega_0^2 = \frac{1}{LC}$$

$$C = \frac{1}{\omega_0^2 L}$$

$$= \frac{1}{4\pi^2(0.52\times10^6\text{ Hz})^2(2.4\times10^{-4}\text{ H})}$$

$$= \boxed{390\text{ pF}}$$

69. The average power supplied by the generator is $P_{av} = 12$ MW. The rms current is given by $I_{rms} = \dfrac{P_{av}}{\mathscr{E}_{rms}}$. So,

$$P_{lost} = I_{rms}^2 R = \frac{P_{av}^2 R}{\mathscr{E}_{rms}^2}.$$

(a) $P_{lost} = \dfrac{(12\times10^6\text{ W})^2(10.0\ \Omega)}{(15\times10^3\text{ V})^2} = \boxed{6.4\text{ MW}}$

(b) $P_{\text{lost}} = \dfrac{(12 \times 10^6 \text{ W})^2 (10.0 \ \Omega)}{(110 \times 10^3 \text{ V})^2} = \boxed{0.12 \text{ MW}}$

Find the percentage of the total power lost for each case.

15 kV: $100\% \times \dfrac{6.4}{12} = \boxed{53\%}$

110 kV: $100\% \times \dfrac{0.12}{12} = \boxed{1.0\%}$

Chapter 22

ELECTROMAGNETIC WAVES

Problems

1. The Ampère-Maxwell law is $\Sigma B_\parallel l = \mu_0\left(I + \varepsilon_0 \dfrac{\Delta\Phi_E}{\Delta t}\right) = \mu_0 I$ since $\dfrac{\Delta\Phi_E}{\Delta t} = 0$.

   By the RHR, the magnetic field lines are circles concentric with the central axis of the wire. At a distance $r \geq R$ from the central axis, the circumference of a circle is $2\pi r$. Thus, $\Sigma B_\parallel l = B(2\pi r) = \mu_0 I$, and $\boxed{B = \dfrac{\mu_0 I}{2\pi r}}$.

3. The Ampère-Maxwell law is $\Sigma B_\parallel l = \mu_0\left(I + \varepsilon_0 \dfrac{\Delta\Phi_E}{\Delta t}\right) = \mu_0 \varepsilon_0 \dfrac{\Delta\Phi_E}{\Delta t}$ since $I = 0$.

   By the RHR, the magnetic field lines are circles concentric with the central axis of the wire. At a distance $r \leq R$ from the central axis, the circumference of a circle is $2\pi r$. Thus, $\Sigma B_\parallel l = B(2\pi r)$.

   Find $\dfrac{\Delta\Phi_E}{\Delta t}$ in terms of I.

   The electric field in the gap is $E = \dfrac{\sigma}{\varepsilon_0} = \dfrac{q}{\varepsilon_0 A_{\text{wire}}} = \dfrac{q}{\varepsilon_0 \pi R^2}$. So, $\dfrac{\Delta\Phi_E}{\Delta t} = \dfrac{\Delta E A_{\text{circle}}}{\Delta t} = \dfrac{\Delta q \pi r^2}{\Delta t \varepsilon_0 \pi R^2} = \dfrac{I r^2}{\varepsilon_0 R^2}$, and the

   Ampère-Maxwell law gives $2\pi r B = \mu_0 \varepsilon_0 \left(\dfrac{I r^2}{\varepsilon_0 R^2}\right)$, or $\boxed{B = \dfrac{\mu_0 I r}{2\pi R^2}}$.

5. A rod-shaped dipole antenna must be an electric dipole antenna. At a point due south of the transmitter, the EM waves are traveling due south. The electric field at this point is oriented vertically, like the antenna. The magnetic field is perpendicular to both the electric field and the direction the EM waves travel, so the magnetic field must be oriented east-west.

7. From Faraday's Law, we have
   $$\mathscr{E} = -N\frac{\Delta\Phi_M}{\Delta t}$$
   The maximum emf will occur when $\Delta\Phi_M$, the change in flux through the coil, is a maximum. The flux through the coil is
   $$\Phi_M = BA\cos\theta = \Phi_{\max}\cos\theta$$
   where θ is the angle between the magnetic field and the normal to the plane of the coil and $\Phi_{\max} = BA$. So,
   $$\Delta\Phi_M = \Delta(BA\cos\theta)$$
   and the emf is
   $$\mathscr{E} = -N\frac{\Delta(BA\cos\theta)}{\Delta t} = -N\frac{\Delta\Phi_{\max}}{\Delta t}\cos\theta = \mathscr{E}_{\max}\cos\theta$$
   The emf is a maximum when $\theta = 0$. Otherwise, the emf is reduced by a factor of $\cos\theta$.

9. The frequency, wavelength, and speed of EM radiation are related by $\lambda f = c$.

   $$\lambda = \frac{c}{f} = \frac{3.00\times10^8 \frac{\text{m}}{\text{s}}}{90.9\times10^6 \text{ Hz}} = \boxed{3.3 \text{ m}}$$

11. (a) The frequency, wavelength, and speed of EM radiation are related by $\lambda f = c$.

$$\lambda = \frac{c}{f} = \frac{3.00 \times 10^8 \ \frac{m}{s}}{60.0 \ Hz} = \boxed{5.00 \times 10^6 \ m}$$

(b) $\boxed{\text{The radius of the Earth is } 6.4 \times 10^6 \ m \text{ , which is close in value to the wavelength.}}$

(c) According to Figure 22.6, the waves are $\boxed{\text{radio waves}}$.

13. (a) $\frac{790 \ THz}{380 \ THz} = 2.1 \approx 2^1$

The human eye can perceive $\boxed{\text{about one octave}}$ of visible light.

(b) Microwaves range from about 1 mm to 30 cm. The corresponding frequencies are

$$f = \frac{c}{\lambda} = \frac{3.00 \times 10^8 \ \frac{m}{s}}{1 \times 10^{-3} \ m} = 3 \times 10^{11} \ Hz$$

and

$$f = \frac{3.00 \times 10^8 \ \frac{m}{s}}{30 \times 10^{-2} \ m} = 1 \times 10^9 \ Hz$$

Then, $\frac{3 \times 10^{11} \ Hz}{1 \times 10^9 \ Hz} = 300 \approx 2^{8.2}$.

So, the microwave region is $\boxed{\text{approximately 8 octaves}}$ wide.

15. The speed of light in matter is given by $v = \frac{c}{n}$, where n is the index of refraction.

$$n = \frac{c}{v} = \frac{3.00 \times 10^8 \ \frac{m}{s}}{1.85 \times 10^8 \ \frac{m}{s}} = \boxed{1.62}$$

17. $\Delta t = \frac{d}{c} = \frac{50.0 \times 10^{-2} \ m}{3.00 \times 10^8 \ \frac{m}{s}} = 1.67 \times 10^{-9} \ s = \boxed{1.67 \ ns}$

19. (a) The wavelength is shorter in matter than it is in vacuum (or air).

$$\lambda_g = \frac{\lambda_v}{n} = \frac{692 \ nm}{1.52} = \boxed{455 \ nm}$$

(b) The frequency in glass is the same as the frequency in air.

$$f_g = f_a = \frac{c}{\lambda_a} = \frac{3.00 \times 10^8 \ \frac{m}{s}}{692 \times 10^{-9} \ m} = \boxed{4.34 \times 10^{14} \ Hz}$$

21. ε_0 and μ_0 are expressed in SI units as

$$[\varepsilon_0] = \frac{C^2}{N \cdot m^2} = \frac{A^2 \cdot s^2}{\frac{kg \cdot m}{s^2} \cdot m^2} = \frac{A^2 \cdot s^4}{kg \cdot m^3}$$

$$[\mu_0] = \frac{T \cdot m}{A} = \frac{N \cdot s}{C \cdot m} \cdot \frac{m}{A} = \frac{kg \cdot m \cdot s \cdot m}{A \cdot s \cdot m \cdot A \cdot s^2} = \frac{kg \cdot m}{A^2 \cdot s^2}$$

The dimensions of speed are m/s. Since ε_0 and μ_0 have different units, they cannot be added. They can be multiplied and raised to powers, and the resulting expression must have units of speed. The general form is then

$$[\varepsilon_0]^M \cdot [\mu_0]^N = \text{m/s}$$

$$\left(\frac{A^2 \cdot s^4}{kg \cdot m^3}\right)^M \left(\frac{kg \cdot m}{A^2 \cdot s^2}\right)^N = m \cdot s^{-1}$$

$$\frac{A^{2M} \cdot s^{4M}}{kg^M \cdot m^{3M}} \cdot \frac{kg^N \cdot m^N}{A^{2N} \cdot s^{2N}} = m \cdot s^{-1}$$

$$A^{2M-2N} \cdot kg^{N-M} \cdot m^{N-3M} \cdot s^{4M-2N} = m^1 \cdot s^{-1}$$

Equating exponents of identical units on the left side and the right side gives
$2M - 2N = 0 \Rightarrow M = N$
$N - M = 0 \Rightarrow M = N$
$N - 3M = 1 \Rightarrow M - 3M = 1 \Rightarrow -2M = 1 \Rightarrow M = -1/2 = N$
$4M - 2N = -1 \Rightarrow 4M - 2M = -1 \Rightarrow 2M = -1 \Rightarrow M = -1/2 = N$
The correct expression is then $\varepsilon_0^{-1/2}\mu_0^{-1/2} = (\varepsilon_0\mu_0)^{-1/2}$.

23. (a) The amplitude of the electric field is

$$E_m = cB_m = 3.00\times10^8 \frac{m}{s}\times2.5\times10^{-11} \text{ T} = \boxed{7.5 \text{ mV/m}}.$$

The frequency of the electric field is $\boxed{3.0 \text{ MHz}}$, the same as the magnetic field.

(b) The magnitude of the electric field is $E = cB = 3.00\times10^8 \frac{m}{s}\times1.5\times10^{-11} \text{ T} = \boxed{4.5 \text{ mV/m}}$.

Since the magnetic field is in the $+z$-direction and the wave is traveling in the $-y$-direction, by $\vec{E}\times\vec{B}$ and the RHR, the electric field at $y = 0$ and $t = 0$ must point $\boxed{\text{in the } +x\text{-direction}}$.

25. (a) Since the electric field depends on the value of y but not on the values of x or z, the wave moves parallel to the y-axis. The direction can be found by noting that as t increases in $ky - \omega t + \pi/6$, y must increase to maintain the relative phase. So, the wave is moving in the $\boxed{+y\text{-direction.}}$

(b) The magnitude of the E and B fields are related by $B_m = E_m/c$. Since the electric field is in the $+z$-direction when $t = 0$ and $y = 0$, and the wave is traveling in the $+y$-direction, by $\vec{E}\times\vec{B}$ and the RHR, the magnetic field at $t = 0$ and $y = 0$ must point in the $+x$-direction. The components are

$$\boxed{B_x = \frac{E_m}{c}\sin(ky - \omega t + \pi/6), B_y = B_z = 0}.$$

27. (a) Intensity is related to average energy density by $I = \langle u \rangle c$.

$$\langle u \rangle = \frac{I}{c} = \frac{1400 \frac{W}{m^2}}{3.00\times10^8 \frac{m}{s}} = \boxed{4.7\times10^{-6} \text{ J/m}^3}$$

(b) The rms values for the electric and magnetic fields are related to the average energy density by

$$\langle u \rangle = \varepsilon_0 E_{rms}^2 = \frac{B_{rms}^2}{\mu_0}.$$

So, $E_{rms} = \sqrt{\dfrac{\langle u \rangle}{\varepsilon_0}} = \sqrt{\dfrac{4.7 \times 10^{-6}\ \dfrac{J}{m^3}}{8.85 \times 10^{-12}\ \dfrac{C^2}{N \cdot m^2}}} = \boxed{730\ V/m}$

and

$B_{rms} = \sqrt{\mu_0 \langle u \rangle} = \sqrt{4\pi \times 10^{-7}\ \dfrac{T \cdot m}{A} \times 4.7 \times 10^{-6}\ \dfrac{J}{m^3}} = \boxed{2.4 \times 10^{-6}\ T}$.

29. Intensity is related to the average power radiated by $I = \dfrac{\langle P \rangle}{A}$ where $A = 4\pi r^2$ and $r = 14 \times 10^6$ ly.

   So, $\langle P \rangle = 4\pi I r^2 = 4\pi \left(4 \times 10^{-21}\ \dfrac{W}{m^2} \right) (14 \times 10^6\ ly)^2 \left(9.461 \times 10^{15}\ \dfrac{m}{ly} \right)^2 = \boxed{9 \times 10^{26}\ W}$.

33. (a) Using Equation (22-14), we have

   $\langle P \rangle = IA \cos \theta = 1.0 \times 10^3\ \dfrac{W}{m^2} \times 2.0\ m \times 6.0\ m \times \cos 0° = 12 \times 10^3\ W$.

   Since the panels are only 35% efficient, the power supplied is

   $12 \times 10^3\ W \times 0.35 = \boxed{4.2\ kW}$.

   (b) $\langle P \rangle = IA \cos \theta \times$ efficiency $= 0.40 \times 10^3\ \dfrac{W}{m^2} \times 2.0\ m \times 6.0\ m \times \cos 60.0° \times 0.35 = \boxed{840\ W}$

   (c) In part (a) the panels provide more than twice the power needed on average, while in part (b) the panels provide less than half the power needed. The excess energy produced at midday should be stored for use at night; in general, a supplemental energy source is necessary.

35. Since the light is initially unpolarized, the intensity of the light after passing through the first polarizer is half the initial intensity.

   $I_1 = \dfrac{1}{2} I_0$

   The intensity after passing through the second polarizer is given by Equation (22-16b).

   $I_2 = I_1 \cos^2 \theta$

   Combining these equations, and using $\theta = 45°$, we have

   $I_2 = \dfrac{1}{2} I_0 \cos^2 45° = \boxed{0.25 I_0}$. So, $\boxed{0.25}$ of the incident intensity is transmitted.

37. (a) If we try to use one sheet, the resulting intensity is

   $\boxed{I_1 = I_0 \cos^2 90.0° = 0,}$

   so at least two sheets must be used.

   (b) The transmitted intensity of the first sheet is

   $I_1 = I_0 \cos^2 45.0° = 0.500 I_0$.

   The transmitted intensity of the second sheet is

   $I_2 = I_1 \cos^2 45.0° = 0.500 I_0 (0.500) = \boxed{0.250 I_0}$.

   (c) The transmitted intensity of the four sheets combined is

   $I_4 = I_0 (\cos^2 22.5°)^4 = I_0 \cos^8 22.5° = \boxed{0.531 I_0}$.

41. First try Equation (22-18). If the resulting velocity is small compared to c, we are done. If the velocity is not small compared to c, we will have to use Equation (22-17).

$$f_o \approx f_s\left(1+\frac{v_{rel}}{c}\right)$$

$$1+\frac{v_{rel}}{c} \approx \frac{f_o}{f_s}$$

$$\frac{v_{rel}}{c} \approx \frac{\lambda_s}{\lambda_o}-1$$

$$v_{rel} \approx c\left(\frac{\lambda_s}{\lambda_o}-1\right)$$

$$\approx \left(3.00\times10^8\ \frac{m}{s}\right)\left(\frac{659.6\ nm}{661.1\ nm}-1\right)$$

$$\approx -680\ km/s$$

This velocity is small compared to c, so the use of Equation (22-18) was justified. $v_{rel}<0$, so the star is moving at 680 km/s away from the Earth.

43. A Doppler shift of this magnitude almost certainly requires a very high (relativistic) relative velocity. To find the relative velocity, solve Equation (22-17) for v_{rel}.

$v_{rel}>0$ since the source of the light is stationary (observer approaching the source). Let $v_{rel}=v$ for simplicity.

$$f_o = f_s\sqrt{\frac{1+\frac{v}{c}}{1-\frac{v}{c}}}$$

$$\left(\frac{f_o}{f_s}\right)^2 = \frac{1+\frac{v}{c}}{1-\frac{v}{c}}$$

$$\left(\frac{f_o}{f_s}\right)^2 - \left(\frac{f_o}{f_s}\right)^2\frac{v}{c} = 1+\frac{v}{c}$$

$$\left(\frac{f_o}{f_s}\right)^2 - 1 = \frac{v}{c}\left[1+\left(\frac{f_o}{f_s}\right)^2\right]$$

$$v = c\frac{\left(\frac{f_o}{f_s}\right)^2-1}{\left(\frac{f_o}{f_s}\right)^2+1}$$

$$= c\frac{\left(\frac{\lambda_s}{\lambda_o}\right)^2-1}{\left(\frac{\lambda_s}{\lambda_o}\right)^2+1}$$

$$= \left(3.00\times10^8\ \frac{m}{s}\right)\frac{\left(\frac{630}{530}\right)^2-1}{\left(\frac{630}{530}\right)^2+1}$$

$$= \boxed{5\times10^7\ m/s}$$

45. The wavelength is

$$\lambda = \frac{c}{f} = \frac{3.00 \times 10^8 \frac{m}{s}}{2.0 \times 10^9 \text{ Hz}} = 0.15 \text{ m} = 15 \text{ cm}.$$

The maximum length is half the wavelength.

$$\frac{1}{2} \times 15 \text{ cm} = \boxed{7.5 \text{ cm}}$$

49. To find the intensity of the transmitted light, use Equation (22-16b) to find the transmitted intensity of each sheet and combine the results. The angle of polarization of the first sheet is θ_1. The transmitted intensity is

$$I_1 = I_0 \cos^2 \theta_1$$

Light exits the first polarizer at an angle θ_1 relative to the original polarization direction. The polarization angle of the second sheet is θ_2 relative to the original polarization direction, so the polarization angle of the second sheet relative to the first polarizer is $\theta_2 - \theta_1$. The transmitted intensity for the second sheet is

$$I_2 = I_1 \cos^2(\theta_2 - \theta_1) = I_1 \cos^2(\theta_1 - \theta_2)$$

Combining the equations gives

$$I_2 = I_0 \cos^2 \theta_1 \cos^2(\theta_1 - \theta_2) = I, \text{ the final transmitted intensity.}$$

53. (a) Just outside the laser, the cross-sectional area of the beam is $A = \pi r^2$ where $r = 2.0$ mm. The intensity of the beam is equal to the power per unit area.

$$I = \frac{P}{A} = \frac{10.0 \text{ W}}{\pi (0.0020 \text{ m})^2} = \boxed{8.0 \times 10^5 \text{ W/m}^2}$$

(b) Similarly, $I = \dfrac{10.0 \text{ W}}{\pi \left(\dfrac{85,000 \text{ m}}{2}\right)^2} = \boxed{1.8 \times 10^{-9} \text{ W/m}^2}$.

Chapter 23

REFLECTION AND REFRACTION OF LIGHT

Problems

1.

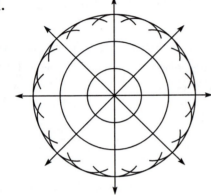

3.

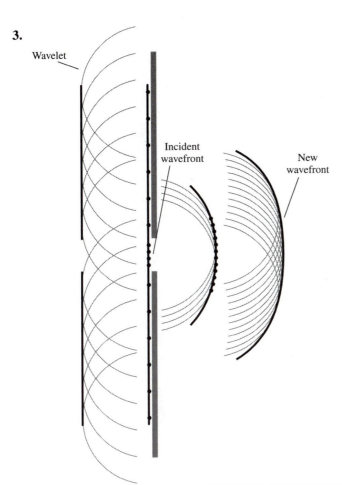

On the incident side are two planar waves. On the transmitted side is one hemispherical wave.

5.

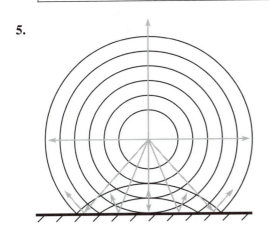

7.

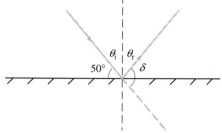

From the figure,
$\theta_i = 90° - 50° = 40°$.
Using the laws of reflection,
$\theta_r = \theta_i = 40°$.
The angles θ_i, θ_r, and δ must add to 180°. Solve for δ.

$$\theta_i + \theta_r + \delta = 180°$$
$$40° + 40° + \delta = 180°$$
$$\delta = \boxed{100°}$$

9.

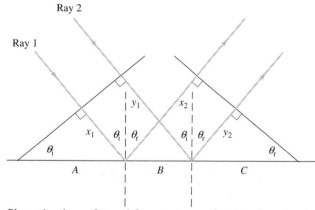

Since the time of travel from one wavefront to the other is the same for both rays, the distance traveled must also be the same.

Distance traveled by ray 1 = Distance traveled by ray 2
$$x_1 + x_2 = y_1 + y_2$$

These distances can be expressed in terms of θ_i, θ_r, A, B, and C.

$x_1 = A \sin \theta_i$
$x_2 = (B+C) \sin \theta_r$
$y_1 = (A+B) \sin \theta_i$
$y_2 = C \sin \theta_r$

Substituting into the previous equation gives
$$A \sin \theta_i + (B+C) \sin \theta_r = (A+B) \sin \theta_i + C \sin \theta_r$$
$$A \sin \theta_i + B \sin \theta_r + C \sin \theta_r = A \sin \theta_i + B \sin \theta_i + C \sin \theta_r$$
$$B \sin \theta_r = B \sin \theta_i$$
$$\sin \theta_r = \sin \theta_i$$
$$\theta_r = \theta_i$$

11. Use Snell's law.

$$n_1 \sin\theta_1 = n_2 \sin\theta_2$$

$$\sin\theta_1 = \frac{n_2}{n_1}\sin\theta_2$$

$$\theta_1 = \sin^{-1}\left(\frac{1.333}{1.000}\sin 42.0°\right)$$

$$= \boxed{63.1°}$$

13. Use the figure below and Snell's law to find θ_1.

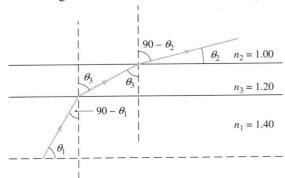

Relate θ_1 and θ_3.

$$n_1 \sin(90° - \theta_1) = n_3 \sin\theta_3$$

Relate θ_2 and θ_3.

$$n_2 \sin(90° - \theta_2) = n_3 \sin\theta_3$$

Eliminate $n_3 \sin\theta_3$ and solve for θ_1.

$$n_1 \sin(90° - \theta_1) = n_2 \sin(90° - \theta_2)$$

$$90° - \theta_1 = \sin^{-1}\left[\frac{n_2}{n_1}\sin(90° - \theta_2)\right]$$

$$\theta_1 = 90° - \sin^{-1}\left[\frac{1.00}{1.40}\sin(90° - 5.00°)\right]$$

$$= \boxed{44.6°}$$

15.

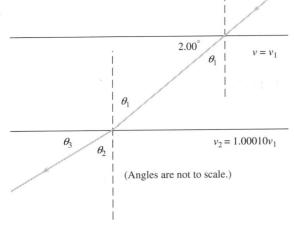

(Angles are not to scale.)

According to the figure,
$\theta_1 = 90° - 2.00° = 88.00°$.

Use Snell's law to find θ_3, the new angle with respect to the horizontal.

$n_2 \sin \theta_2 = n_1 \sin \theta_1$

$$\theta_2 = \sin^{-1}\left(\frac{n_1}{n_2}\sin\theta_1\right)$$

$$90° - \theta_2 = 90° - \sin^{-1}\left(\frac{v_2}{v_1}\sin\theta_1\right)$$

$$\theta_3 = 90° - \sin^{-1}\left(\frac{1.00010v_1}{v_1}\sin 88.00°\right)$$

$$= \boxed{1.83°}$$

17.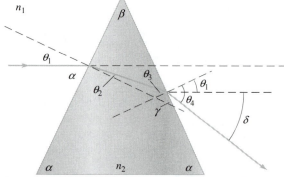

Using the figure above, find θ_1 in terms of β.

$$\beta + 2\alpha = 180° \rightarrow \alpha = \frac{180° - \beta}{2} = 90° - \frac{\beta}{2}$$

$$\theta_1 = 90° - \alpha = 90° - \left(90° - \frac{\beta}{2}\right) = \frac{\beta}{2}$$

Now use Snell's law to find θ_2.

$n_1 \sin \theta_1 = n_2 \sin \theta_2$

$$\sin \theta_2 = \frac{n_1}{n_2}\sin\theta_1 = \frac{n_1}{n_2}\sin\frac{\beta}{2}$$

Since β is small, use the approximation $\sin \theta \cong \theta$.

$$\sin \theta_2 \approx \frac{n_1}{n_2}\frac{\beta}{2}$$

Since $n_1 \sim n_2$ and $\frac{\beta}{2}$ is small, $\sin\theta_2$ is small, so apply the approximation for θ_2.

$$\theta_2 \approx \frac{n_1}{n_2}\frac{\beta}{2}$$

Using $n_1 = 1$ and $n_2 = n$ gives $\theta_2 = \frac{\beta}{2n}$.

Find θ_3 in terms of n and β.

From the figure, $90° + \beta + \gamma = 180°$, which implies $\gamma = 90° - \beta$.

$$\gamma + (90° + \theta_3) + \theta_2 = 180°$$
$$90° - \beta + 90° + \theta_3 + \theta_2 = 180°$$
$$\theta_3 = \beta - \theta_2$$
$$= \beta - \frac{\beta}{2n}$$
$$= \beta\left(1 - \frac{1}{2n}\right)$$

Use Snell's law to find θ_4, with $n_1 = 1$ and $n_2 = n$.

$$\sin\theta_4 = n\sin\theta_3 = n\sin\left[\beta\left(1 - \frac{1}{2n}\right)\right]$$

Now, $\beta\left(1 - \frac{1}{2n}\right) < \beta$, so it is small, as well as θ_4. Thus, $\theta_4 \approx n\beta\left(1 - \frac{1}{2n}\right) = \beta\left(n - \frac{1}{2}\right)$.

Now find δ.

$$\delta + \theta_1 = \theta_4$$
$$\delta = \theta_4 - \theta_1$$
$$= \beta\left(n - \frac{1}{2}\right) - \frac{\beta}{2}$$
$$= \beta n - \frac{\beta}{2} - \frac{\beta}{2}$$
$$= \boxed{\beta(n-1)}$$

19. $n_1 = 1.000$

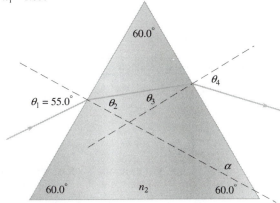

For the longest visible wavelengths, $n_2 = 1.517$, and by Snell's law

$$n_1\sin\theta_1 = n_2\sin\theta_2$$
$$\sin\theta_2 = \frac{n_1}{n_2}\sin\theta_1$$
$$\theta_2 = \sin^{-1}\left(\frac{1.000}{1.517}\sin 55.0°\right) = 32.7°$$

Find θ_3.

$$60.0° + 90.0° + \alpha = 180.0° \rightarrow \alpha = 30.0°$$
$$\theta_2 + (90.0° + \theta_3) + \alpha = 180.0°$$
$$\theta_2 + \theta_3 + 30.0° = 90.0°$$
$$\theta_3 = 60.0° - \theta_2$$
$$= 60.0° - 32.7° = 27.3°$$

Use Snell's law again.

$$n_2 \sin \theta_3 = n_1 \sin \theta_4$$

$$\sin \theta_4 = \frac{n_2}{n_1} \sin \theta_3$$

$$\theta_4 = \sin^{-1}\left(\frac{1.517}{1.000} \sin 27.3°\right) = 44.1°$$

For the shortest visible wavelengths, set $n_2 = 1.538$ and follow the same process. Find θ_2.

$$\theta_2 = \sin^{-1}\left(\frac{1.000}{1.538} \sin 55.0°\right) = 32.18°$$

Find θ_3.

$$\theta_3 = 60.0° - 32.18° = 27.82°$$

Find θ_4.

$$\theta_4 = \sin^{-1}\left(\frac{1.538}{1.000} \sin 27.82°\right) = 45.9°$$

The range of refraction angles is $\boxed{44.1° \le \theta \le 45.9°}$.

21. From Table 23.1, the index of refraction for diamond is 2.419, for air it is 1.000, and for water it is 1.333.

   (a) The critical angle for diamond in air is
   $$\theta_c = \sin^{-1}\frac{n_t}{n_i} = \sin^{-1}\frac{1.000}{2.419} = \boxed{24.42°}.$$

   (b) The critical angle for diamond in water is
   $$\theta_c = \sin^{-1}\frac{n_t}{n_i} = \sin^{-1}\frac{1.333}{2.419} = \boxed{33.44°}.$$

   (c) Under water, the larger critical angle means that fewer light rays are totally reflected at the bottom surfaces of the diamond. Thus, less light is reflected back toward the viewer.

23. The angle of incidence on the back of the prism is 45°. The critical angle is
   $$\theta_c = \sin^{-1}\frac{n_t}{n_i} = \sin^{-1}\frac{1.0}{1.6} = 39°.$$

   Since the angle of incidence (45°) is greater than the critical angle (39°), no light exits the back of the prism. The light is totally reflected downward, and then passes through the bottom surface ($\theta_i < \theta_c$), with a small amount reflected back into the prism.

25. When the light is incident on the Plexiglas tank, some is transmitted at angle θ_1. Use Snell's law.
   $$n \sin \theta_i = n_1 \sin \theta_1$$
   where $n = 1.00$ for air and $n_1 = 1.51$ for Plexiglas. At the Plexiglas carbon tetrachloride interface, θ_1 is the incident angle and θ_2 is the transmitted angle.
   $$n_2 \sin \theta_2 = n_1 \sin \theta_1$$
   where $n_2 = 1.461$ for carbon tetrachloride. The ray passes through the carbon tetrachloride and is incident on the bottom tank-liquid interface at angle θ_2. Here the light must experience total internal reflection, so
   $$\theta_2 = \theta_c = \sin^{-1}\frac{n_1}{n_2}, \text{ or } \frac{n_1}{n_2} = \sin \theta_2. \text{ Find } \theta_1.$$

$n \sin \theta_i = n_1 \sin \theta_1 = n_2 \sin \theta_2 = n_2 \dfrac{n_1}{n_2} = n_1$, so $\theta_i = \sin^{-1} \dfrac{n_1}{n} = \sin^{-1} \dfrac{1.51}{1.00} = \sin^{-1} 1.51$, or $\sin \theta_i = 1.51$, which is

impossible since $\sin \theta \leq 1$ for all θ. Thus, there is $\boxed{\text{no}}$ angle θ for which light is transmitted into the carbon tetrachloride but not into the Plexiglas at the bottom of the tank.

27. (a) The reflected light is totally polarized when the angle of incidence equals Brewster's angle.

$$\theta_B = \tan^{-1} \frac{n_t}{n_i} = \tan^{-1} \frac{1.333}{1.000} = 53.12°$$

The angle below the horizontal is the complement of this angle.

$$90° - 53.12° = \boxed{36.88°}$$

(b) For Brewster's angle, the reflected light is polarized $\boxed{\text{perpendicular to the plane of incidence.}}$

(c) When the angle of incidence is Brewster's angle, the incident and transmitted rays are complementary.

$$\theta_t = 90° - \theta_i = 90° - 53.12° = 36.88°$$

The angle below the horizontal is the complement of this angle.

$$90° - 36.88° = \boxed{53.12°}$$

29. (a) At Brewster's angle, the reflected and transmitted rays are perpendicular to each other. However, at angles greater than or equal to the critical angle, no rays are transmitted. So $\boxed{\text{the critical angle is always greater than}}$ $\boxed{\text{Brewster's angle, regardless of } n_1 \text{ and } n_2}$ (assuming $n_2 < n_1$).

(b) For $n_1 < n_2$ there is $\boxed{\text{no critical angle}}$, and

$$\theta_B = \tan^{-1} \frac{n_2}{n_1} > \tan^{-1} 1 = 45°$$

So, $\boxed{\theta_B > 45°}$.

31. The equation derived in Example 23.4 can be used for this problem (with $n_{amber} = n_w$) since $n_{amber} > n_{air}$.

$$\frac{\text{apparent depth}}{\text{actual depth}} = \frac{n_{air}}{n_{amber}} = \frac{1.000}{1.546}$$

$$\begin{aligned}
\text{actual depth} &= \text{apparent depth} \cdot 1.546 \\
&= 7.00 \text{ mm} \cdot 1.546 \\
&= \boxed{10.8 \text{ mm}}
\end{aligned}$$

33. As seen in Conceptual Example 23.5, the mirror must be at least half as tall as Norah.

$$\frac{1.64 \text{ m}}{2} = \boxed{0.82 \text{ m}}$$

35. Since the rose is 0.250 m in front of the mirror, the image will be 0.250 m behind the mirror. If Nagar is looking straight into the mirror, the distance to the image will be the distance from Nagar to the mirror plus the distance from the mirror to the image.

$$2.00 \text{ m} + 0.250 \text{ m} = \boxed{2.25 \text{ m}}$$

37. He sees three images by looking straight into each mirror. He sees three other images by looking where each pair of mirrors meet (left wall and right wall, left wall and ceiling, right wall and ceiling). He sees one more image by looking at the corner where all three mirrors meet. $\boxed{\text{He sees 7 images total.}}$

41. The mirror is concave, so $p = 20.0$ cm and $f = 5.00$ cm. Find the image distance q using the mirror equation.

$$\frac{1}{p} + \frac{1}{q} = \frac{1}{f}$$

$$\frac{1}{q} = \frac{1}{f} - \frac{1}{p}$$

$$q = \frac{pf}{p - f}$$

$$= \frac{(20.0 \text{ cm})(5.00 \text{ cm})}{20.0 \text{ cm} - 5.00 \text{ cm}}$$

$$= 6.67 \text{ cm}$$

The image is formed $\boxed{6.67 \text{ cm in front of the mirror}}$.

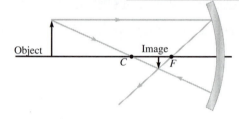

43. The mirror is convex, so $f = -\dfrac{R}{2}$. The image is virtual, so $q < 0$. Use the magnification equation to find q in terms of p using the fact that $|m| = \dfrac{1}{2}$ and $q < 0$.

$|m| = \dfrac{1}{2} = \left|-\dfrac{q}{p}\right|$, so $|q| = \dfrac{1}{2}|p|$. Then, $q = -\dfrac{1}{2}p$, since $p > 0$. Use the mirror equation.

$$\frac{1}{q} + \frac{1}{p} = \frac{1}{f}$$

$$-\frac{2}{p} + \frac{1}{p} = -\frac{2}{R}$$

$$-\frac{1}{p} = -\frac{2}{R}$$

$$p = \frac{1}{2}R$$

$$= \frac{1}{2}(25.0 \text{ cm})$$

$$= 12.5 \text{ cm}$$

The object is $\boxed{12.5 \text{ cm in front of the mirror}}$.

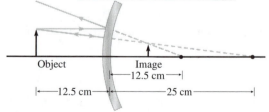

45.

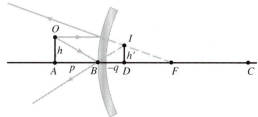

In the figure, the two right triangles OAB and IDB are similar, so

$$\frac{h}{p} = \frac{h'}{-q}$$

$$\frac{h'}{h} = \frac{-q}{p}$$

The negative sign is included since $h/p > 0$; $q < 0$ since the image is behind the mirror, so $h'/q < 0$, and $-h'/q > 0$.

Combining this with the magnification definition $h' = mh$ gives

$$m = \frac{h'}{h} = -\frac{q}{p}.$$

49.

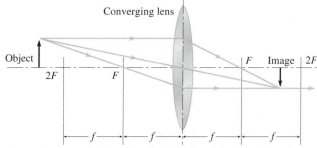

Converging lens

Object   2F   F   F   Image   2F

As can be seen in the figure, when an object is placed more than twice the focal length away from a converging lens, an inverted, real, and diminished image is formed.

51.

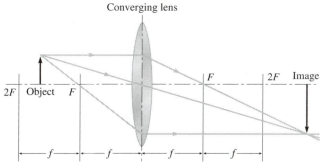

Converging lens

2F   Object   F   F   2F   Image

As can be seen in the figure, when an object is placed between twice the focal length and the focal length from a converging lens, an inverted, real, and enlarged image is formed.

53. The object distance is $p = 6.0 \text{ m}$. Since the image is virtual, the image distance is $q = -9.0 \text{ cm}$. Use the Thin lens equation.

$$\frac{1}{p} + \frac{1}{q} = \frac{1}{f}$$

$$f = \frac{1}{\frac{1}{p} + \frac{1}{q}} = \frac{1}{\frac{1}{6.0 \text{ cm}} - \frac{1}{9.0 \text{ cm}}} = \boxed{18 \text{ cm}}$$

55. (a) Solving the thin lens equation for q gives

$$\frac{1}{p} + \frac{1}{q} = \frac{1}{f}$$

$$q = \frac{1}{\frac{1}{f} - \frac{1}{p}}$$

Substituting the given values yields

$$q = \frac{1}{-\frac{1}{8.00 \text{ cm}} - \frac{1}{5.00 \text{ cm}}} = -3.08 \text{ cm for } p = 5.00 \text{ cm.}$$

$$q = \frac{1}{-\frac{1}{8.00 \text{ cm}} - \frac{1}{8.00 \text{ cm}}} = -4.00 \text{ cm for } p = 8.00 \text{ cm.}$$

Likewise for p-values of 14.0 cm, 16.0 cm, and 20.0 cm. The corresponding q values are -5.09 cm, -5.33 cm, and -5.71 cm, respectively. All images are virtual, since a diverging lens is used. The magnification determines the size and orientation of the image. The results are summarized in the table.

p (cm)	q (cm)	$m = -\dfrac{q}{p}$	Real or virtual	Orientation	Relative size
5.00	−3.08	0.615	virtual	upright	diminished
8.00	−4.00	0.500	virtual	upright	diminished
14.0	−5.09	0.364	virtual	upright	diminished
16.0	−5.33	0.333	virtual	upright	diminished
20.0	−5.71	0.286	virtual	upright	diminished

(b) Solving the magnification equation for the image height yields $h' = mh$.

For $p = 5.00$ cm, $h = 4.00$ cm, and $m = 0.616$, we have

$$h' = 0.616 \cdot 4.00 \text{ cm} = \boxed{2.46 \text{ m}}$$

For $p = 20.0$ cm, $h = 4.00$ cm, and $m = 0.286$, we have

$$h' = 0.286 \cdot 4.00 \text{ cm} = \boxed{1.14 \text{ cm}}$$

57.

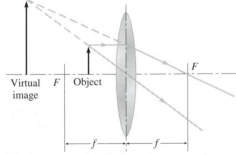

The image is virtual since the rays only *seem* to come from the image.

61.

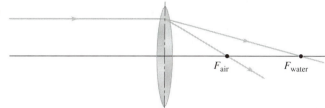

In the figure, F_{air} is the focal point of the lens in air, and F_{water} is the focal point of the lens in water. The focal length in water is longer than the focal length in air. The indices of refraction of water and glass are closer than those for air and glass, so rays refract less in water than in air.

65. Since the indices of refraction are different, the red light and blue light will have different focal points. The focal point for blue light will be closer to the lens, since blue light refracts more than red light.

69. Since the mirror is fixed to the car, the speed relative to the car is the same as the speed relative to the mirror. Since the object and image are equidistant for a plane mirror, the image speed will equal the object speed, which is 8.0 km/h relative to the car.

73.

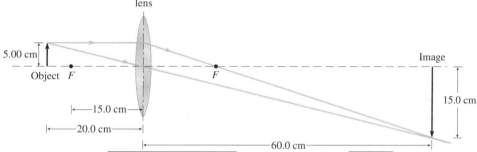

The image is about 60.0 cm behind the lens. The image is about 15.0 cm tall.

77. For the two right triangles ABC and ACD, we have $\tan\beta = \dfrac{d}{p}$ and $\tan\gamma = \dfrac{d}{q}$.

Using the small angle approximation $\tan\theta \approx \theta$ gives $\beta = \dfrac{d}{p}$ and $\gamma = \dfrac{d}{q}$.

From the figure, $\delta = \beta + \gamma$, so $\delta = \dfrac{d}{p} + \dfrac{d}{q} = d\left(\dfrac{1}{p} + \dfrac{1}{q}\right)$.

According to the thin lens equation, $\dfrac{1}{f} = \dfrac{1}{p} + \dfrac{1}{q}$, so $\delta = \dfrac{d}{f}$.

81. The critical angles are

$$\theta_{c\ (red)} = \sin^{-1}\frac{n_t}{n_i} = \sin^{-1}\frac{1.0003}{1.6182} = 38.182°$$

$$\theta_{c\ (yellow)} = \sin^{-1}\frac{1.0003}{1.6276} = 37.922°$$

$$\theta_{c\ (blue)} = \sin^{-1}\frac{1.0003}{1.6523} = 37.258°$$

$\theta_{c\ (red)}$ and $\theta_{c\ (yellow)}$ are greater than $\theta_i = 37.5°$, so red and yellow reach the detector.

85. Draw two principal rays for each end of the object.

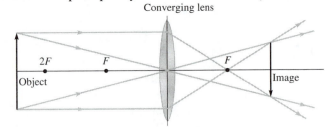

87.

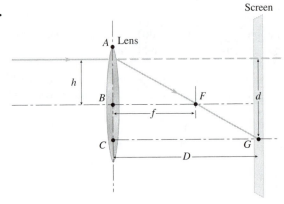

In the figure, triangle ABF and triangle ACG are similar, so

$$\frac{h}{f} = \frac{-d}{D}$$

$$f = -\frac{h}{d}D$$

For paraxial rays, the slope of the d vs. h graph is constant. The middle three data points reflect this case. Find the slope.

$$m = \frac{\Delta d}{\Delta h} = \frac{-1.0-1.0}{0.5-(-0.5)} = \frac{-2.0}{1.0} = -2.0$$

For a constant slope, $\dfrac{\Delta d}{\Delta h} = \dfrac{d}{h}$, so $f = -\dfrac{1}{-2.0}D = 0.50(1.0 \text{ m}) = \boxed{50 \text{ cm}}$.

Chapter 24

OPTICAL INSTRUMENTS

Problems

1. (a) To find the final image position, use the thin lens equation on each lens. For lens 1,

$$\frac{1}{p_1} + \frac{1}{q_1} = \frac{1}{f_1}$$

$$q_1 = \frac{1}{\frac{1}{f_1} - \frac{1}{p_1}} = \frac{1}{\frac{1}{5.0 \text{ cm}} - \frac{1}{12.0 \text{ cm}}} = 8.6 \text{ cm}$$

For lens 2, first find the object distance.

$$p_2 = s - q_1 = 2.0 \text{ cm} - 8.6 \text{ cm} = -6.6 \text{ cm}$$

Find the location of the final image.

$$\frac{1}{p_2} + \frac{1}{q_2} = \frac{1}{f_2}$$

$$q_2 = \frac{1}{\frac{1}{f_2} - \frac{1}{p_2}} = \frac{1}{\frac{1}{4.0 \text{ cm}} - \frac{1}{-6.6 \text{ cm}}} = 2.5 \text{ cm}$$

The final image is $\boxed{2.5 \text{ cm past the 4.0-cm lens}}$. The image is $\boxed{\text{real}}$ since q_2 is positive.

(b) $\quad m = m_1 m_2 = -\frac{q_1}{p_1}\left(-\frac{q_2}{p_2}\right) = -\frac{8.6 \text{ cm}}{12.0 \text{ cm}} \times -\frac{2.5 \text{ cm}}{-6.6 \text{ cm}} = \boxed{-0.27}$

3.

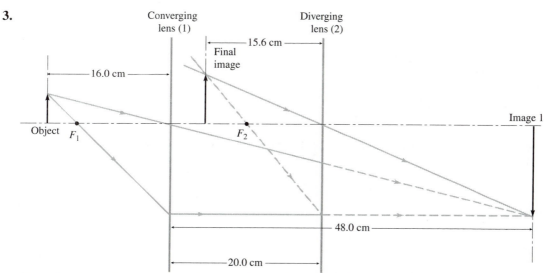

From the figure, the final image is about 15.6 cm left of lens 2. Verify using the lens equations. Find q_1 using the thin lens equation.

$$\frac{1}{p_1} + \frac{1}{q_1} = \frac{1}{f_1}$$

$$q_1 = \frac{1}{\frac{1}{f_1} - \frac{1}{p_1}} = \frac{1}{\frac{1}{12.0 \text{ cm}} - \frac{1}{16.0 \text{ cm}}} = 48.0 \text{ cm}$$

For the diverging lens (2), the object distance is

$$p_2 = s - q_1 = 20.0 \text{ cm} - 48.0 \text{ cm} = -28.0 \text{ cm}.$$

Find q_2.

$$q_2 = \frac{1}{\frac{1}{f_2} - \frac{1}{p_2}} = \frac{1}{\frac{1}{-10.0 \text{ cm}} - \frac{1}{-28.0 \text{ cm}}} = -15.6 \text{ cm}$$

The final image is located $\boxed{15.6 \text{ cm to the left of the diverging lens}}$.

5. Find q_1 using the thin lens equation.

$$\frac{1}{p_1} + \frac{1}{q_1} = \frac{1}{f_1}$$

$$q_1 = \frac{1}{\frac{1}{f_1} - \frac{1}{p_1}} = \frac{1}{\frac{1}{4.00 \text{ cm}} - \frac{1}{6.00 \text{ cm}}} = \boxed{12.0 \text{ cm}}$$

Now find the object distance for lens 2.

$$p_2 = s - q_1 = 8.00 \text{ cm} - 12.0 \text{ cm} = -4.0 \text{ cm}$$

Use the thin lens equation to find q_2.

$$q_2 = \frac{1}{\frac{1}{f_2} - \frac{1}{p_2}} = \frac{1}{\frac{1}{-2.00 \text{ cm}} - \frac{1}{-4.0 \text{ cm}}} = \boxed{-4.0 \text{ cm}}$$

The image heights are found from the magnification equation.

$$\frac{h'}{h} = \frac{-q}{p}$$

$$h' = -\frac{qh}{p}$$

For image 1, $h_1' = -\dfrac{12.0 \text{ cm} \cdot 2.00 \text{ mm}}{6.00 \text{ cm}} = \boxed{-4.00 \text{ mm}}$.

For image 2, $h_2' = -\dfrac{-4.0 \text{ cm} \cdot (-4.0 \text{ mm})}{-4.0 \text{ cm}} = \boxed{4.0 \text{ mm}}$.

9. The largest possible image size is 36 mm. To find p, solve the magnification equation for q and substitute this into the thin lens equation.

$$-\frac{q}{p} = \frac{h'}{h}$$

$$q = -\frac{h'p}{h}$$

Substitute for q.

$$\frac{1}{p} + \frac{1}{q} = \frac{1}{f}$$

$$\frac{1}{p} - \frac{h}{h'p} = \frac{1}{f}$$

$$\frac{1}{p}\left(1 - \frac{h}{h'}\right) = \frac{1}{f}$$

$$p = f\left(1 - \frac{h}{h'}\right)$$

Using $f = 50.0$ mm, $h = 52$ m, and $h' = -36$ mm (inverted image) yields

$$p = (50.0 \text{ mm})\left(1 - \frac{52 \text{ m}}{-36 \text{ mm}}\right) = (0.0500 \text{ m})\left(1 + \frac{52 \text{ m}}{0.036 \text{ m}}\right) = \boxed{72 \text{ m}}.$$

11. First find p using the magnification equation. The slide is inverted with respect to the image, so h is negative.

$$-\frac{q}{p} = \frac{h'}{h}$$

$$p = -\frac{qh}{h'} = -\frac{12.0 \text{ m} \cdot (-36 \text{ mm})}{1.50 \text{ m}} = 290 \text{ mm}$$

Now find the focal length f using the thin lens equation.

$$\frac{1}{f} = \frac{1}{p} + \frac{1}{q}$$

$$f = \frac{1}{\frac{1}{p} + \frac{1}{q}} = \frac{1}{\frac{1}{290 \text{ mm}} + \frac{1}{12{,}000 \text{ mm}}} = \boxed{280 \text{ mm}}$$

13. Solve the thin lens equation for the focal length f.

$$\frac{1}{f} = \frac{1}{p} + \frac{1}{q}$$

$$= \frac{p + q}{pq}$$

$$f = \frac{pq}{p + q}$$

For $p = 25.0$ cm and $q = 2.00$ cm, the focal length is

$$f = \frac{25.0 \text{ cm} \cdot 2.00 \text{ cm}}{25.0 \text{ cm} + 2.00 \text{ cm}} = 1.85 \text{ cm}.$$

For $p = \infty$, $\frac{1}{p} = 0$, so $\frac{1}{f} = \frac{1}{q}$. With $q = 2.00$ cm, $f = 2.00$ cm.

Thus, the focal length of the lens system must vary between 1.85 cm and 2.00 cm to see objects from 25.0 cm to infinity.

15. Solve the thin lens equation for q using $\dfrac{1}{f} = 3.0 \text{ m}^{-1}$ and $p = N = 0.25 \text{ m}$.

$$\frac{1}{q} + \frac{1}{p} = \frac{1}{f}$$

$$q = \left(\frac{1}{f} - \frac{1}{p} \right)^{-1}$$

$$= \left(3.0 \text{ m}^{-1} - \frac{1}{0.25 \text{ m}} \right)^{-1}$$

$$= -1.0 \text{ m}$$

So, the uncorrected nearpoint is $\boxed{1.0 \text{ m}}$.

17. Solve the thin lens equation for the focal length f. The object distance is $p = 25.0$ cm and the image distance is $q = 1.75$ cm.

$$\frac{1}{f} = \frac{1}{p} + \frac{1}{q}$$

$$f = \frac{1}{\frac{1}{p} + \frac{1}{q}} = \frac{1}{\frac{1}{25.0 \text{ cm}} + \frac{1}{1.75 \text{ cm}}} = \boxed{1.64 \text{ cm}}$$

21. **(a)** A refractive power of $+40.0$ D means $P = \dfrac{1}{f} = 40.0 \text{ m}^{-1}$. Substitute this value and

$q = -25.0 \text{ cm} = -0.250 \text{ m}$ into the thin lens equation and solve for object distance p.

$$p = \frac{1}{\frac{1}{f} - \frac{1}{q}} = \frac{1}{40.0 \text{ m}^{-1} - \frac{1}{-0.250 \text{ m}}} = \boxed{2.27 \text{ cm}}$$

(b) Assuming the nearpoint $N = 25$ cm, the angular magnification is

$$M = \frac{N}{p} = \frac{25 \text{ cm}}{2.27 \text{ cm}} = \boxed{11}.$$

(c) The size of the image is given by M times the object height, so $11(3.00 \text{ cm}) = \boxed{33 \text{ cm}}$.

25. At the near point, the wing subtends an angle of $\theta_1 \approx \dfrac{h}{N} = \dfrac{0.10 \text{ cm}}{25 \text{ cm}} = 0.0040$. The image subtends an angle

of $\theta_2 \approx \dfrac{h'}{q} = \dfrac{1.0 \text{ m}}{5.0 \text{ m}} = 0.20$. The angular magnification is $M = \dfrac{\theta_2}{\theta_1} = \dfrac{0.20}{0.0040} = \boxed{50}$.

27. Since the final image is not at infinity, the image from the objective lens is not at the focal point of the eyepiece. To find the position of the objective lens image, first find the object distance for the eyepiece.

$$M_e = \frac{N}{p_e}$$

$$p_e = \frac{N}{M_e} = \frac{25.0 \text{ cm}}{5.00} = 5.00 \text{ cm}$$

The focal length of the eyepiece can be calculated using the thin lens equation.

$$\frac{1}{p_e} + \frac{1}{q_e} = \frac{1}{f_e}$$

$$f_e = \frac{1}{\frac{1}{p_e} + \frac{1}{q_e}} = \frac{1}{\frac{1}{5.00 \text{ cm}} + \frac{1}{-25.0 \text{ cm}}} = 6.25 \text{ cm}$$

Now find the image distance for the objective lens, q_o.

$$q_o + p_e = f_o + L + f_e$$
$$q_o = f_o + L + f_e - p_e$$
$$= 1.50 \text{ cm} + 16.0 \text{ cm} + 6.25 \text{ cm} - 5.00 \text{ cm}$$
$$= 18.8 \text{ cm}$$

The object distance for the objective lens can be found from the thin lens equation.

$$\frac{1}{p_o} + \frac{1}{q_o} = \frac{1}{f_o}$$
$$p_o = \frac{1}{\frac{1}{f_o} - \frac{1}{q_o}} = \frac{1}{\frac{1}{1.50 \text{ cm}} - \frac{1}{18.8 \text{ cm}}} = \boxed{1.63 \text{ cm}}$$

29. **(a)** First find the object distance for the eyepiece, using the thin lens equation.

$$\frac{1}{p_e} + \frac{1}{q_e} = \frac{1}{f_e}$$
$$p_e = \frac{f_e q_e}{q_e - f_e} = \frac{2.80 \text{ cm} \times (-25.0 \text{ cm})}{-25.0 \text{ cm} - 2.80 \text{ cm}} = 2.52 \text{ cm}$$

The distance between the lenses is

$$q_o + p_e = 16.5 \text{ cm} + 2.52 \text{ cm} = \boxed{19.0 \text{ cm}}.$$

(b) The angular magnification of the eyepiece is $M_e = \dfrac{N}{p_e}$. The transverse magnification for the objective is

$$m_o = -\frac{q_o}{p_o} = -q_o\left(\frac{1}{p_o}\right) = -q_o\left(\frac{1}{f_o} - \frac{1}{q_o}\right).$$

The total magnification is

$$M_{\text{total}} = m_o M_e = -q_o\left(\frac{1}{f_o} - \frac{1}{q_o}\right) \times \frac{N}{p_e} = -(16.5 \text{ cm})\left(\frac{1}{0.500 \text{ cm}} - \frac{1}{16.5 \text{ cm}}\right) \times \frac{25.0 \text{ cm}}{2.518 \text{ cm}} = \boxed{-318}.$$

(c) Use the thin lens equation to find the object distance for the objective lens.

$$\frac{1}{p_o} + \frac{1}{q_o} = \frac{1}{f_o}$$
$$p_o = \frac{1}{\frac{1}{f_o} - \frac{1}{q_o}} = \frac{1}{\frac{1}{5.00 \text{ mm}} - \frac{1}{165 \text{ mm}}} = \boxed{5.16 \text{ mm}}$$

33. **(a)** The moon is far enough away that we can approximate its distance as infinite. Then we can use the equation

barrel length $= f_o + f_e = 2.40 \text{ m} + 0.160 \text{ m} = \boxed{2.56 \text{ m}}$.

(b) Using $h = 3480 \text{ km}$, $p = 385,000 \text{ km}$, and $q \approx f_o = 2.40 \text{ m}$ in the transverse magnification equation yields

$$\frac{h'}{h} = -\frac{q}{p}$$
$$h' = -\frac{qh}{p} = -\frac{2.40 \text{ m} \cdot 3480 \text{ km}}{385,000 \text{ km}} = -0.0217 \text{ m} = -2.17 \text{ cm}$$

The diameter of the image is $\boxed{2.17 \text{ cm}}$.

(c) $M = -\dfrac{f_o}{f_e} = -\dfrac{2.40 \text{ m}}{0.160 \text{ m}} = \boxed{-15}$

37. (a) Using $M = -5.0$ in the astronomical telescope magnification equation yields

$$M = -\frac{f_o}{f_e}$$
$$f_o = -Mf_e$$
$$= 5.0 f_e$$

The focal length of the objective must be 5 times the focal length of the eyepiece. The focal length of lens 1 is 5 times the focal length of lens 2, so lens 1 is the objective and lens 2 is the eyepiece.

(b) The distance separating the lenses should be the sum of the focal lengths.

$$25.0 \text{ cm} + 5.0 \text{ cm} = \boxed{30.0 \text{ cm}}$$

41. (a) A large magnitude magnification is desired. Since $M = -f_o / f_e$, the objective lens should have the long focal length. So, the lens with the 30.0-cm focal length should be the objective.

(b) $M = -\dfrac{f_o}{f_e} = -\dfrac{30.0 \text{ cm}}{3.0 \text{ cm}} = \boxed{-10}$

(c) The distance between the lenses is the sum of the focal lengths.

$$30.0 \text{ cm} + 3.0 \text{ cm} = \boxed{33.0 \text{ cm}}$$

45. (a) Light must be incident on the film to expose it and create a photograph, so the image must be real.

(b) Diverging lenses only form virtual images, so the lens must be converging.

(c) Use the thin lens equation with $p = 3.0 \text{ m} = 3.0 \times 10^3 \text{ mm}$ and $f = 50.0 \text{ mm}$ to find the image distance q.

$$q = \frac{fp}{p-f} = \frac{50.0 \text{ mm} \times 3.0 \times 10^3 \text{ mm}}{3.0 \times 10^3 \text{ mm} - 50.0 \text{ mm}} = \boxed{51 \text{ mm}}$$

(d) Use the transverse magnification equation with $h = 1.0 \text{ m}$, $p = 3.0 \text{ m}$, and $q = 51 \text{ mm}$ to solve for the image height h'.

$$\frac{h'}{h} = -\frac{q}{p}$$
$$h' = -\frac{qh}{p} = -\frac{51 \text{ mm} \times 1.0 \text{ m}}{3.0 \text{ m}} = -17 \text{ mm}$$

The image is $\boxed{17 \text{ mm}}$ tall.

(e) For objects at infinity, the lens-film distance must be 50.0 mm since the parallel rays converge at the focal point of the lens. For an object distance of 1.00 m, the image distance is

$$q = \frac{fp}{p-f} = \frac{50.0 \text{ mm} \times 1.00 \times 10^3 \text{ mm}}{1.00 \times 10^3 \text{ mm} - 50.0 \text{ mm}} = 52.6 \text{ mm}$$

The lens must travel a distance of

$$52.6 \text{ mm} - 50.0 \text{ mm} = \boxed{2.6 \text{ mm}}.$$

49. (a) Referring to Figure 24.5a, we see that rays from the top of the object are incident at the bottom of the image and rays from the bottom of the object are incident at the top of the image, so the image is inverted.

(b) The magnification is $m = -\dfrac{q}{p} = -\dfrac{2.8 \text{ m}}{6.6 \text{ m}} = \boxed{-0.42}$.

(c) The pinhole admits a narrow cone of rays diverging from each point on the object; the cone of rays makes a small circular spot on the film or screen. If the spot is small enough, the image appears clear to the eye. A larger spot results in the spot being spread out and blurry. Thus, the eye can detect that the rays do not converge to a single point.

(d) The image must be real to expose the film or project the image on a screen, and to focus the image. Only converging lenses form real images.

(e) Using $p = 6.6$ m and $q = 2.8$ m in the thin lens equation yields

$$f = \frac{pq}{p+q} = \frac{6.6 \text{ m} \times 2.8 \text{ m}}{6.6 \text{ m} + 2.8 \text{ m}} = \boxed{2.0 \text{ m}}.$$

53. (a) For an image at infinity, the magnification is

$$M = \frac{N}{f} = NP = 25 \text{ cm} \times 12 \text{ D} = 0.25 \text{ m} \times 12 \text{ m}^{-1} = \boxed{3.0}.$$

(b) For an image at 25 cm, use the thin lens equation with $q = -25$ cm and $\frac{1}{f} = 12$ D to find p.

$$\frac{1}{p} + \frac{1}{q} = \frac{1}{f}$$

$$\frac{1}{p} = \frac{1}{f} - \frac{1}{q} = 12 \text{ m}^{-1} - \frac{1}{-0.25 \text{ m}} = 16 \text{ m}^{-1}$$

The magnification is

$$M = \frac{N}{p} = N \cdot \frac{1}{p} = 0.25 \text{ m} \times 16 \text{ m}^{-1} = \boxed{4.0}.$$

Chapter 25

INTERFERENCE AND DIFFRACTION

Problems

1. Since the light from the two lamps is incoherent, the intensity of the lamps together is just the sum of the intensities.

$$I = I_0 + 4I_0 = \boxed{5I_0}$$

3.

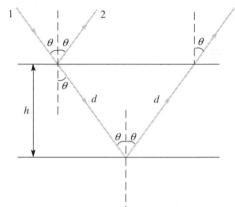

Ray 1 is incident at the first step and reflected (2) and at the second step and again reflected (3). When rays 2 and 3 reach an observer, ray 3 has traveled a distance $2d$ farther than ray 2.

For constructive interference to happen, this distance must be an integer number of wavelengths.

$$m\lambda = 2d$$

d and h are the hypotenuse and adjacent leg of a right triangle, respectively, so $h = d\cos\theta = \dfrac{m\lambda}{2}\cos\theta$, or

$$\lambda = \frac{2h}{m\cos\theta} = \frac{446 \text{ nm}}{m\cos\theta}.$$

θ	λ (nm) ($m = 1$)	λ (nm) ($m = 2$)
0°	446	223
10.0°	453	226
30.0°	515	257

The $m = 2$ values are below the visible wavelength range, so the wavelengths are those given in the table above for $m = 1$.

5. (a) As in Example 25.1, the formula relating the path length difference to the wavelength is
$$2\Delta x = \lambda$$
The maxima in Figure 25.51 are at $x = 0.7$ cm and $x = 2.3$ cm, so $\Delta x = 1.6$ cm and the wavelength is
$$2 \cdot 1.6 \text{ cm} = \lambda$$
$$\lambda = \boxed{3.2 \text{ cm}}$$

(b) The maxima have power readings of 3.4 units and 2.6 units. The ratio is $\frac{7}{5}$. Amplitude is proportional to the square root of intensity and intensity is proportional to power, so amplitude is proportional to the square root of power. The ratio of the amplitudes is $\sqrt{\dfrac{3.4}{2.6}} = \boxed{1.1}$.

7. As the mirror is moved a distance d, the path length through the arm changed by $2d$, which is equal to 274 wavelengths.
$$274\lambda = 2d$$
$$d = 137\lambda = 137 \cdot 633 \text{ nm} = \boxed{86.7 \text{ } \mu\text{m}}$$

9. Since the film appears red, red light must be experiencing constructive interference. At the air-oil boundary, reflected light is 180° out of phase, since $n_{oil} > n_{air}$. For transmitted light reflected at the oil-water boundary, the reflective ray is not phase shifted since $n_{water} < n_{oil}$. The two reflected rays are 180° out of phase, so constructive interference occurs when the relative path length difference, $2t$, is an odd multiple of one half the wavelength in the oil, $\lambda = \lambda_0 / n_{oil}$.
$$2t = \left(m + \frac{1}{2}\right)\lambda = \left(m + \frac{1}{2}\right)\frac{\lambda_0}{n_{oil}}$$
The minimum thickness, t, occurs when $m = 0$.
$$t = \frac{1}{4}\frac{\lambda_0}{n_{oil}} = \frac{1}{4}\frac{630 \text{ nm}}{1.50} = \boxed{105 \text{ nm}}$$

11. The reflected rays at both boundaries are inverted, since $n_{air} < n_{film}$ and $n_{film} < n_{glass}$. To minimize reflection, the rays should interfere destructively. So, the path length difference, $2t$, must be equal to an odd multiple of one half the wavelength in the film, $\lambda = \lambda_0 / n_{film}$.
$$2t = \left(m + \frac{1}{2}\right)\lambda = \left(m + \frac{1}{2}\right)\frac{\lambda_0}{n_{film}}$$
Solving for t, and substituting $n_{film} = 1.3$, $\lambda_0 = 500.0$ nm, and $m = 0$ yields the minimum thickness.
$$t = \left(m + \frac{1}{2}\right)\frac{\lambda_0}{2n_{film}} = \left(0 + \frac{1}{2}\right)\frac{500.0 \text{ nm}}{2 \cdot 1.3} = \boxed{96 \text{ nm}}$$

13. (a) Rays reflected off the front of the film will be inverted since $n_{air} < n_{film}$, but rays reflected off the back of the film are not inverted, so the reflected rays will be 180° out of phase plus the phase shift caused by the path length difference. Destructive interference occurs when the path length difference, $2t$, is equal to an integral number of wavelengths in the film, $\lambda = \lambda_0 / n_{film}$.
$$2t = m\lambda = m\frac{\lambda_0}{n_{film}}$$
Solving for λ_0 with $t = 910.0$ nm and $n_{film} = 1.50$ gives
$$\lambda_0 = \frac{2tn_{film}}{m} = \frac{2730 \text{ nm}}{m}.$$
Substituting $m = 4$, 5, and 6 gives wavelengths in the visible spectrum: $\lambda_0 = \boxed{683 \text{ nm, 546 nm, and 455 nm}}$.

(b) The condition for constructive interference is used to find the strongest wavelengths in reflected light. This occurs when the path length difference, $2t$, is an odd multiple of half the wavelength in the film.

$$2t = \left(m + \frac{1}{2}\right)\lambda = \left(m + \frac{1}{2}\right)\frac{\lambda_0}{n_{\text{film}}}$$

Solving for λ_0 with $t = 910.0$ nm and $n_{\text{film}} = 1.50$ gives

$$\lambda_0 = \frac{2tn_{\text{film}}}{m + \frac{1}{2}} = \frac{2730 \text{ nm}}{m + \frac{1}{2}}.$$

Substituting $m = 4$, 5, and 6 gives wavelengths in the visible spectrum: $\lambda_0 = \boxed{607 \text{ nm, } 496 \text{ nm, and } 420 \text{ nm.}}$

17. Let n_i be the index of refraction for the incident side and n_t be the index for the transmitted side.

First case: $n > n_i$ and $n > n_t$

Ray 1 is inverted upon reflection and ray 2 is not. Constructive interference occurs for rays 1 and 2 when the path length difference, $2t$, is equal to an odd multiple of the wavelength in the film, $\lambda = \lambda_0 / n$.

$$2t = \left(m + \frac{1}{2}\right)\lambda = \left(m + \frac{1}{2}\right)\frac{\lambda_0}{n} \qquad (1)$$

The path length difference between rays 3 and 4 is $2t$, and ray 4 is not inverted by either of its two reflections within the film. So, destructive interference occurs if $2t$ is equal to an odd multiple of the wavelength in the film.

Thus, $2t = \left(m + \frac{1}{2}\right)\frac{\lambda_0}{n}$, which is the same as the condition for constructive interference for rays 1 and 2.

For rays 1 and 2 to interfere destructively, $2t$ must equal an integral number of wavelengths in the film, so

$$2t = \frac{m\lambda_0}{n} \qquad (2).$$

For rays 3 and 4 to interfere constructively, $2t$ must equal an integral number of wavelengths in the film, so

$$2t = \frac{m\lambda_0}{n}, \text{ which is the same as the condition for destructive interference for rays 1 and 2.}$$

Second case: $n < n_i$ and $n < n_t$

Now, ray 2 is inverted but ray 1 is not. The path length difference must still equal an odd multiple of the wavelength in the film for constructive interference. The condition is given by (1). The condition for destructive interference is still given by (2). Ray 4 is now inverted by both reflections, but two 180° phase changes result in no net change. Therefore, the conditions for constructive and destructive interference are the same as before. So, when rays 1 and 2 interfere constructively/destructively, rays 3 and 4 interfere destructively/constructively.

Third case: $n_t < n < n_i$

Neither ray 1 nor ray 2 is inverted. For constructive interference, the path length difference must be equal to an integral number of wavelengths in the film, so $2t = \frac{m\lambda_0}{n}$.

For destructive interference, the path length difference must be an odd multiple of the wavelength in the film, so

$$2t = \left(m + \frac{1}{2}\right)\frac{\lambda_0}{n}.$$

Ray 4 is inverted by its second reflection, so the path length difference between rays 3 and 4 must be equal to an odd multiple of the wavelength in the film for constructive interference, $2t = \left(m + \frac{1}{2}\right)\frac{\lambda_0}{n}$, and for destructive

interference, $2t = \frac{m\lambda_0}{n}$. So, when rays 1 and 2 interfere constructively/destructively, rays 3 and 4 interfere

destructively/constructively.

Fourth case: $n_i < n < n_t$

Both rays 1 and 2 are inverted, so the conditions for constructive and destructive interference are the same as found in the third case; 180° phase change for both is the same as no phase change at all. Ray 4 is inverted by its first reflection, so the conditions for constructive and destructive interference for rays 3 and 4 are the same as found in the third case. So, as in the previous three cases, when rays 1 and 2 interfere constructively/destructively, rays 3 and 4 interfere destructively/constructively.

21. $\dfrac{D}{x} = \dfrac{2.50 \text{ m}}{0.760\times10^{-2} \text{ m}} = 329$, so $x \ll D$ and the small angle approximation is justified. From Example 25.4,

$$\lambda = \dfrac{dx}{D} = \dfrac{(0.0150\times10^{-2} \text{ m})(0.760\times10^{-2} \text{ m})}{2.50 \text{ m}} = \boxed{456 \text{ nm}}$$

23. $x \ll D$, so the small angle approximation is valid. Then, from Example 25.4, $d = \dfrac{\lambda D}{x}$. So, for fixed D and d,

$\lambda \propto x$. Form a proportion.

$$\dfrac{\lambda_2}{\lambda_1} = \dfrac{x_2}{x_1}$$

$$\lambda_2 = \dfrac{0.640 \text{ cm}}{0.530 \text{ cm}}(589 \text{ nm})$$

$$= \boxed{711 \text{ nm}}$$

25. Solve Equation (25-10) for θ and use the fact that $d = \dfrac{1}{N}$.

$$d \sin\theta = m\lambda$$

$$\theta = \sin^{-1}\left(\dfrac{m\lambda}{d}\right)$$

$$= \sin^{-1}(m\lambda N)$$

$$= \sin^{-1}\left[3(546\times10^{-7} \text{ cm})\dfrac{8000 \text{ lines}}{2.54 \text{ cm}}\right]$$

$$= \boxed{31.1°}$$

27. Since the third-order line is the last to appear, the angle for this line must be approaching 90°. Solving Equation (25-10) for d, and using $m = 3$, $\theta = 90°$, and $\lambda = 650 \text{ nm}$ gives

$$d \sin\theta = m\lambda$$

$$d = \dfrac{m\lambda}{\sin\theta} \approx \dfrac{3\cdot650\times10^{-9} \text{ m}}{\sin 90°} = 2\times10^{-6} \text{ m}$$

So, $N = \dfrac{1}{d} = \dfrac{1}{2\times10^{-6} \text{ m}} = \dfrac{1}{2\times10^{-4} \text{ cm}} = \boxed{5000 \text{ lines/cm}}$.

29. (a) Solve Equation (25-10) for m. $d = 1.20 \text{ μm}$, $\lambda = 0.600 \text{ μm}$, and $\theta = 90°$.

$$d \sin\theta = m\lambda$$

$$m = \dfrac{d \sin\theta}{\lambda} = \dfrac{1.50 \text{ μm} \cdot \sin 90°}{0.600 \text{ μm}} = 2.50$$

The maxima visible on the screen will be associated with $m = 0, \pm1, \pm2$, so $\boxed{\text{five}}$ maxima are seen.

(b) Referring to Figure 25.21 and Example 25.4, we have

$$\tan\theta_1 = \frac{x}{D}.$$

Find θ_1.

$d\sin\theta_1 = \lambda$ for $m = 1$, so $\theta_1 = \sin^{-1}\dfrac{\lambda}{d}$.

Substitute for θ_1 and solve for x_1.

$$x_1 = D\tan\left(\sin^{-1}\frac{\lambda}{d}\right) = (3.0 \text{ m})\tan\left(\sin^{-1}\frac{0.600 \text{ μm}}{1.50 \text{ μm}}\right) = 1.3 \text{ m}$$

Solve for x_2.

$$\theta_2 = \sin^{-1}\frac{2\lambda}{d} \text{ since } m = 2.$$

$$x_2 = (3.0 \text{ m})\tan\left[\sin^{-1}\frac{2(0.600 \text{ μm})}{1\ 50 \text{ μm}}\right] = 4.0 \text{ m}$$

The maxima are shown below.

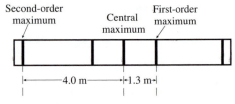

31. **(a)** The line at 12.98° must be a first-order line, since it is the smallest angle. Solve Equation (25-10) for λ using $\theta = 12.98°$, $m = 1$, and

$$d = \frac{1}{5000.0 \text{ slits/cm}} = 2.0000\times10^{-6} \text{ m.}$$

$$d\sin\theta = m\lambda$$

$$\lambda = \frac{d\sin\theta}{m}$$

$$= \frac{2.0000\times10^{-6} \text{ m}\cdot\sin 12.98°}{1}$$

$$= 449.2 \text{ nm}$$

Now, the angles for the second-, third-, and fourth-order lines for this wavelength can be found.

$$d\sin\theta = m\lambda, \text{ so } \theta = \sin^{-1}\left(\frac{m\lambda}{d}\right).$$

$$\theta_2 = \sin^{-1}\left(\frac{2\cdot449.2\times10^{-9} \text{ m}}{2.0000\times10^{-6} \text{ m}}\right) = 26.69°$$

$$\theta_3 = \sin^{-1}\left(\frac{3\cdot449.2\times10^{-9} \text{ m}}{2.0000\times10^{-6} \text{ m}}\right) = 42.36°$$

$$\theta_4 = \sin^{-1}\left(\frac{4\cdot449.2\times10^{-9} \text{ m}}{2.0000\times10^{-6} \text{ m}}\right) = 63.95°$$

Next, the line at 19.0° must be a first-order line for a different wavelength. Solve Equation (25-10) for λ using $\theta = 19.0°$, $m = 1$, and $d = 2.0000\times10^{-6}$ m.

$$\lambda = \frac{d\sin\theta}{m} = \frac{2.0000\times10^{-6} \text{ m}\cdot\sin 19.0°}{1} = 651 \text{ nm}$$

And now the angles for the second- and third-order lines for this wavelength can be found.

$$\theta_2 = \sin^{-1}\left(\frac{2 \cdot 651 \times 10^{-9} \text{ m}}{2.0000 \times 10^{-6} \text{ m}}\right) = 40.6°$$

$$\theta_3 = \sin^{-1}\left(\frac{3 \cdot 651 \times 10^{-9} \text{ m}}{2.0000 \times 10^{-6} \text{ m}}\right) = 77.6°$$

All the spectral lines are accounted for by $\boxed{\text{two}}$ wavelengths, $\boxed{449.2 \text{ nm and } 651 \text{ nm}}$.

(b) To find the total number of lines seen on the screen to one side of the central maximum, solve

Equation (25-10) for m (for both wavelengths) using $\theta = 90°$ and $d = \dfrac{1}{2000.0 \text{ slits/cm}} = 5.0000 \times 10^{-6}$ m,

making sure to round m down to the nearest whole number.

$$d \sin \theta = m\lambda$$

$$m = \frac{d \sin \theta}{\lambda}$$

$$= \frac{5.0000 \times 10^{-6} \text{ m} \cdot \sin 90°}{449 \times 10^{-9} \text{ m}}$$

$$= 11$$

$$\text{and } m = \frac{5.0000 \times 10^{-6} \text{ m} \cdot \sin 90°}{651 \times 10^{-9} \text{ m}} = 7$$

The total is $11 + 7 = \boxed{18 \text{ lines}}$.

33. (a) Solve Equation (25-10) for m using $\lambda = 440.936$ nm, $\theta = 90°$, and $d = \dfrac{1.600 \text{ cm}}{12,000 \text{ slits}}$.

$$d \sin \theta = m\lambda$$

$$m = \frac{d \sin \theta}{\lambda}$$

$$= \frac{1.600 \times 10^{-2} \text{ m}}{12,000} \cdot \frac{\sin 90°}{440.936 \times 10^{-9} \text{ m}}$$

$$= 3.024$$

Since m must be an integer, we have $m = 3$, and $\boxed{\text{three}}$ orders of lines can be seen.

(b) For order 0, both angles are at 0°, so the separation is $0 - 0 = 0$.

For orders 1, 2, and 3, solve Equation (25-10) for θ for each pair of lines, and subtract to find the difference.

$$d \sin \theta = m\lambda$$

$$\theta = \sin^{-1}\left(m \cdot \lambda \cdot \frac{1}{d}\right)$$

Here, $\dfrac{1}{d} = \dfrac{12,000 \text{ slits}}{1.600 \times 10^{-2} \text{ m}} = 7.500 \times 10^5$ slits/m.

The angles are

$$\theta_{a1} = \sin^{-1}\left(1 \cdot 440.000 \times 10^{-9} \text{ m} \cdot 7.500 \times 10^5 \text{ m}^{-1}\right) = 19.27°$$

$$\theta_{b1} = \sin^{-1}\left(1 \cdot 440.936 \times 10^{-9} \text{ m} \cdot 7.500 \times 10^5 \text{ m}^{-1}\right) = 19.31°$$

$$\theta_{a2} = \sin^{-1}\left(2 \cdot 440.000 \times 10^{-9} \text{ m} \cdot 7.500 \times 10^5 \text{ m}^{-1}\right) = 41.30°$$

$$\theta_{b2} = \sin^{-1}\left(2 \cdot 440.936 \times 10^{-9} \text{ m} \cdot 7.500 \times 10^5 \text{ m}^{-1}\right) = 41.41°$$

$$\theta_{a3} = \sin^{-1}\left(3 \cdot 440.000 \times 10^{-9} \text{ m} \cdot 7.500 \times 10^5 \text{ m}^{-1}\right) = 81.89°$$

$$\theta_{b3} = \sin^{-1}\left(3 \cdot 440.936 \times 10^{-9} \text{ m} \cdot 7.500 \times 10^5 \text{ m}^{-1}\right) = 82.80°$$

So, the angular separations are:

$$\boxed{\theta_{b1} - \theta_{a1} = 0.04°, \ \theta_{b2} - \theta_{a2} = 0.11°, \ \theta_{b3} - \theta_{a3} = 0.91°}.$$

(c) $\boxed{\text{The two lines are best resolved by the third-order spectra, since the angular separation is the largest.}}$

37. The distance s is given by the position of the second minima. To find this position, combine Equation (25-12) with the equation relating s, θ, and D (the screen-slit distance), $\tan\theta = \dfrac{s}{D}$. First solve Equation (25-12) for $\sin\theta$.

$$a \sin\theta = m\lambda$$

$$\sin\theta = \frac{m\lambda}{a}$$

Assuming θ is small, replace $\sin\theta$ with $\tan\theta$.

$$\tan\theta = \frac{m\lambda}{a}$$

Substitute this expression into the equation relating s, θ, and D.

$$\frac{m\lambda}{a} = \frac{s}{D}$$

Now solve for s using $m = 2$, $\lambda = 630$ mm, $a = 0.40$ mm, and $D = 2.0$ m.

$$s = \frac{m\lambda L}{a} = \frac{2 \cdot 630 \times 10^{-9} \text{ m} \cdot 2.0 \text{ m}}{0.40 \times 10^{-3} \text{ m}} = \boxed{6.3 \text{ mm}}$$

$s \ll D$, so using the small angle approximation was justified.

39. (a) Equation (25-12) is $d \sin\theta = m\lambda$. Since we are concerned about the width of the central maximum, $m = 1$. For a fixed d, $\sin\theta \propto \lambda$. So, larger wavelengths give larger angles for first-order minima. Since the width of the central bright fringe is twice the distance from the center of the screen to the first-order minima, the fringe is wider for greater wavelengths. Since $\lambda_{red} > \lambda_{blue}$, the central maximum is $\boxed{\text{wider}}$ for red light than it is for blue.

(b) Call the width of the central maximum W. Referring to Figure 25.33, we have $W = 2x$, and by trigonometry, $x = D \tan\theta$, so $W = 2x = 2D \tan\theta$.

Assuming θ is small, replace $\tan\theta$ with $\sin\theta$.

$$W = 2D \sin\theta$$

From Equation (25-12), we have $\sin\theta = \dfrac{\lambda}{a}$ since $m = 1$, so W becomes

$$W = \frac{2L\lambda}{a}.$$

Applying this equation to the current problem gives

$$W_R = \frac{2L\lambda_R}{a} \quad \text{and} \quad W_B = \frac{2L\lambda_B}{a}.$$

Dividing these equations gives

$$\frac{W_R}{W_B} = \frac{\frac{2L\lambda_R}{a}}{\frac{2L\lambda_B}{a}} = \frac{\lambda_R}{\lambda_B}.$$

Now solve for W_R when $W_B = 2.0$ cm, $\lambda_R = 0.70$ μm, and $\lambda_B = 0.43$ μm.

$$W_R = W_B \frac{\lambda_R}{\lambda_B} = (2.0 \text{ cm})\frac{0.70 \text{ μm}}{0.43 \text{ μm}} = \boxed{3.3 \text{ cm}}$$

41. The angular width of the central diffraction maximum is two times the angular position of the first minimum. Solving Equation (25-13) for θ, and using $\lambda = 590$ nm and $a = 7.0$ mm gives

$$a\sin\theta = 1.22\lambda$$

$$\theta = \sin^{-1}\left(\frac{1.22\lambda}{a}\right)$$

$$= \sin^{-1}\left(\frac{1.22 \cdot 590 \times 10^{-9} \text{ m}}{7.0 \times 10^{-3} \text{ m}}\right)$$

$$= 0.0059°$$

Double this angle to get the answer: $\boxed{0.012°}$.

45. (a) By Snell's law, we have $n_{air}\sin\Delta\theta = n\sin\beta$ for ray 2. Using $n_{air} = 1$ yields $\boxed{\sin\Delta\theta = n\sin\beta}$.

(b) If $\beta \geq \phi$ then $\sin\beta \geq \sin\phi$. Applying Equation (25-13) to image 1 and solving for $\sin\theta$ gives

$$a\sin\phi = 1.22\lambda$$

$$a\sin\phi = 1.22\frac{\lambda_0}{n}$$

$$\sin\phi = \frac{1.22\lambda_0}{an}$$

Taking the result from part (a) and solving for $\sin\beta$ gives $\sin\beta = \dfrac{\sin\Delta\theta}{n}$. Substituting this expression for $\sin\beta$ and the previous expression for $\sin\phi$ into the inequality $\sin\beta \geq \sin\phi$ yields

$$\frac{\sin\Delta\theta}{n} \geq \frac{1.22\lambda_0}{an}$$

$$a\sin\Delta\theta \geq 1.22\lambda_0$$

which is equivalent to Equation (25-14), Rayleigh's criterion.

49.

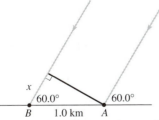

The signal from the pulsar arrives first at antenna A and then a short time later at antenna B. The signal arrives at antenna B later because of the extra distance x that the signal must travel. The time difference is

$$\Delta t = \frac{x}{c} = \frac{1.0 \times 10^3 \text{ m} \cdot \cos 60.0°}{3.00 \times 10^8 \text{ m}} = \boxed{1.7 \text{ μs}}.$$

51. (a) All points on the line $\theta = 0$ are equidistant from the two antennas. The difference in the path lengths is $\boxed{0}$.

(b) At $\theta = 90°,$ the difference in the path lengths is just the distance between the antennas, $\boxed{0.30 \text{ km.}}$

(c) The wavelength is $\lambda = \dfrac{c}{f} = \dfrac{3.00 \times 10^8 \text{ m/s}}{3.0 \times 10^6 \text{ Hz}} = 100 \text{ m} = 0.10 \text{ km},$ which is $\dfrac{1}{3}d.$ Thus, the double-slit maxima

equation will have solutions for $m = 0, \pm 1, \pm 2, \pm 3,$ yielding 7 angles between $-90°$ and $90°$. By symmetry, there will be 5 maxima in the ranges beyond $90°$ and $-90°$. $\boxed{\text{There will be 12 maxima total.}}$

(d) Solve Equation (25-10) for θ using $d = 0.30$ km, $\lambda = 0.10$ km, and $m = 0, 1, 2,$ and 3.

$d \sin \theta = m\lambda$

$$\theta = \sin^{-1}\left(\frac{m\lambda}{d}\right)$$

$$\theta_0 = \sin^{-1}\left(\frac{0 \cdot \lambda}{d}\right) = \boxed{0}$$

$$\theta_1 = \sin^{-1}\left(\frac{1 \cdot 0.10 \text{ km}}{0.30 \text{ km}}\right) = \boxed{19°}$$

$$\theta_2 = \sin^{-1}\left(\frac{2 \cdot 0.10 \text{ km}}{0.30 \text{ km}}\right) = \boxed{42°}$$

$$\theta_3 = \sin^{-1}\left(\frac{3 \cdot 0.10 \text{ km}}{0.30 \text{ km}}\right) = \boxed{90°}$$

(e) $\boxed{\text{The answers in parts (a), (b), and (c) will be unchanged. The angles calculated in part (d) for } \theta_0 \text{ and } \theta_3 \text{ will be unchanged, but } \theta_1 \text{ and } \theta_2 \text{ will be different from before.}}$

53. (a) Light reflects off the top and bottom of the film. Since $n_{\text{film}} > n_{\text{air}}$, the ray that reflects from the top is inverted. Since $n_{\text{lens}} > n_{\text{film}}$, the ray that reflects from the bottom is also inverted. So, destructive interference between the two rays must be due to the path length difference $2t$, which must equal one half the wavelength of the ray in the film for the minimum thickness.

$$2t = \frac{1}{2}\lambda$$

$$t = \frac{1}{4}\frac{\lambda_0}{n_{\text{film}}}$$

$$= \frac{1}{4}(560 \text{ nm})\left(\frac{1}{1.38}\right)$$

$$= \boxed{100 \text{ nm}}$$

(b) Constructive interference in this case is given by $2t = m\lambda = \dfrac{m\lambda_0}{n_{\text{film}}}$; the phase difference must be equal to an integral multiple of the wavelength. Solve for $\lambda_{0,m}.$

$$\lambda_{0,m} = \frac{2tn_{\text{film}}}{m} = \frac{2(101.4 \text{ nm})(1.38)}{m} = \frac{280 \text{ nm}}{m}$$

So, $\lambda_1 = \boxed{280 \text{ nm}}$ and $\lambda_2 = \boxed{140 \text{ nm}}$ are the closest wavelengths to 560 nm giving constructive interference.

(c) Yes; although perfectly constructive interference does not occur for any visible wavelength, some visible light is reflected at all visible wavelengths except 560 nm (the only wavelength with perfectly destructive interference).

57. Let n be the index of refraction of the mica sheet. Since $n > 1$, rays reflected from the front of the mica will be inverted, while rays reflected from the back of the mica will not be inverted. The phase difference for the reflected rays is $180°$, plus the phase shift caused by the path length difference $2t$ in the mica. Destructive interference (gaps in the spectrum) occurs when $2t$ is equal to an integral multiple of the wavelength in mica, $\lambda = \lambda_0 / n$.

$$2t = m\lambda$$
$$2t = m\frac{\lambda_0}{n}$$
$$2tn = m\lambda_0$$

The expression on the left-hand side is constant, so the right-hand side must also be constant, so we can write $m_1\lambda_1 = m_2\lambda_2$, where λ_1 and λ_2 are the wavelengths of two gaps in the spectrum, and m_1 and m_2 are their respective m-values. Substituting $\lambda_1 = 630$ nm, $\lambda_2 = 525$ nm, and $m_2 = m_1 + 1$ (adjacent minima; $\lambda_1 > \lambda_2$) yields

$$m_1 \cdot 630 \text{ nm} = (m_1 + 1) \cdot 525 \text{ nm}$$
$$m_1 \cdot 630 \text{ nm} = m_1 \cdot 525 \text{ nm} + 525 \text{ nm}$$
$$m_1 \cdot 105 \text{ nm} = 525 \text{ nm}$$
$$m_1 = 5.0$$

Finally, solve the equation for destructive interference given above for n, and use $m_1 = 5.0$, $\lambda_1 = 630$ nm, and $t = 0.500 \text{ } \mu\text{m}$ to find the value of n.

$$n = \frac{m_1\lambda_1}{2t} = \frac{5.0 \cdot 630 \times 10^{-9} \text{ m}}{2 \cdot 1.00 \times 10^{-6} \text{ m}} = \boxed{1.6}$$

61. First solve the equation for the maxima of a grating for θ.

$$d\sin\theta = m\lambda$$
$$\theta = \sin^{-1}\left(\frac{m\lambda}{d}\right)$$

The relationship between the diffraction angle θ, the grating-screen distance D, and the position x on the screen is $\tan\theta = \frac{x}{D}$. Solving for x, and using $d = \dfrac{1}{10,000.0 \text{ slits/cm}} = 1.00000 \times 10^{-6} \text{ m/slit}$, and $D = 2.0$ m gives

$$x = D \cdot \tan\theta$$
$$x = 2.0 \text{ m} \cdot \tan\left[\sin^{-1}\left(\frac{m \cdot \lambda}{1.00000 \times 10^{-6} \text{ m}}\right)\right]$$

Using $\lambda = 690$ nm and $m = 0, \pm 1$ gives the location of the red lines.

$$x_{R0} = 2.0 \text{ m} \cdot \tan\left[\sin^{-1}(0)\right] = 0$$
$$x_{R\pm 1} = 2.0 \text{ m} \cdot \tan\left[\sin^{-1}\left(\frac{\pm 1 \cdot 690 \times 10^{-9} \text{ m}}{1.00000 \times 10^{-6} \text{ m}}\right)\right] = \pm 1.9 \text{ m}$$

Using $\lambda = 460$ nm and $m = 0, \pm1, \pm2$ gives the location of the blue lines.

$x_{B0} = 0$

$$x_{B\pm1} = 2.0 \text{ m} \cdot \tan\left[\sin^{-1}\left(\frac{\pm1 \cdot 460 \times 10^{-9} \text{ m}}{1.00000 \times 10^{-6} \text{ m}}\right)\right] = \pm1.0 \text{ m}$$

$$x_{B\pm2} = 2.0 \text{ m} \cdot \tan\left[\sin^{-1}\left(\frac{\pm2 \cdot 460 \times 10^{-9} \text{ m}}{1.00000 \times 10^{-6} \text{ m}}\right)\right] = \pm4.7 \text{ m}$$

The only overlap is at $x = 0$, where the lines combine to make purple. The pattern is shown below.

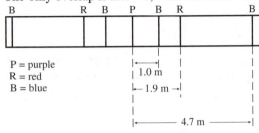

P = purple
R = red
B = blue

65. First find the anglar separation $\Delta\theta$ of the two craters, using $x = 499$ km and $D = 3.85 \times 10^8$ m.

$$\tan\Delta\theta = \frac{x}{D}$$

$$\Delta\theta = \tan^{-1}\left(\frac{x}{D}\right)$$

$$= \tan^{-1}\left(\frac{499 \times 10^3 \text{ m}}{3.85 \times 10^8 \text{ m}}\right)$$

$$= 0.0743°$$

Now solve the Rayleigh's criterion inequality (25-14) for λ_0, using $\Delta\theta = 0.0743°$ and $a = 305$ m.

$$a\sin\Delta\theta \geq 1.22\lambda_0$$

$$\lambda_0 \leq \frac{a\sin\Delta\theta}{1.22}$$

$$\leq \frac{305 \text{ m} \cdot \sin 0.0743°}{1.22}$$

$$\leq 32.4 \text{ cm}$$

The wavelength of the radio waves must be $\boxed{\text{shorter than 32.4 cm}}$.

Chapter 26

RELATIVITY

Problems

1. The time required for the optical signal to reach the station, as measured by an observer at rest relative to the station (the stationmaster) is

$$\frac{d}{c} = \frac{1.0 \text{ km}}{3.00 \times 10^5 \frac{\text{km}}{\text{s}}} = 3.3 \text{ μs}$$

Measured by the same observer, the time needed for the train to arrive is

$$\frac{d}{v} = \frac{d}{0.60c} = \frac{1.0 \text{ km}}{0.60 \cdot 3.00 \times 10^5 \frac{\text{km}}{\text{s}}} = 5.6 \text{ ms}$$

The difference in the arrival times is

$$5.56 \text{ μs} - 3.33 \text{ μs} = \boxed{2.2 \text{ μs}}.$$

5. (a) The proper time interval is the lifetime of the pion in its own rest frame, so $\Delta t_0 = 25$ ns. The time interval measured in the lab frame is calculated using the time-dilation equation.

$$\Delta t = \gamma \Delta t_0 = \frac{1}{\sqrt{1 - \frac{v^2}{c^2}}} \Delta t_0 = \frac{1}{\sqrt{1 - \frac{(0.60c)^2}{c^2}}} \cdot 25 \text{ ns} = \boxed{31 \text{ ns}}.$$

   (b) As measured by the laboratory observers, the distance traveled is

$$d = v \Delta t = 0.60 \times 3.00 \times 10^8 \frac{\text{m}}{\text{s}} \cdot 31 \times 10^{-9} \text{ s} = \boxed{5.6 \text{ m}}.$$

7. (a) The age of the passenger at the end of the trip is found by adding the elapsed time Δt_0, as measured by the ship's clock, to the passenger's age at the start of the trip. To find the elapsed time Δt_0, use the time dilation equation with

$$\Delta t = \frac{\text{distance relative to Earth}}{\text{speed relative to Earth}} = \frac{710 \text{ ly}}{0.9999c} = 710 \text{ y}$$

Find Δt.

$$\Delta t_0 = \frac{\Delta t}{\gamma} = \Delta t \cdot \sqrt{1 - \frac{v^2}{c^2}} = 710 \text{ y} \cdot \sqrt{1 - \frac{(0.9999c)^2}{c^2}} = 10 \text{ y}$$

The passenger's age at the end of the trip is 20 years old + 10 years = $\boxed{30 \text{ years old}}$.

   (b) The spaceship takes slightly more than 710 years to reach its destination, as measured by an observer on Earth. The radio signal takes 710 years to reach Earth. The total elapsed time between the departure of the ship and the arrival of the signal back on Earth is 710 years + 710 years = 1420 years. The year will be

$$2000 + 1420 = \boxed{3420}.$$

9. The proper time interval is 8.0 h. The time interval Δt measured by the clock on the ground is given by the time dilation equation $\Delta t = \gamma \Delta t_0$. The time difference is

$$\Delta t - \Delta t_0 = \gamma \Delta t_0 - \Delta t_0 = (\gamma - 1)\Delta t_0 = \left[\left(1 - \frac{v^2}{c^2}\right)^{-1/2} - 1 \right] \Delta t_0$$

Since $v \ll c$, by the binomial approximation, $\gamma = \left(1 - \frac{v^2}{c^2}\right)^{-1/2} \approx 1 + \frac{v^2}{2c^2}$.

The previous equation becomes

$$\Delta t - \Delta t_0 \approx \left(1 + \frac{v^2}{2c^2} - 1\right)\Delta t_0 = \frac{v^2}{2c^2} \cdot \Delta t_0 = \frac{\left(220\,\frac{m}{s}\right)^2}{2 \cdot \left(3.00 \times 10^8\,\frac{m}{s}\right)^2} \cdot 8.0\text{ h} = \boxed{7.7\text{ ns}}.$$

11. **(a)** The proper length is $L_0 = 91.5$ m. The length observed by the pilot is

$$L = \frac{L_0}{\gamma} = L_0\sqrt{1 - \frac{v^2}{c^2}} = (91.5\text{ m})\sqrt{1 - \frac{(0.50c)^2}{c^2}} = \boxed{79\text{ m}}.$$

(b) Since the speed of the UFO is constant relative to the Earth, the time is found using the equation $x = vt$.

$$t = \frac{x}{v} = \frac{91.5\text{ m}}{0.50 \times 3.00 \times 10^8\,\frac{m}{s}} = 6.1 \times 10^{-7}\text{ s} = \boxed{610\text{ ns}}$$

(c) As seen by the pilot, the distance traveled is 79 m and the speed is 0.50c, so the time required is

$$t = \frac{x}{v} = \frac{79\text{ m}}{0.50 \times 3.00 \times 10^8\,\frac{m}{s}} = 5.3 \times 10^{-7}\text{ s} = \boxed{530\text{ ns}}.$$

13. The length measured from the other ship is contracted by a factor

$$\gamma = \left(1 - \frac{v^2}{c^2}\right)^{-1/2} = \left[1 - \frac{(0.90c)^2}{c^2}\right]^{-1/2} = 2.3.$$

The contracted length is

$$L = \frac{L_0}{\gamma} = \frac{30.0\text{ m}}{2.3} = \boxed{13\text{ m}}.$$

15. **(a)** Length contraction occurs only along the direction of motion. Since the rod is held perpendicular to the direction of motion, the Earth observer will measure the same length for the rod as the pilot of the ship did, $\boxed{1.0\text{ m}}$.

(b) The pilot still measures the proper length of the rod as $L_0 = 1.0$ m. To the Earth observer, the rod is now contracted, and its length is

$$L = \frac{L_0}{\gamma} = L_0\sqrt{1 - \frac{v^2}{c^2}} = 1.0\text{ m} \times \sqrt{1 - \frac{(0.40c)^2}{c^2}} = \boxed{0.92\text{ m}}.$$

17. (a) The observer on the ground measures the proper length between the towers as $L_0 = 3.0$ km. Relative to the passenger on the train, the distance between the towers is

$$L = \frac{L_0}{\gamma} = L_0\sqrt{1 - \frac{v^2}{c^2}} = 3.0 \text{ km} \times \sqrt{1 - \frac{(0.80c)^2}{c^2}} = 1.8 \text{ km}.$$

The time interval measured by the passenger is

$$\Delta t = \frac{L}{v} = \frac{1.8 \text{ km}}{0.80 \times 3.00 \times 10^5 \frac{\text{km}}{\text{s}}} = 7.5 \times 10^{-6} \text{ s} = \boxed{7.5 \text{ } \mu\text{s}}.$$

(b) The observer on the ground measures the time interval

$$\Delta t = \frac{L_0}{v} = \frac{3.0 \text{ km}}{0.80 \times 3.00 \times 10^5 \frac{\text{km}}{\text{s}}} = 1.3 \times 10^{-5} \text{ s} = \boxed{13 \text{ } \mu\text{s}}.$$

21. Since the ships are approaching the Moon from opposite directions, we use a coordinate system relative to the Moon such that one ship (ship A) approaches from the left at a speed $0.60c$, and the other ship (ship B) approaches from the right at speed $0.80c$. The velocity of ship A relative to ship B is written v_{AB}. The velocity of ship A relative to the Moon is $v_{AM} = 0.60c$, then the velocity of ship B relative to the Moon is $v_{BM} = -0.80c$, so $v_{MB} = -v_{BM} = 0.80c$. Using the relativistic velocity transformation equation, we have

$$v_{AB} = \frac{v_{AM} + v_{MB}}{1 + \frac{v_{AM} \cdot v_{MB}}{c^2}} = \frac{0.60c + 0.80c}{1 + \frac{0.60c \cdot 0.80c}{c^2}} = 0.946c.$$

$v_{BA} = -v_{AB} = -0.946c$, so the relative speed measured by a passenger on either ship is $\boxed{0.946c}$.

23. The velocity of the electron relative to the lab, v_{EL}, is given by

$$v_{EL} = \frac{v_{EP} + v_{PL}}{1 + \frac{v_{EP} \cdot v_{PL}}{c^2}}.$$

$v_{PL} = \frac{4}{5}c$ is the velocity of the proton relative to the lab. $v_{EP} = -\frac{5}{7}c$ is the velocity of the electron relative to the proton. The velocity of the electron relative to the proton is negative since the electron moves to the left and positive direction is chosen to be to the right. Substitute.

$$v_{EL} = \frac{-\frac{5}{7}c + \frac{4}{5}c}{1 + \frac{\left(-\frac{5}{7}c\right)\cdot\left(\frac{4}{5}c\right)}{c^2}} = \boxed{\frac{1}{5}c}$$

The speed of the electron relative to the lab is $\boxed{\frac{1}{5}c}$.

25. The speed of electron B in any frame of reference in which electron A is at rest is the same as the speed of electron B relative to electron A, v_{BA}. v_{BA} is given by

$$v_{BA} = \frac{v_{BL} + v_{LA}}{1 + \frac{v_{BL} \cdot v_{LA}}{c^2}}.$$

The coordinate system relative to the lab is chosen so that objects traveling west have a positive velocity. Then the velocity of electron B relative to the lab is $v_{BL} = \frac{4}{5}c$ and the velocity of electron A relative to the lab is

$v_{AL} = \frac{3}{5}c$, so $v_{LA} = -v_{AL} = -\frac{3}{5}c$. Using these values in the equation for v_{BA} yields

$$v_{BA} = \frac{\frac{4}{5}c + \left(-\frac{3}{5}c\right)}{1 + \frac{\left(\frac{4}{5}c\right)\left(-\frac{3}{5}c\right)}{c^2}} = \frac{5}{13}c.$$

The speed of electron B in a frame of reference in which electron A is at rest is $\boxed{\dfrac{5}{13}c}$.

27. The magnitude of the momentum is given by $p = \gamma mv$.

$$p = \gamma mv$$

$$= \left(1 - \frac{v^2}{c^2}\right)^{-1/2} \times m_p \times v$$

$$= \left(1 - \frac{(0.90c)^2}{c^2}\right)^{-1/2} \times 1.673 \times 10^{-27} \text{ kg} \times 0.90 \times 3.00 \times 10^8 \, \frac{\text{m}}{\text{s}}$$

$$= \boxed{1.04 \times 10^{-18} \text{ kg} \cdot \text{m/s}}$$

29. (a) The magnitude of the momentum is calculated using the component form of Equation (26-6).

$$p = \gamma mv = \left[1 - \frac{(0.87c)^2}{c^2}\right]^{-1/2} \times 12.6 \text{ kg} \times 0.87 \times 3.00 \times 10^8 \, \frac{\text{m}}{\text{s}} = \boxed{6.7 \times 10^9 \text{ kg} \cdot \text{m/s}}$$

(b) To find the time needed to bring the body to rest, use the equation relating the impulse to the change in momentum, $F_{net} \Delta t = \Delta p$.

$$\Delta t = \frac{\Delta p}{F_{net}} = \frac{0 - 6.7 \times 10^9 \, \frac{\text{kg} \cdot \text{m}}{\text{s}}}{-16.4 \times 10^8 \text{ N}} = \boxed{4.1 \text{ s}}$$

31. The change in mass is related to the energy released by Equation (26-7).

$$\Delta E = \Delta mc^2 = 1.0 \times 10^{-3} \text{kg} \times \left(3.00 \times 10^8 \, \frac{\text{m}}{\text{s}}\right)^2 = \boxed{9.0 \times 10^{13} \text{ J}}$$

33. The mass-energy must be conserved. So, rest energy before decay = rest energy after decay + kinetic energy.

$m_{\Lambda^0} c^2 = m_n c^2 + m_{\pi^0} c^2 +$ kinetic energy, so

$$\text{kinetic energy} = (m_{\Lambda^0} - m_n - m_{\pi^0}) \cdot c^2 = \left(1115 \frac{\text{MeV}}{c^2} - 940 \frac{\text{MeV}}{c^2} - 135 \frac{\text{MeV}}{c^2}\right) \cdot c^2 = \boxed{40 \text{ MeV}}.$$

35. (a) The total energy is

$$E = \gamma mc^2 = \left(1 - \frac{v^2}{c^2}\right)^{-1/2} \times E_0 = \left[1 - \frac{(0.980c)^2}{c^2}\right]^{-1/2} \times 106 \text{ MeV} = \boxed{530 \text{ MeV}}.$$

(b) The muon is at rest in its own frame of reference. Its total energy is just its rest energy, $\boxed{106 \text{ MeV}}$.

37. Calculate the total energy of the electron.

$$E = \gamma mc^2$$

$$= \left(1 - \frac{v^2}{c^2}\right)^{-1/2} mc^2$$

$$= \left[1 - \frac{(0.60c)^2}{c^2}\right]^{-1/2} \times 9.109 \times 10^{-31} \text{ kg} \times \left(3.00 \times 10^8 \frac{\text{m}}{\text{s}}\right)^2 \times \left(\frac{1 \text{ eV}}{1.602 \times 10^{-19} \text{ J}}\right)$$

$$= \boxed{0.64 \text{ MeV}}$$

39. $1 \text{ MeV} = 1 \times 10^6 \text{ eV} \cdot \dfrac{1.602 \times 10^{-19} \text{ J}}{1 \text{ eV}} = 1.602 \times 10^{-13} \text{ J}$

So, $\dfrac{1 \text{ MeV}}{c^2} = \dfrac{1.602 \times 10^{-13} \text{ J}}{\left(2.998 \times 10^8 \frac{\text{m}}{\text{s}}\right)^2} = 1.782 \times 10^{-30} \text{ kg}.$

The conversion is $\boxed{1 \text{ MeV}/c^2 = 1.782 \times 10^{-30} \text{ kg}}$.

41. Solve Equation (26-10) for p using $E_0 = 0.511 \text{ MeV}$ and $E = 3.00E_0$.

$$E^2 = E_0^2 + (pc)^2$$

$$9.00E_0^2 = E_0^2 + p^2c^2$$

$$8.00E_0^2 = p^2c^2$$

$$p = \sqrt{8.00}\,\frac{E_0}{c}$$

$$= \sqrt{8.00}\,\frac{0.511 \text{ MeV}}{c}$$

$$= \boxed{1.45 \text{ MeV}/c}$$

45. The total energy is

$E = K + E_0.$

Squaring both sides gives

$E^2 = (K + E_0)^2 = K^2 + 2KE_0 + E_0^2.$

Combining this with the energy-momentum relation $E^2 = E_0^2 + (pc)^2$ yields

$E_0^2 + (pc)^2 = K^2 + 2KE_0 + E_0^2$, or $(pc)^2 = K^2 + 2KE_0$, which is Equation (26-11).

49. (a) To calculate when the signal will arrive at Earth, we must first find the elapsed time (as measured by an observer on the Earth) before the signal leaves the ship, then add the amount of time the signal takes to travel back to the Earth. The elapsed time before the signal leaves the ship is

$$\Delta t_1 = \gamma \Delta t_0 = \left(1 - \frac{(0.750c)^2}{c^2}\right)^{-1/2} \times 48.0 \text{ h} = 72.6 \text{ h}.$$

The time needed for the signal to travel back to Earth is

$$\Delta t_2 = \frac{x}{v} = \frac{0.750 \times c \times \Delta t_1}{c} = 0.750 \times \Delta t_1.$$

The total time is

$$\Delta t = \Delta t_1 + \Delta t_2 = 1.750 \times \Delta t_1 = \boxed{127 \text{ h}}.$$

(b) The situations in parts (a) and (b) are symmetric. So, the time required is the same, $\boxed{127 \text{ h}}$.

53. **(a)** Let T be the reading on the Earth clock, as seen by an observer on Earth, when the signal reaches the ship. The distance traveled by the ship according to an Earth observer, is $d = 0.80cT$, so the time reading is $T = d/(0.80c)$. The distance traveled by the light signal is the same as the distance traveled by the ship, and can be written $d = c(T - 1.0 \times 10^4 \text{ s})$.

Now substitute the previous value for T into this equation and solve for d.

$$d = c\left(\frac{d}{0.80c} - 1.0 \times 10^4 \text{ s}\right) = \frac{d}{0.80} - (1.0 \times 10^4 \text{ s})c$$

$$0.80d = d - (8.0 \times 10^3 \text{ s})c$$

$$0.20d = (8.0 \times 10^3 \text{ s})c$$

$$d = \frac{8.0 \times 10^3 \text{ s} \times 3.00 \times 10^8 \frac{\text{m}}{\text{s}}}{0.20}$$

$$= \boxed{1.2 \times 10^{13} \text{ m}}$$

(b) The clock reading T is $T = \dfrac{d}{0.80c} = \dfrac{1.2 \times 10^{13} \text{ m}}{0.80 \times 3.00 \times 10^8 \frac{\text{m}}{\text{s}}} = \boxed{5.0 \times 10^4 \text{ s}}$.

57. **(a)** For an observer on the ground, the distance traveled by the muons is just the difference between the initial and final altitudes.

$$4500 \text{ m} - 0 \text{ m} = \boxed{4500 \text{ m}}$$

(b) For an observer on the ground, the time of flight is

$$t = \frac{x}{v} = \frac{4500 \text{ m}}{0.9950 \times 3.00 \times 10^8 \frac{\text{m}}{\text{s}}} = 1.5 \times 10^{-5} \text{ s} = \boxed{15 \text{ μs}}.$$

(c) The proper time interval for the half-life of a muon is measured in the reference frame of the muon itself, so $\Delta t_0 = 1.5$ μs. An observer on the ground sees the half-life as

$$\Delta t = \gamma \Delta t_0 = \left[1 - \frac{(0.9950c)^2}{c^2}\right]^{-1/2} \times 1.5 \text{ μs} = \boxed{15 \text{ μs}}.$$

(d) The time of flight is equal to the half-life, so during the flight half of the muons decay. So, $\boxed{500,000}$ muons reach sea level.

61. **(a)** The proper length is $L_0 = 30.0$ ly. In the astronaut's frame of reference, this distance is

$$L = \frac{L_0}{\gamma} = \frac{30.0 \text{ ly}}{\left[1 - \frac{(0.800c)^2}{c^2}\right]^{-1/2}} = \boxed{18.0 \text{ ly}}.$$

(b) The time needed to travel this distance is

$$\Delta t = \frac{\Delta x}{v} = \frac{18.0 \text{ ly}}{0.800c} = \boxed{22.5 \text{ yr}}.$$

This is consistent with the results of Example 26.1.

65. If K is much larger than E_0, then E is also much larger than E_0, since

$$E = K + E_0 > K \gg E_0.$$

Using Equation (26-10), we have

$$E^2 = E_0{}^2 + (pc)^2$$

$$E^2 - E_0{}^2 = (pc)^2$$

Since $E \gg E_0$, $E^2 \gg E_0^2$, so $E^2 - E_0{}^2 \approx E^2$. The equation becomes

$$E^2 \approx (pc)^2, \text{ or } E \approx pc.$$

67. The relativistic energies are given by $(p_n c)^2 = K_n^2 + 2K_n E_{0n}$ and $(p_\pi c)^2 = K_\pi^2 + 2K_\pi E_{0\pi}$.

By conservation of momentum, $p_n = p_\pi$, so $K_n^2 + 2K_n E_{0n} = K_\pi^2 + 2K_\pi E_{0\pi}$ (1).

The total energy of the system is conserved, so

$$m_\Lambda c^2 = m_n c^2 + m_\pi c^2 + K_n + K_\pi$$

$$(m_\Lambda - m_n - m_\pi)c^2 = K_n + K_\pi$$

$$= K$$

where K is the total kinetic energy. Substitute $K_n = K - K_\pi$ into (1) and solve for K_π.

$$K^2 - 2KK_\pi + K_\pi^2 + 2KE_{0n} - 2K_\pi E_{0n} = K_\pi^2 + 2K_\pi E_{0\pi}$$

$$2KK_\pi + 2K_\pi E_{0n} + 2K_\pi E_{0\pi} = 2KE_{0n} + K^2$$

$$2K_\pi(K + E_{0n} + E_{0\pi}) = K(K + 2E_{0n})$$

$$K_\pi = \frac{K(K + 2E_{0n})}{2(K + E_{0n} + E_{0\pi})}$$

$$= \frac{(m_\Lambda - m_n - m_\pi)c^2[(m_\Lambda - m_n - m_\pi)c^2 + 2m_n c^2]}{2[(m_\Lambda - m_n - m_\pi)c^2 + m_n c^2 + m_\pi c^2]}$$

$$= \frac{\begin{array}{c}(115.7 \text{ MeV} - 939.6 \text{ MeV} - 135.0 \text{ MeV})\times \\ [(1115.7 \text{ MeV} - 939.6 \text{ MeV} - 135.0 \text{ MeV}) + 2(939.6 \text{ MeV})]\end{array}}{2[(1115.7 \text{ MeV} - 939.6 \text{ MeV} - 135.0 \text{ MeV}) + 939.6 \text{ MeV} + 135.0 \text{ MeV}]}$$

$$= \boxed{35.4 \text{ MeV}}$$

Calculate K_n.

$$K_n = (1115.7 \text{ MeV} - 939.6 \text{ MeV} - 135.0 \text{ MeV}) - 35.4 \text{ MeV} = \boxed{5.7 \text{ MeV}}$$

Chapter 27

EARLY QUANTUM PHYSICS AND THE PHOTON

Problems

1. The energy of a photon with $\lambda = 0.70\ \mu m$ is

$$E = hf = \frac{hc}{\lambda} = \frac{1240\ eV \cdot nm}{7.0 \times 10^2\ nm} = \boxed{1.8\ eV}.$$

3. The minimum energy required to remove an electron from silver is called the work function for silver. The work function is related to the threshold frequency f_0 by $\phi = hf_0$.

$$\phi = hf_0 = 4.136 \times 10^{-15}\ eV \cdot s \times 1.04 \times 10^{15}\ Hz = \boxed{4.30\ eV}$$

5. (a) The threshold wavelength is $\lambda_0 = 288\ nm$. The work function is given by

$$\phi = hf_0 = \frac{hc}{\lambda_0} = \frac{1240\ eV \cdot nm}{288\ nm} = \boxed{4.31\ eV}.$$

(b) Calculate the maximum kinetic energy using Einstein's photoelectric equation.

$$K_{max} = hf - \phi = \frac{hc}{\lambda} - \phi = \frac{1240\ eV \cdot nm}{140\ nm} - 4.306\ eV = \boxed{4.6\ eV}$$

9. The frequency intercept gives the threshold frequency, so $f_0 = 43.9 \times 10^{13}\ Hz$. The stopping potential is related to the maximum kinetic energy of the ejected electrons by $K_{max} = eV_s$. Einstein's photoelectric equation is

$$K_{max} = hf - \phi,\ \text{so}\ V_s = \frac{hf}{e} - \frac{\phi}{e}.$$

(a) The slope of the graph is $m = h/e$. Find the slope.

$$m = \frac{1.50\ V - 0\ V}{80.0 \times 10^{13}\ Hz - 43.9 \times 10^{13}\ Hz} = 4.155 \times 10^{-15}\ V \cdot s$$

So Planck's constant is $h = em = (1.602 \times 10^{-19}\ C)(4.155 \times 10^{-15}\ V \cdot s) = \boxed{6.66 \times 10^{-34}\ J \cdot s}$.

(b) The work function ϕ is given by the stopping potential intercept $V_0 = -\phi/e$, where $V_s = mf + V_0$. $V_s = 0$ when $f = f_0$. Calculate ϕ_0.

$$0 = mf_0 - \frac{\phi}{e}$$

$$\phi = emf_0$$

$$= e(4.155 \times 10^{-15}\ V \cdot s)(43.9 \times 10^{13}\ Hz)$$

$$= \boxed{1.82\ eV}$$

11. The minimum potential difference is found by equating the energy of an x-ray photon and the electron's kinetic energy.

$$hf = K$$

$$\frac{hc}{\lambda} = eV_{min}$$

$$V_{min} = \frac{hc}{\lambda e} = \frac{1240 \text{ eV} \cdot \text{nm}}{0.250 \text{ nm} \cdot e} = \boxed{4.96 \text{ kV}}$$

13. The minimum wavelength can be found by equating the photon's energy and the electron's kinetic energy.

$$hf_{max} = K$$

$$\frac{hc}{\lambda_{min}} = eV$$

$$\lambda_{min} = \frac{hc}{eV}$$

$$= \frac{1240 \text{ eV} \cdot \text{nm}}{40.0 \times 10^3 \text{ eV}}$$

$$= \boxed{31 \text{ pm}}$$

17. (a) Calculate the Compton shift in wavelength.

$$\lambda' - \lambda = \frac{h}{m_e c}(1 - \cos\theta) = (2.43 \text{ pm})(1 - \cos 80.0°) = \boxed{2.01 \text{ pm}}$$

(b) $\lambda' - \lambda = \Delta\lambda$

$$\lambda' = \lambda + 2.01 \text{ pm}$$

$$= 150 \times 10^2 \text{ pm} + 2.01 \text{ pm} = \boxed{152 \text{ pm}}$$

21. The change in kinetic energy of the electron is the difference in the energies of the incident photon and the scattered photon.

$$K_e = E - E' = \frac{hc}{\lambda} - \frac{hc}{\lambda'} = \frac{1240 \text{ eV} \cdot \text{nm}}{0.0100 \text{ nm}} - \frac{1240 \text{ eV} \cdot \text{nm}}{0.0124 \text{ nm}} = \boxed{2.4 \times 10^4 \text{ eV}}$$

23. The orbital radius in the nth state is given by $r_n = n^2 a_0$.

$$r_3 = 3^2 \cdot 52.9 \text{ pm} = 476 \text{ pm} = \boxed{0.476 \text{ nm}}$$

25. The ground state energy is $E_1 = -13.6 \text{ eV}$. The energy of a hydrogen atom in the $n = 4$ state is

$$E_4 = \frac{E_1}{4^2} = \frac{-13.6 \text{ eV}}{16} = -0.850 \text{ eV}.$$

The difference between these two is the amount of energy needed to cause a transition from the ground state to the $n = 4$ state.

$$E_4 - E_1 = -0.850 \text{ eV} - (-13.6 \text{ eV}) = \boxed{12.8 \text{ eV}}$$

29. The minimum energy for an ionized atom is $E_{ionized} = 0$. The energy needed to ionize a hydrogen atom initially in the $n = 2$ state is

$$E = E_{ionized} - E_2 = E_{ionized} - \frac{E_1}{2^2} = 0 - \left(\frac{-13.6 \text{ eV}}{4}\right) = \boxed{3.40 \text{ eV}}.$$

31. The amount of energy released when a hydrogen atom makes a transition from the $n = 6$ to the $n = 3$ state is

$$E = E_6 - E_3 = \frac{-13.6 \text{ eV}}{6^2} - \frac{-13.6 \text{ eV}}{3^2} = 1.13 \text{ eV } (1.133 \text{ eV}).$$

The energy of a photon is related to its wavelength by $E = hf = \dfrac{hc}{\lambda}$.

So, $\lambda = \dfrac{hc}{E} = \dfrac{1240 \text{ eV} \cdot \text{nm}}{1.133 \text{ eV}} = \boxed{1.09 \text{ } \mu\text{m}}$.

33. **(a)** Use the classical kinetic energy.

$$K = \frac{1}{2} m_e v^2 = \frac{1}{2} m_e \left(\sqrt{\frac{ke^2}{m_e r}} \right)^2 = \frac{1}{2} m_e \frac{ke^2}{m_e r} = \boxed{\frac{ke^2}{2r}}$$

(b) $U = q_0 V$ gives the potential energy of the electron.

Here, $V = \dfrac{ke}{r}$ is the electric potential of the proton (a point charge), and q_0 is the charge on an electron.

The electric potential energy is $U = -e\left(\dfrac{ke}{r}\right) = \boxed{-\dfrac{ke^2}{r}}$.

(c) $E = K + U = \dfrac{ke^2}{2r} - \dfrac{ke^2}{r} = \dfrac{ke^2}{2r} - \dfrac{2ke^2}{2r} = -\dfrac{ke^2}{2r}$

(d) Substituting $r_n = \dfrac{n^2 \hbar^2}{mke^2}$ into the result for part (c) gives the result.

$$E = \frac{-ke^2}{2\frac{n^2\hbar^2}{mke^2}} = -\frac{mk^2e^4}{2n^2\hbar^2}$$

37. The Bohr equation for angular momentum is

$m_e v r_n = n\hbar.$

Solving for v with $n = 1$ gives

$$v = \frac{\hbar}{m_e r_1} = \frac{h}{2\pi m_e r_1}.$$

In this case, r_1 is the radius of the ground state of singly-ionized helium. The atomic number for helium is $Z = 2$. The orbital radii equation is

$$r_n = \frac{n^2}{Z} a_0.$$

For the ground state of He$^+$, $n = 1$ and $Z = 2$.

$$r_1 = \frac{1^2}{2} a_0 = \frac{a_0}{2}$$

Substituting this value of r_1 into the speed equation gives the result.

$$v = \frac{h}{\pi m_e a_0} = \frac{6.626 \times 10^{-34} \text{ J} \cdot \text{s}}{\pi \times 9.11 \times 10^{-31} \text{ kg} \times 5.29 \times 10^{-11} \text{ m}} = \boxed{4.38 \times 10^6 \text{ m/s}}$$

41. (a) A photon with the longest wavelength will have the least energy. The transition from the $n = 4$ state to the $n = 3$ state will release the least energy.

$$E = E_4 - E_3 = \frac{E_1}{4^2} - \frac{E_1}{3^2} = \frac{-13.60 \text{ eV}}{16} - \frac{-13.60 \text{ eV}}{9} = 0.6611 \text{ eV}$$

Calculate the wavelength.

$$E = hf = \frac{hc}{\lambda}, \text{ so } \lambda = \frac{hc}{E} = \frac{(6.626 \times 10^{-34} \text{ J} \cdot \text{s})\left(2.998 \times 10^8 \frac{\text{m}}{\text{s}}\right)}{(0.6611 \text{ eV})\left(\frac{1.602 \times 10^{-19} \text{ J}}{\text{eV}}\right)} = \boxed{1876 \text{ nm}}.$$

(b) The energy released by a transition from the $n = \infty$ state to the $n = 3$ state is

$$E = 0 - \frac{-13.60 \text{ eV}}{3^2} = 1.511 \text{ eV}.$$

The wavelength of a photon with this energy is

$$\lambda = \frac{hc}{E} = \frac{(6.626 \times 10^{-34} \text{ J} \cdot \text{s})\left(2.998 \times 10^8 \frac{\text{m}}{\text{s}}\right)}{(1.511 \text{ eV})\left(\frac{1.602 \times 10^{-19} \text{ J}}{\text{eV}}\right)} = \boxed{820.6 \text{ nm}}.$$

(c) The range of wavelengths from 820.6 nm to 1876 nm is in the $\boxed{\text{IR}}$ (infrared) part of the EM spectrum.

43. For a photon, the maximum wavelength corresponds to the minimum energy. The minimum energy needed is just the rest energy of an electron-positron pair.

$$E = 2m_e c^2 = 2 \times 9.109 \times 10^{-31} \text{ kg} \times \left(3.00 \times 10^8 \frac{\text{m}}{\text{s}}\right)^2 = 1.64 \times 10^{-13} \text{ J}$$

The wavelength of a photon is related to its energy by

$$E = hf = \frac{hc}{\lambda}.$$

Solving for λ gives the result.

$$\lambda = \frac{hc}{E} = \frac{6.626 \times 10^{-34} \text{ J} \cdot \text{s} \times 3.00 \times 10^8 \frac{\text{m}}{\text{s}}}{1.64 \times 10^{-13} \text{ J}} = \boxed{1.21 \text{ pm}}$$

45. The rest energies of the electron and positron are converted into the combined energy of the two photons. The energies of the photons are the same, since the frequencies of the photons are identical. Thus, the energy of each photon will equal the rest energy of an electron.

$$E = m_e c^2 = 511 \text{ keV}$$

The energy of a photon is related to its wavelength by

$$E = hf = \frac{hc}{\lambda}.$$

So, $\lambda = \dfrac{hc}{E} = \dfrac{1240 \text{ eV} \cdot \text{nm}}{511 \times 10^3 \text{ eV}} = 0.00243 \text{ nm} = \boxed{2.43 \text{ pm}}.$

49. (a) The energy of each photon is equal to $E = hf$.

$$E = (6.626 \times 10^{-34} \text{ J} \cdot \text{s})(89.3 \times 10^6 \text{ Hz})\left(\frac{1 \text{ eV}}{1.602 \times 10^{-19} \text{ J}}\right) = \boxed{3.69 \times 10^{-7} \text{ eV}}.$$

(b) The ratio of the total radiated power to the energy per photon is the rate of photons emitted.

$$\frac{P}{E} = \frac{50.0 \times 10^3 \text{ W}}{\frac{(6.626 \times 10^{-34} \text{ J} \cdot \text{s})(89.3 \times 10^6 \text{ Hz})}{1 \text{ photon}}} = \boxed{8.45 \times 10^{29} \text{ photons/s}}$$

53. After the collision the electron recoils in the direction of motion of the incident photon. Its motion has no component perpendicular to the motion of the incident photon. Conservation of momentum requires the scattering angle must be 180°. Solving the Compton shift formula for λ gives

$$\lambda' - \lambda = \frac{h}{m_e c}(1 - \cos\theta)$$

$$\lambda = \lambda' - \frac{h}{m_e c}(1 - \cos 180°)$$
$$= \lambda' - 2(2.43 \text{ pm})$$
$$= \lambda' - 4.86 \text{ pm}$$

The kinetic energy of the electron is

$$K_e = E - E' = \frac{hc}{\lambda} - \frac{hc}{\lambda'}.$$

Substituting $\lambda = \lambda' - 4.86$ pm and $K_e = 0.20$ keV, and solving for λ' gives the wavelength of the scattered x-ray.

$$\frac{K_e}{hc} = \frac{1}{\lambda' - 4.86 \text{ pm}} - \frac{1}{\lambda'}$$

$$\frac{0.20 \times 10^3 \text{ eV}}{1240 \text{ eV} \cdot \text{nm} \times 1000 \text{ pm/nm}} = \frac{1}{\lambda' - 4.86 \text{ pm}} - \frac{1}{\lambda'}$$

$$(1.613 \times 10^{-4} \text{ pm}^{-1})(\lambda' - 4.86 \text{ pm})\lambda' = \lambda' - (\lambda' - 4.86 \text{ pm})$$

$$\lambda'^2 - (4.86 \text{ pm})\lambda' = 3.01 \times 10^4 \text{ pm}^2$$

$$\lambda'^2 - (4.86 \text{ pm})\lambda' - 3.01 \times 10^4 \text{ pm}^2 = 0$$

Solve for λ' using the quadratic formula.

$$\lambda' = \frac{4.86 \text{ pm} \pm \sqrt{(-4.86 \text{ pm})^2 - 4 \cdot 1 \cdot (-3.01 \times 10^4 \text{ pm}^2)}}{2 \cdot 1} = \boxed{176 \text{ pm}} \text{ or } -171 \text{ pm, which is extraneous.}$$

The wavelength of the incident x-ray can now be calculated.

$$\lambda = \lambda' - 4.86 \text{ pm} = 176 \text{ pm} - 4.86 \text{ pm} = \boxed{171 \text{ pm}}$$

57. **(a)** The work function for sodium is found from Einstein's photoelectric equation.

$$K_{\max} = hf - \phi$$
$$\phi = hf - K_{\max}$$
$$\phi = \frac{hc}{\lambda} - eV_s$$

Now substitute $\lambda = 570$ nm and $V_s = 0.28$ V.

$$\phi = \frac{1240 \text{ eV} \cdot \text{nm}}{570 \text{ nm}} - 0.28 \text{ eV} = 1.9 \text{ eV}$$

The stopping potential for $\lambda = 400.0$ nm is

$$eV_s = hf - \phi$$
$$V_s = \frac{hc}{e} \cdot \frac{1}{\lambda} - \frac{\phi}{e}$$
$$= \frac{1240 \text{ eV} \cdot \text{nm}}{e \cdot 400.0 \text{ nm}} - 1.9 \text{ V} = \boxed{1.2 \text{ V}}$$

(b) The stopping potential does not depend upon the intensity of the light, so it is still $\boxed{0.28 \text{ V}}$.

(c) $\phi = \boxed{1.9 \text{ eV}}$ as found in part (a).

61. The minimum wavelength corresponds to the maximum frequency, which occurs when the energy of the photon is equal to the electron's kinetic energy.

$$hf_{max} = K_e$$

$$\frac{hc}{\lambda_{min}} = eV$$

Solving for V and using $\lambda_{min} = 45.0 \text{ pm} = 45.0\times10^{-3} \text{ nm}$ gives the result.

$$V = \frac{hc}{e\lambda_{min}} = \frac{1240 \text{ eV}\cdot\text{nm}}{e\times45.0\times10^{-3} \text{ nm}} = \boxed{27.6 \text{ kV}}$$

65. (a) The momentum of the atom must equal the momentum of the incident photon.

$$p_H = p_{photon}$$

$$m_H v = \frac{h}{\lambda}$$

$$v = \frac{h}{m_H\lambda} = \frac{6.626\times10^{-34} \text{ J}\cdot\text{s}}{1.673\times10^{-27} \text{ kg}\times97\times10^{-9} \text{ m}} = \boxed{4.1 \text{ m/s}}$$

(b) The energy of the incident photon is

$$E = \frac{hc}{\lambda} = \frac{1240 \text{ eV}\cdot\text{nm}}{97 \text{ nm}} = 12.8 \text{ eV}$$

This energy corresponds to a transition from the $n = 1$ state to the $n = 4$ state.

$$E = |E_1| - \frac{|E_1|}{4^2} = 13.6 \text{ eV} - 0.85 \text{ eV} = 12.8 \text{ eV}$$

The transition from the $n = 4$ state back to the $n = 1$ state can occur in 4 ways emitting six different photons: $4 \to 1, 4 \to 2 \to 1, 4 \to 3 \to 1,$ and $4 \to 3 \to 2 \to 1.$

(c) There are six photons possible. The wavelengths are given by

$$\lambda = \frac{1}{R\left(\frac{1}{n_f^2} - \frac{1}{n_i^2}\right)} = \frac{1}{(1.097\times10^7 \text{ m}^{-1})\left(\frac{1}{n_f^2} - \frac{1}{n_i^2}\right)}.$$

The classifications are UV for $\lambda < 400$ nm, visible for $400 \text{ nm} \le \lambda \le 700$ nm, and IR for $\lambda > 700$ nm. The results are given in the table below.

Transition	λ (nm)	Class
$4 \to 3$	1875	IR
$4 \to 2$	486	visible
$4 \to 1$	97	UV
$3 \to 2$	656	visible
$3 \to 1$	103	UV
$2 \to 1$	122	UV

69. The minimum wavelength corresponds to the maximum frequency, which occurs when the photon's energy equals the kinetic energy of the electron.

$$hf_{max} = K_e$$

$$\frac{hc}{\lambda_{min}} = K_e$$

$$\lambda_{min} = \frac{hc}{K_e} = \frac{1240 \text{ eV} \cdot \text{nm}}{2.0 \times 10^3 \text{ eV}} = \boxed{0.62 \text{ nm}}$$

73. **(a)** The *Balmer series* ($n_f = 2$) gives visible wavelengths. The wavelengths are given by

$$\lambda = \frac{1}{(1.097 \times 10^7 \text{ m}^{-1})\left(\frac{1}{2^2} - \frac{1}{n_i^2}\right)}.$$

$n_i = 3$ gives 656.3 nm and $n_i = 4$ gives 486.2 nm, both of which are visible. So, the incident radiation excites the ground-state atoms into the $n = 4$ state. The energy difference between these states is equal to the energy of the incident radiation.

$$\Delta E = E_4 - E_1 = E_1\left(\frac{1}{4^2} - 1\right) = (-13.6 \text{ eV})\left(\frac{1}{16} - 1\right) = 12.75 \text{ eV}$$

Calculate the wavelength.

$$\lambda = \frac{hc}{E} = \frac{1240 \text{ eV} \cdot \text{nm}}{12.75 \text{ eV}} = \boxed{97.3 \text{ nm}}$$

(b) Since $\lambda \propto \frac{1}{E_{photon}}$, the longest wavelength corresponds to the smallest energy for the incident radiation. So,

the incident radiation must excite the ground-state atom to its $n = 3$ state for visible light to be emitted. Calculate the wavelength of the incident radiation.

$$\lambda = \frac{1}{R\left(1 - \frac{1}{3^2}\right)} = \frac{1}{(1.097 \times 10^7 \text{ m}^{-1})\left(1 - \frac{1}{9}\right)} = \boxed{102.6 \text{ nm}}$$

As found in part (a), the wavelength of the emitted radiation for the $n = 3$ to the $n = 2$ state is $\boxed{656.3 \text{ nm}}$.

(c) The incident photon must be energetic enough to excite an electron from any finite state to $n_f = \infty$. The case where the electron is in the ground state, $n_i = 1$, represents the minimum energy required, 13.6 eV.

$$E \geq 13.6 \text{ eV}$$

$$\frac{hc}{\lambda} \geq 13.6 \text{ eV}$$

$$\lambda \leq \frac{1240 \text{ eV} \cdot \text{nm}}{13.6 \text{ eV}}$$

$$\boxed{\lambda \leq 91.2 \text{ nm}}$$

Chapter 28

QUANTUM PHYSICS

Problems

1. $\lambda = \dfrac{h}{p} = \dfrac{h}{mv} = \dfrac{6.626\times10^{-34}\ \text{J}\cdot\text{s}}{0.50\ \text{kg}\times10\,\frac{\text{m}}{\text{s}}} = \boxed{1\times10^{-34}\ \text{m}}$

$\boxed{\text{The wavelength is much too small compared to the diameter of the hoop}}$ for any appreciable diffraction to occur—for a diameter of ~ 1 m, its a factor 10^{-34} smaller!

3. (a) The electron's kinetic energy is small compared to its rest energy, so the electron is nonrelativistic, and we can use $p = mv$ and $K = \dfrac{1}{2}mv^2$. First solve for v in terms of K.

$$K = \frac{1}{2}mv^2$$

$$v^2 = \frac{2K}{m}$$

$$v = \sqrt{\frac{2K}{m}}$$

The momentum is then

$$p = mv = m\sqrt{\frac{2K}{m}} = \sqrt{2Km}.$$

Calculate the de Broglie wavelength.

$$\lambda = \frac{h}{p} = \frac{h}{\sqrt{2Km}} = \frac{6.626\times10^{-34}\ \text{J}\cdot\text{s}}{\sqrt{2\times1.0\ \text{eV}\times1.6\times10^{-19}\,\frac{\text{J}}{\text{eV}}\times9.11\times10^{-31}\ \text{kg}}} = \boxed{1.2\ \text{nm}}$$

(b) This electron is also nonrelativistic. The wavelength is

$$\lambda = \frac{6.626\times10^{-34}\ \text{J}\cdot\text{s}}{\sqrt{2\times1.0\times10^3\,\text{eV}\times1.6\times10^{-19}\,\frac{\text{J}}{\text{eV}}\times9.11\times10^{-31}\ \text{kg}}} = \boxed{39\ \text{pm}}.$$

5. Find the electron's momentum in terms of its de Broglie wavelength.

$$p = \frac{h}{\lambda} = \frac{6.626\times10^{-34}\ \text{J}\cdot\text{s}}{0.40\times10^{-9}\ \text{m}} = \boxed{1.7\times10^{-24}\ \text{kg}\cdot\text{m/s}}$$

9. (a) The neutrons are nonrelativistic. Calculate the wavelength range.

$$\lambda_{\text{min}} = \frac{h}{p} = \frac{h}{mv} = \frac{6.626\times10^{-34}\ \text{J}\cdot\text{s}}{1.675\times10^{-27}\ \text{kg}\times2.0\times10^4\,\frac{\text{m}}{\text{s}}} = 2.0\times10^{-11}\ \text{m}$$

For $v = 0$, λ_{max} is infinite.

For neutrons between 0 and 2.0×10^4 m/s, the de Broglie wavelengths are $\lambda \geq 2.0\times10^{-11}$ m.
Solving Equation (25-15) for λ, and using $\theta = 10.0°$, $d = 0.20$ nm, and $m = 1, 2, 3,$ and 4 gives

$$2d \sin \theta = m\lambda$$

$$\lambda = \frac{2d \sin \theta}{m}$$

$$\lambda_1 = \frac{2 \times 0.20 \times 10^{-9} \text{ m} \times \sin 10.0°}{1} = 6.9 \times 10^{-11} \text{ m}$$

$$\lambda_2 = \frac{2 \times 0.20 \times 10^{-9} \text{ m} \times \sin 10.0°}{2} = 3.5 \times 10^{-11} \text{ m}$$

$$\lambda_3 = \frac{2 \times 0.20 \times 10^{-9} \text{ m} \times \sin 10.0°}{3} = 2.3 \times 10^{-11} \text{ m}$$

$$\lambda_4 = \frac{2 \times 0.20 \times 10^{-9} \text{ m} \times \sin 10.0°}{3} = 1.7 \times 10^{-11} \text{ m}$$

Of these wavelengths, only λ_1, λ_2, and λ_3 are greater than $\lambda_{\min}$. The strongly reflected wavelengths are 69 pm, 35 pm, and 23 pm.

(b) The reflected beam is at the same angle with respect to the planes as the incident beam, 10.0°. The incident beam is directed at 10.0° below the plane and the reflected beam is 10.0° above the plane, so the angle of emergence with respect to the incident beam is 10.0° + 10.0° = 20.0° for all three wavelengths.

13. **(a)** Substitute $p = mv$ into the equation for the deBroglie wavelength and solve for v.

$$\lambda = \frac{h}{p}$$

$$\lambda = \frac{h}{mv}$$

$$v = \frac{h}{m\lambda}$$

Calculate the kinetic energy.

$$K = \frac{1}{2}mv^2$$

$$= \frac{1}{2}m\frac{h^2}{m^2\lambda^2}$$

$$= \frac{h^2}{2m\lambda^2}$$

$$= \frac{(6.626 \times 10^{-34} \text{ J} \cdot \text{s})^2}{2 \times 9.11 \times 10^{-31} \text{ kg} \times (5.0 \times 10^{-9} \text{ m})^2} \times \frac{1 \text{ eV}}{1.60 \times 10^{-19} \text{ J}}$$

$$= \boxed{0.060 \text{ eV}}$$

The kinetic energy is small compared to the rest energy of an electron, so the electrons are nonrelativistic. The use of nonrelativistic equations for p and K in the preceding derivation was justified.

(b) The kinetic energy of the electrons is related to the potential difference by $K = eV$.

$$V = \frac{K}{e} = \frac{0.060 \text{ eV}}{e} = \boxed{0.060 \text{ V}}$$

(c) A light microscope using 5-nm light would be rather impractical, since a wavelength of 5 nm is an x-ray wavelength.

15. The fractional uncertainty in the momentum is

$$\frac{\Delta p}{p} = 10^{-6}.$$

$$\Delta p = p \cdot 10^{-6} = mv \cdot 10^{-6} = 0.50 \text{ kg} \times 10\frac{\text{m}}{\text{s}} \times 10^{-6} = 5 \times 10^{-6} \text{ kg} \cdot \text{m/s}$$

The uncertainty in the basketball's position is found using the uncertainty principle.

$$\Delta x \cdot \Delta p \geq \frac{\hbar}{2}$$

$$\Delta x \geq \frac{\hbar}{2\Delta p} = \frac{6.626 \times 10^{-34} \text{ J} \cdot \text{s}}{4\pi \times 5 \times 10^{-6} \frac{\text{kg} \cdot \text{m}}{\text{s}}} = \boxed{1 \times 10^{-29} \text{ m}}$$

17. The single-slit diffraction minima are given by $a \sin\theta = m\lambda$.
The central fringe corresponds to $m = 1$. Using the small angle approximations $\theta \approx \tan\theta = x/D$ and

$\theta \approx \sin\theta = \frac{\lambda}{a}$, the equation becomes $\lambda = ax/D$, where x is half the width of the central fringe and D is the

distance from the slit to the screen. The wavelength of an electron can also be expressed as $\lambda = h/p$. Equate these two wavelengths and solve for p.

$$\frac{h}{p} = \frac{ax}{D}$$

$$p = \frac{Dh}{ax}$$

Now substitute $p = \sqrt{2Km_e}$ and solve for K.

$$\sqrt{2Km_e} = \frac{Dh}{ax}$$

$$2Km_e = \frac{D^2 h^2}{a^2 x^2}$$

$$K = \frac{D^2 h^2}{2a^2 x^2 m_e}$$

$$= \frac{(1.0 \text{ m})^2 \times (6.626 \times 10^{-34} \text{ J} \cdot \text{s})^2}{2 \times (40.0 \times 10^{-9} \text{ m})^2 \times (0.031 \text{ m})^2 \times 9.11 \times 10^{-31} \text{ kg}} \times \frac{1 \text{ eV}}{1.6 \times 10^{-19} \text{ J}}$$

$$= \boxed{0.98 \text{ eV}}$$

19. (a) The uncertainty of the x-component of the electron's position is $\Delta x = 0.05$ nm. The uncertainty in the x-component of the momentum is given by the uncertainty principle.

$$\Delta x \Delta p \geq \frac{\hbar}{2}$$

$$\Delta x \geq \frac{\hbar}{2\Delta p} = \frac{6.626 \times 10^{-34} \text{ J} \cdot \text{s}}{4\pi \times 0.05 \times 10^{-9} \text{ m}} = \boxed{1 \times 10^{-24} \text{ kg} \cdot \text{m/s}}$$

(b) $K = \frac{1}{2}mv^2 = \frac{m^2v^2}{2m} = \frac{p^2}{2m}$, so

$$K = \frac{p^2}{2m} = \frac{\left(1.055 \times 10^{-24}\ \frac{\text{kg} \cdot \text{m}}{\text{s}}\right)^2}{2 \times 9.11 \times 10^{-31}\ \text{kg}} \times \frac{1\ \text{eV}}{1.6 \times 10^{-19}\ \text{J}} = \boxed{4\ \text{eV}}.$$

(c) $\boxed{\text{Yes}}$; 13.6/4 = 3.4, so the estimate is reasonable.

21. Use the energy-time uncertainty principle to find ΔE.

$$\Delta E \Delta t \geq \frac{\hbar}{2}$$

$$\Delta E \geq \frac{\hbar}{2\Delta t}$$

$$\approx \frac{1 \times 10^{-34}\ \text{J} \cdot \text{s}}{2 \times 0.1 \times 10^{-9}\ \text{s}} = 5 \times 10^{-25}\ \text{J}$$

Calculate the fractional uncertainty.

$$\frac{\Delta E}{E} \approx \frac{5 \times 10^{-25}\ \text{J} \times \frac{1\ \text{eV}}{1.6 \times 10^{-19}\ \text{J}}}{1672 \times 10^6\ \text{eV}} = \boxed{2 \times 10^{-15}}$$

25. The momentum is given by $p_n = \frac{h}{\lambda_n} = \frac{nh}{2L}$.

Set $n = 4$.

$$p_4 = \frac{4h}{2L} = \frac{2h}{L} = \frac{2 \times 6.626 \times 10^{-34}\ \text{J} \cdot \text{s}}{1.0 \times 10^{-9}\ \text{m}} = \boxed{1.3 \times 10^{-24}\ \text{kg} \cdot \text{m/s}}$$

27. (a) Calculate the wavelength.

$$\lambda = \frac{hc}{E} = \frac{hc}{E_2 - E_1} = \frac{hc}{2^2 E_1 - E_1} = \frac{hc}{3E_1} = \frac{1240\ \text{eV} \cdot \text{nm}}{3(40.0\ \text{eV})} = \boxed{10.3\ \text{nm}}$$

(b) Since $E \propto \frac{1}{L^2}$, doubling the length of the box would reduce the energy to $\boxed{\text{one fourth as much}}$ as before.

29. (a) The graphs are the same as those in Figure 28.11, with $L = 10$ cm.

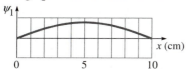

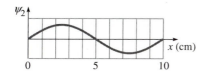

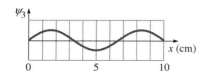

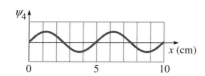

(b) Find the energy difference between the ground state and the first excited state.

$$\Delta E = E_2 - E_1 = n^2 E_1 - E_1 = (2^2 - 1)E_1 = 3E_1$$

$E_1 = \dfrac{h^2}{8mL^2}$ for a particle in a box, so

$$\Delta E = \frac{3h^2}{8mL^2} = \frac{3(6.626\times10^{-34}\ \text{J}\cdot\text{s})^2}{8(9.109\times10^{-31}\ \text{kg})(0.1\ \text{m})^2} \times \frac{1\ \text{eV}}{1.602\times10^{-19}\ \text{J}} = \boxed{1\times10^{-16}\ \text{eV}}.$$

31. (a) The figure below shows the wave function for the $n = 5$ state of an electron in a finite box of length L.

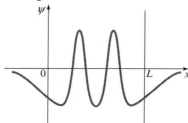

(b) Assume that the energy is the same as that for an infinite box, $E_n = \dfrac{n^2 h^2}{8mL^2}$. Solve for n.

$$n = \sqrt{\frac{8mL^2 E_n}{h^2}} = \sqrt{\frac{8(9.11\times10^{-31}\ \text{kg})(1.0\times10^{-9}\ \text{m})^2(1.0\times10^3\ \text{eV})}{(6.626\times10^{-34}\ \text{J}\cdot\text{s})^2\left(\frac{1\ \text{eV}}{1.6\times10^{-19}\ \text{J}}\right)}} = 51.5$$

$n = 52$ would give an energy greater than U_0, so there are approximately $\boxed{51}$ bound states.

33. There are $4l + 2$ electron states in a subshell. Since $l = 1$, there are $4(1) + 2 = \boxed{6}$ electron states. Since $l = 1$, $m_l = -1, 0,$ and $1,$ and for each m_l, $m_s = +\dfrac{1}{2}$ and $-\dfrac{1}{2}$. The states are given in the table below.

n	3	3	3	3	3	3
l	1	1	1	1	1	1
m_l	−1	−1	0	0	1	1
m_s	$-\dfrac{1}{2}$	$+\dfrac{1}{2}$	$-\dfrac{1}{2}$	$+\dfrac{1}{2}$	$-\dfrac{1}{2}$	$+\dfrac{1}{2}$

37. Since $n = 7$, l can have values from 0 to 6. For each value of l, there are $2(2l + 1)$ states. So, $\boxed{\text{for } l = 0, 1, 2, 3, 4, 5,}$ $\boxed{\text{and } 6, \text{ there are } 2, 6, 10, 14, 18, 22, \text{ and } 26 \text{ electron states, respectively}}$. The total is $\boxed{98}$.

39. Nickel has atomic number 28, so it has 28 electrons in a neutral atom. It does not appear on the list of exceptions, so the ground state electron configuration is

$$\boxed{1s^2 2s^2 2p^6 3s^2 3p^6 4s^2 3d^8}.$$

41. (a) Fluorine and chlorine have 9 and 17 electrons in a neutral atom, respectively. Neither of these elements appears in the list of exceptions. The ground state electron configurations are

$$\boxed{\begin{aligned} &\text{F: } 1s^2 2s^2 2p^5 \\ &\text{Cl: } 1s^2 2s^2 2p^6 3s^2 3p^5 \end{aligned}}$$

(b) Both neutral atoms have valence −1. Their outermost electrons are in the $\boxed{p^5 \text{ subshell}}$.

45. Stimulated emission can occur between the energy levels 20.66 eV and 18.70 eV. The associated wavelength is

$$\lambda = \frac{hc}{\Delta E} = \frac{1240 \text{ eV} \cdot \text{nm}}{20.66 \text{ eV} - 18.70 \text{ eV}} = \boxed{633 \text{ nm}}.$$

49. (a) The tunneling probability is proportional to $e^{-2\kappa a}$, where

$$\kappa = \sqrt{\frac{2m}{\hbar^2}(U_0 - E)}.$$

$\kappa \propto \sqrt{m}$ and $e^{-2\kappa a}$ is greater for smaller κ. So, the particle with the smaller mass has the higher tunneling probability. That particle is the $\boxed{\text{proton}}$.

(b) $\dfrac{P_p}{P_d} = \dfrac{e^{-2\kappa_p a}}{e^{-2\kappa_d a}} = e^{2a(\kappa_d - \kappa_p)}$, where $a = 10.0$ fm and $\kappa_d - \kappa_p$ is

$$\sqrt{\dfrac{2m_d}{\hbar^2}(U_0 - E)} - \sqrt{\dfrac{2m_p}{\hbar^2}(U_0 - E)} = \sqrt{\dfrac{2}{\hbar^2}(U_0 - E)}\left(\sqrt{2.0m_p} - \sqrt{m_p}\right) = \left(\sqrt{2.0} - 1\right)\sqrt{\dfrac{2m_p}{\hbar^2}(U_0 - E)}$$

Calculate the probability ratio.

$$\dfrac{P_p}{P_d} = e^{2(10.0\times10^{-15}\ \text{m})\left(\sqrt{2.0}-1\right)\sqrt{\frac{8\pi^2(1.673\times10^{-27}\ \text{kg})}{(6.626\times10^{-34}\ \text{J}\cdot\text{s})^2}(10.0\ \text{MeV}-3.0\ \text{MeV})\left(\frac{1.602\times10^{-13}\ \text{J}}{1\ \text{MeV}}\right)}}$$

$$\boxed{\dfrac{P_p}{P_d} = 120}$$

53. For a neutron, $E_n^2 = E_0^2 + p_n^2 c^2$, and for a photon, $E_\gamma = p_\gamma c$.

The de Broglie wavelength is given by $\lambda = \dfrac{h}{p}$, and since $\lambda_n = \lambda_\gamma$, $p_n = p_\gamma$.

Solve each energy equation for momentum and set the momenta equal.

$$\dfrac{\sqrt{E_n^2 - E_0^2}}{c} = \dfrac{E_\gamma}{c}$$

$$E_n^2 - E_0^2 = E_\gamma^2$$

Now, for a neutron,

$$K_n = E_n - E_0$$
$$E_n = K_n + E_0$$

Substitute.

$$(K_n + E_0)^2 - E_0^2 = E_\gamma^2$$
$$K_n^2 + 2K_n E_0 - E_\gamma^2 = 0$$

Set $K_n = E_\gamma$ and solve for E_γ.

$$E_\gamma^2 + 2E_\gamma E_0 - E_\gamma^2 = 0$$
$$2E_\gamma E_0 = 0$$
$$E_\gamma = 0$$

So, $E_\gamma = K_n = 0$ is the only case that $E_\gamma = K_n$, which implies that the neutron is motionless and the photon does not exist! Therefore, the answer is $\boxed{\text{no}}$, it is not possible that the energy of each photon is equal to the kinetic energy of each neutron if $\lambda_n = \lambda_\gamma$.

57. The wavelength of the electrons must equal the wavelength of the photons to give the same diffraction pattern.

$$\lambda_{\text{ph}} = \lambda_{\text{e}}$$

$$\frac{hc}{E} = \frac{h}{\sqrt{2Km}}$$

$$2Km = \frac{E^2}{c^2}$$

$$K = \frac{E^2}{2mc^2}$$

$$= \frac{(2.0 \text{ eV})^2}{2 \times 511 \times 10^3 \text{ eV}}$$

$$= \boxed{3.9 \times 10^{-6} \text{ eV}}$$

61. Calculate the ratio of the ground states.

$$\frac{E_{2L}}{E_{1L}} = \frac{\frac{h^2}{8m(2L)^2}}{\frac{h^2}{8mL^2}} = \boxed{\frac{1}{4}}$$

65. The energy-time uncertainty principle is $\Delta E \Delta t \geq \frac{1}{2}\hbar$.

Calculate the minimum uncertainty in the energy.

$$(\Delta E)_{\text{min}} = \frac{\hbar}{2\Delta t} = \frac{6.626 \times 10^{-34} \text{ J} \cdot \text{s}}{4\pi \times 15 \times 60 \text{ s}} = 5.86 \times 10^{-38} \text{ J}$$

$E_0 = mc^2$, so the inherent uncertainty in the mass of the free electron is

$$\Delta m = \frac{5.86 \times 10^{-38} \text{ J}}{\left(3.0 \times 10^8 \frac{\text{m}}{\text{s}}\right)^2} = \boxed{6.5 \times 10^{-55} \text{ kg}}.$$

$$\frac{6.5 \times 10^{-55} \text{ kg}}{1.67 \times 10^{-27} \text{ kg}} = 3.9 \times 10^{-28}$$

So, $\boxed{\dfrac{\Delta m}{m} = 3.9 \times 10^{-28}}$.

Chapter 29

NUCLEAR PHYSICS

Problems

1. Calculate the mass density of a nucleus with mass number A using $r = r_0 A^{1/3}$.

$$\rho = \frac{M}{V} = \frac{M}{\frac{4}{3}\pi r^3} = \frac{A\,u}{\frac{4}{3}\pi(r_0 A^{1/3})^3} = \frac{1\,u}{\frac{4}{3}\pi r_0^3} = \frac{1.66\times10^{-27}\ \text{kg}}{\frac{4}{3}\pi(1.2\times10^{-15}\ \text{m})^3} = \boxed{2.3\times10^{17}\ \text{kg/m}^3}$$

3. $Z = $ # of protons $= 38$; the element is Sr.
   $N = $ # of neutrons $= 50$
   Find the nucleon number.
   $A = Z + N = 38 + 50 = 88$

   So, the symbol is $\boxed{{}^{88}_{38}\text{Sr}}$.

5. Cl has atomic number 17, so $Z = 17$. The nucleon number is 35.
   So, $N = A - Z = 35 - 17 = \boxed{18}$ neutrons.

9. The ${}^4\text{He}$ nucleus has 2 protons and 2 neutrons. The mass defect is
   $\Delta m = $ (mass of 2 protons and 2 neutrons) $-$ (mass of nucleus)
   $\qquad = 2\times1.0072765\ \text{u} + 2\times1.0086649\ \text{u} - 4.00151\ \text{u}$
   $\qquad = 0.03037\ \text{u}$
   The binding energy is
   $$E_B = \Delta mc^2 = 0.03037\ \text{u} \times 931.494\ \text{MeV/u} = \boxed{28.29\ \text{MeV}}$$

13. The ${}^{31}_{15}\text{P}$ atom has 15 protons and 16 neutrons. Its mass is 30.973762 u. The mass defect is

    $\Delta m = $ (mass of 15 ${}^1\text{H}$ atoms and 16 neutrons) $-$ (mass of ${}^{31}_{15}\text{P}$ atom)
    $\qquad = 15\times1.007825\ \text{u} + 16\times1.0086649\ \text{u} - 30.973762\ \text{u}$
    $\qquad = 0.282251\ \text{u}$
    The binding energy per nucleon is
    $$\frac{E_B}{A} = \frac{\Delta mc^2}{A} = \frac{0.2822514\ \text{u} \times 931.494\ \text{MeV/u}}{31\ \text{nucleons}} = \boxed{8.48114\ \text{MeV/nucleon}}$$

17. **(a)** Calculate the mass defect using $E_B = \Delta mc^2$.

    $$\Delta m = \frac{E_B}{c^2} = \frac{13.6\ \text{eV}}{931.494\times10^6\ \text{eV/u}} = \boxed{1.46\times10^{-8}\ \text{u}}$$

    (b) The ratio of this mass defect to the mass of the electron is $\dfrac{1.46\times10^{-8}\ \text{u}}{5.49\times10^{-4}\ \text{u}} = 2.7\times10^{-5}$. This is small enough to

    be ignored. There is $\boxed{\text{no}}$ reason to worry when calculating the mass of the ${}^1\text{H}$ nucleus, especially since its mass is 1836 times that of the electron.

19. In beta-minus decay (29-11), the atomic number Z increases by 1 while the mass number A remains constant. For the parent $\left(^{40}_{19}K\right)$ $Z = 19$, so the daughter nuclide will have $Z = 19 + 1 = 20$, which is the element Ca. The symbol for the daughter is $\boxed{^{40}_{20}Ca}$.

21. In electron-capture decay, the atomic number Z is decreased by 1 while the mass number A stays the same. In this case, $Z = 11$ and $A = 22$ for the parent $\left(^{22}_{11}Na\right)$, so the daughter will have $Z = 10$ and $A = 22$, which is Ne. The symbol is $\boxed{^{22}_{10}Ne}$.

25. The neutron to proton ratio is $\dfrac{31-14}{14} = 1.2$. This ratio is low, so we would expect that the nuclide has too many neutrons. Also, stable isotopes of silicon have fewer neutrons than $^{31}_{14}Si$, so the expected decay should convert a neutron into a proton. $\boxed{\beta^-}$ decay has the desired effect.

27. In Problem 19, the daughter nuclide in this decay was found to be $^{40}_{20}Ca$. The reaction is

$$^{40}_{19}K \rightarrow \,^{40}_{20}Ca + \,^{0}_{-1}e + \bar{\nu}$$

The atomic masses of $^{40}_{19}K$ and $^{40}_{20}Ca$ are 39.963999 u and 39.962591 u, respectively. To get the masses of the nuclei, we subtract Zm_e from each. The masses of the electron is 0.0005486 u, and the neutrino's mass is negligible. The mass difference is
$$\Delta m = [(M_{Ca} - 20m_e) + m_e] - (M_K - 19m_e) = M_{Ca} - M_K = 39.962591\ u - 39.963999\ u = -0.001408\ u$$
The disintegration energy is
$$E = |\Delta m|c^2 = 0.001408\ u \times 931.494\ MeV/u = \boxed{1.312\ MeV}$$

This is also the maximum kinetic energy of the β^- particle (electron).

29. (a) Find the number of half-lives.
$$600.0\ s = \frac{600.0\ s}{200.0\ s/half\text{-}life} = 3.000\ half\text{-}lives$$
The activity after 3.000 half-lives will be
$$R = \left(\frac{1}{2}\right)^{3.000} \times R_0 = \frac{1}{8.000} \times 80{,}000.0\ s^{-1} = \boxed{10{,}000\ s^{-1}}$$

(b) Find the initial number of nuclei N_0, using $R_0 = \lambda N_0$.
$$N_0 = \frac{1}{\lambda} R_0 = \tau R_0 = \frac{R_0 T_{1/2}}{\ln 2} = 80{,}000.0\ s^{-1} \times \frac{200.0\ s}{\ln 2} = \boxed{2.308 \times 10^7}$$

(c) The probability per second is
$$\lambda = \frac{1}{\tau} = \frac{\ln 2}{T_{1/2}} = \frac{\ln 2}{200.0\ s} = \boxed{3.466 \times 10^{-3}\ s^{-1}}$$

31. The half-life of ^{238}U is 4.468×10^9 yr $\times 3.156 \times 10^7$ s/yr $= 1.410 \times 10^{17}$ s.

The time constant is $\tau = \dfrac{T_{1/2}}{\ln 2} = \dfrac{1.410 \times 10^{17} \text{ s}}{\ln 2} = 2.034 \times 10^{17}$ s.

The number of nuclei in 1.0 kg of ^{238}U is

$$N = \frac{\text{mass}}{\text{mass per mole}} \times N_A$$

$$= \frac{1.0 \times 10^3 \text{ g}}{238.051 \text{ g/mole}} \times 6.022 \times 10^{23} \text{ nuclei/mole}$$

$$= 2.5 \times 10^{24} \text{ nuclei}$$

The activity is

$$R = \frac{N}{\tau} = \frac{2.5 \times 10^{24} \text{ nuclei}}{2.034 \times 10^{17} \text{ s}} = \boxed{1.2 \times 10^7 \text{ Bq}}$$

33. The activity as a function of time is given by

$$R = R_0 e^{-t/\tau}$$

Solving for t and using $\dfrac{0.242 \text{ Bq/g}}{0.25 \text{ Bq/g}} = 0.968 = \dfrac{R}{R_0}$, and $\tau = \dfrac{T_{1/2}}{\ln 2} = \dfrac{5730 \text{ yr}}{\ln 2}$ gives the result.

$$e^{-t/\tau} = \frac{R}{R_0}$$

$$-\frac{t}{\tau} = \ln \frac{R}{R_0}$$

$$t = -\tau \ln \frac{R}{R_0}$$

$$= -\frac{5730 \text{ yr}}{\ln 2} \times \ln 0.968$$

$$= \boxed{270 \text{ yr}}$$

35. The ratio of C-14 to C-12 in the bone is $\dfrac{1}{4}$ as much as in a living sample. Since $\left(\dfrac{1}{2}\right)^2 = \dfrac{1}{4}$, we conclude that the age of the bone is 2 half-lives, or 2×5730 yr $= \boxed{11,500 \text{ yr.}}$

37. The activity as a function of time is given by

$$R = R_0 e^{-t/\tau} = R_0 e^{-t \ln 2/T_{1/2}}$$

Solving for $T_{1/2}$ and using $R = 2.0 \times 10^3$ Bq, $R_0 = 6.4 \times 10^4$ Bq, and $t = 12$ minutes gives the result.

$$e^{-t \ln 2/T_{1/2}} = \frac{R}{R_0}$$

$$-\frac{t \ln 2}{T_{1/2}} = \ln \frac{R}{R_0}$$

$$T_{1/2} = \frac{-t \ln 2}{\ln \frac{R}{R_0}}$$

$$= -\frac{12 \text{ min} \times \ln 2}{\ln \left(\dfrac{2.0 \times 10^3 \text{ Bq}}{6.4 \times 10^4 \text{ Bq}}\right)} = \boxed{2.4 \text{ min}}$$

41. (a) Calculate the energy absorbed.

$$\frac{\text{energy }(E)}{\text{mass }(m)} = \text{absorbed dose}$$

$$E = m(\text{absorbed dose})$$
$$= 0.30 \text{ kg} \times 2000.0 \text{ Gy}$$
$$= 6.0 \times 10^2 \text{ J}$$

Calculate the number of photons.

$$\# \text{ of photons} = \frac{\text{total energy }(E)}{\text{energy per photon}}$$

$$= \frac{6.0 \times 10^2 \text{ J} \cdot \frac{1 \text{ eV}}{1.6 \times 10^{-19} \text{ J}}}{100.0 \times 10^3 \text{ eV/photon}}$$

$$= \boxed{3.8 \times 10^{16} \text{ photons}}$$

(b) Solving Equation (14-5) for ΔT, and using $Q = 6.0 \times 10^2$ J, $m = 0.30$ kg, and $c = 4186 \dfrac{\text{J}}{\text{kg} \cdot {}^\circ\text{C}}$ gives the result.

$$mc\Delta T = Q$$
$$\Delta T = \frac{Q}{mc}$$

$$= \frac{6.0 \times 10^2 \text{ J}}{0.30 \text{ kg} \times 4186 \frac{\text{J}}{\text{kg} \cdot {}^\circ\text{C}}}$$

$$= \boxed{0.48^\circ\text{C}}$$

45. (a) Find the fractional change in the number of counts for each photon energy.

$$\frac{\Delta N_1}{N_1} = \frac{15,028 - 15,730}{15,730} = -0.0446$$

$$\frac{\Delta N_2}{N_2} = \frac{20,102 - 87,103}{87,103} = -0.76922$$

$$\frac{\Delta N_3}{N_3} = \frac{13,318 - 15,258}{15,258} = -0.1271$$

$$\frac{\Delta N_4}{N_4} = \frac{1594 - 6907}{6907} = -0.7692$$

$\dfrac{\Delta N_2}{N_2} = \dfrac{\Delta N_4}{N_4}$, so the $\boxed{662 \text{ keV and } 1345 \text{ keV}}$ photons could be emitted by the same nuclide (have the same half-life).

(b) Determine the half-lives using the number of counts.

$$\frac{\Delta N}{N_0} = \frac{N - N_0}{N_0} = \frac{N}{N_0} - 1 = 2^{-t/T_{1/2}} - 1$$

Solve for $T_{1/2}$.

$$2^{-t/T_{1/2}} = 1 + \frac{\Delta N}{N_0}$$

$$\frac{-t}{T_{1/2}} \ln 2 = \ln\left(1 + \frac{\Delta N}{N_0}\right)$$

$$T_{1/2} = -\frac{t \ln 2}{\ln\left(1 + \frac{\Delta N}{N_0}\right)}$$

So, for nuclides A and B,

$$T_A = -\frac{(332.0 \text{ s}) \ln 2}{\ln(1 - 0.044628)} = 5040.6 \text{ s}$$

$$T_B = -\frac{(332.0 \text{ s}) \ln 2}{\ln(1 - 0.769216)} = 156.95 \text{ s}$$

The number of counts measured in the first 300.0-s interval is proportional to the change in the number of nuclides during that interval.

$$\Delta N = N - N_0 = N_0 2^{-t/T_{1/2}} - N_0 = N_0(2^{-t/T_{1/2}} - 1)$$

Find N_{0A}/N_{0B} for the counts. This is the same as the ratio of the nuclides.

$$\frac{N_{0A}}{N_{0B}} = \frac{(\Delta N)_A (2^{-t/T_B} - 1)}{(\Delta N)_B (2^{-t/T_A} - 1)} = \frac{15,730\left[2^{-(300.0 \text{ s})/(156.95 \text{ s})} - 1\right]}{87,103\left[2^{-(300.0 \text{ s})/5040.6 \text{ s}} - 1\right]} = \boxed{3.28}$$

49. From Figure 29.4, the binding energies per nucleon for $^{235}_{92}$U, $^{139}_{54}$Xe, and $^{95}_{38}$Sr are approximately 7.6 MeV, 8.3 MeV, and 8.7 MeV, respectively. The binding energies are as follows:

$^{235}_{92}$U: $235 \times 7.6 \text{ MeV} = 1786 \text{ MeV}$

$^{139}_{54}$Xe: $139 \times 8.3 \text{ MeV} = 1154 \text{ MeV}$

$^{95}_{38}$Sr: $95 \times 8.7 \text{ MeV} = 827 \text{ MeV}$

The energy released is equal to the increase in the binding energy.

$1154 \text{ MeV} + 827 \text{ MeV} - 1786 \text{ MeV} = 195 \text{ MeV} \approx \boxed{200 \text{ MeV}}$

53. The radii of the ^{2}H and ^{3}H nuclei are approximately $1.2 \text{ fm} \times 2^{1/3} = 1.51 \text{ fm}$ and $1.2 \text{ fm} \times 3^{1/3} = 1.73 \text{ fm}$, respectively. To estimate the electric potential energy when the two nuclei are just "touching," we find the electric potential energy of two point charges, both with charge $+e$, at a distance of 3.24 fm; this is equal to the minimum required kinetic energy.

$$U_E = \frac{ke^2}{r} = \frac{\left(8.99 \times 10^9 \ \frac{\text{N} \cdot \text{m}^2}{\text{C}}\right)(1.602 \times 10^{-19} \text{ C})^2}{3.24 \times 10^{-15} \text{ m}} \times \frac{1 \text{ eV}}{1.602 \times 10^{-19} \text{ J}} = 0.44 \times 10^6 \text{ eV}$$

The minimum total kinetic energy required of the two nuclei is about $\boxed{0.44 \text{ MeV}}$.

57. The four excited states of $^{208}_{81}\text{Ti}$ shown have excitation energies of 40 keV, 327 keV, 472 keV, and 492 keV. The alpha particle will have maximum kinetic energy when the $^{208}_{81}\text{Ti}$ nucleus is in the ground state. If the $^{208}_{81}\text{Ti}$ nucleus ends up in one of the excited states, the kinetic energy of the alpha particle will be its maximum value minus the excitation energy of the state. The four possible kinetic energies are:

$6.090 \text{ MeV} - 0.040 \text{ MeV} = \boxed{6.050 \text{ MeV}}$
$6.090 \text{ MeV} - 0.327 \text{ MeV} = \boxed{5.763 \text{ MeV}}$
$6.090 \text{ MeV} - 0.472 \text{ MeV} = \boxed{5.618 \text{ MeV}}$
$6.090 \text{ MeV} - 0.492 \text{ MeV} = \boxed{5.598 \text{ MeV}}$

61. (a) The reaction is

$$^4_2\alpha + ^{14}_7\text{N} \rightarrow ^1_1\text{p} + ^a_b\text{X}$$

$$4 + 14 = 1 + a \rightarrow a = 17$$
$$2 + 7 = 1 + b \rightarrow b = 8$$

So X must be $^{17}_8\text{O}$.

(b) The radii of $^4_2\alpha$ and $^{17}_7\text{N}$ are $1.2 \text{ fm} \times 4^{1/3} = 1.9 \text{ fm}$ and $1.2 \text{ fm} \times 14^{1/3} = 2.9 \text{ fm}$, respectively. The distance between their centers when they touch is $1.9 \text{ fm} + 2.9 \text{ fm} = \boxed{4.8 \text{ fm.}}$

(c) The minimum kinetic energy required is equal to the electric potential energy when the two particles touch.

$$K_{min} = U_E = \frac{kq_\alpha q_N}{r} = \frac{k \times 2e \times 7e}{d} = \boxed{\frac{14ke^2}{d}}$$

(d) The mass defect is
$$\Delta m = 16.999132 \text{ u} + 1.007825 \text{ u} - 14.003074 \text{ u} - 4.002603 \text{ u} = 0.001280 \text{ u}$$
The mass of the products is greater than the mass of the reactants. The total kinetic energy of the products will be $\boxed{\text{less than}}$ the initial kinetic energy of the reactants by an amount

$$E = \Delta mc^2 = 0.001280 \text{ u} \times 931.5 \text{ MeV/u} = \boxed{1.192 \text{ MeV}}$$

65. (a) Assuming the particles are nonrelativistic, we have

$$K = \frac{1}{2}mv^2$$

$$v = \sqrt{2K/m}$$

$$= \sqrt{\frac{2 \times 4.17 \times 10^6 \text{ eV} \times 1.60 \times 10^{-19} \text{ J/eV}}{4.00 \text{ u} \times 1.66 \times 10^{-27} \text{ kg/u}}}$$

$$= \boxed{1.42 \times 10^7 \text{ m/s}}$$

$\gamma \approx 1.001$, so using the nonrelativistic form of the kinetic energy is reasonable.

(b) To pass through undeflected, the net force on the alpha particles must be zero. The magnetic and electric forces must be equal in magnitude.

$$F_M = F_E$$
$$qvB = qE$$
$$E = Bv$$
$$= 0.30 \text{ T} \times 1.42 \times 10^7 \text{ m/s}$$
$$= \boxed{4.3 \times 10^6 \text{ V/m}}$$

(c) Using $F = ma$, with $F = qvB$ and $a = \dfrac{v^2}{r}$ (uniform circular motion), and solving for r, gives

$$F = ma$$

$$qvB = m\frac{v^2}{r}$$

$$qrB = mv$$

$$r = \frac{mv}{Bq}$$

$$= \frac{4.00 \text{ u} \times 1.66 \times 10^{-27} \text{ kg/u} \times 1.42 \times 10^7 \text{ m/s}}{0.30 \text{ T} \times 2 \times 1.60 \times 10^{-19} \text{ C}}$$

$$= \boxed{98 \text{ cm}}$$

(d) Rearranging the equation in part (c) gives

$$r = \frac{mv}{Bq}$$

$$\frac{q}{m} = \frac{v}{Br}$$

B, v, and r are the only quantities that can be measured in this experiment, so only the ratio q/m can be determined—$\boxed{\text{both } m \text{ and } q \text{ affect the radius of the trajectory}}$.

Chapter 30

PARTICLE PHYSICS

Problems

1. The difference in the rest mass of the particles before and after the decay is related to the energy released by the decay. Neglect the relatively small mass of the neutrino.

    $\Delta m = (\text{mass of muon}) - (\text{mass of pion})$

    $= 0.106 \ \text{GeV}/c^2 - 0.140 \ \text{GeV}/c^2 = -0.034 \ \text{GeV}/c^2$

    The energy released by this decay is $E = |\Delta m| c^2 = \boxed{34 \ \text{MeV}}$.

5. The mass defect is

    $\Delta m = 2(0.14 \ \text{GeV}/c^2) - 2(0.938 \ \text{GeV}/c^2) = -1.6 \ \text{GeV}/c^2$

    The energy released in the decay is

    $E = |\Delta m| c^2 = 1.6 \ \text{GeV}$

    Conservation of energy requires that $E = K_{\pi^-} + K_{\pi^+}$. Conservation of momentum requires that the magnitude of the momenta of the two pions be the same. Since the pions have the same mass, their velocities must be equal and opposite, so $K_{\pi^-} = K_{\pi^+} = \dfrac{E}{2} = \dfrac{1.6 \ \text{GeV}}{2} = \boxed{0.80 \ \text{GeV}}$.

7. Since π^+ is the antiparticle of π^-, the decay products of π^+ must be antiparticles of the decay products of π^-. The decay modes of π^+ are then

    $\boxed{\pi^+ \rightarrow \mu^+ + v_\mu \text{ and } \pi^+ \rightarrow e^+ + v_e}$.

9. The quarks in a proton are uud. Therefore, the quarks in an antiproton are $\boxed{\overline{\text{uud}}.}$

11. The rest energy of a proton is 938 MeV, so a proton with energy 1.0 TeV is extremely relativistic. So, we have

    $E \approx pc$ and $p = \dfrac{E}{c} = \dfrac{h}{\lambda}$.

    Calculate the de Broglie wavelength.

    $\lambda = \dfrac{hc}{E} = \dfrac{1240 \times 10^{-9} \ \text{eV} \cdot \text{m}}{1.0 \times 10^{12} \ \text{eV}} = \boxed{1.2 \times 10^{-18} \ \text{m}}$

13. Assuming the products—protons and antiprotons—all have zero kinetic energy, the maximum possible number of proton-antiproton pairs produced is $\dfrac{2 \times 6.0 \ \text{GeV}}{2 \times 0.938 \ \text{GeV}} = 6.4$, or $\boxed{6}$ pairs.

Notes

Notes

Notes

Notes

Notes

Notes

Notes

Notes